내신 및 시·도 교육청 영어듣기평가 완벽 대비

Listening 올리고

Level 2

중학영어듣기 모의고사

DARAKWON

중학영어듣기 모의고사

지은이 정수진, 한길연, 박선화
펴낸이 정규도
펴낸곳 (주)다락원

초판 1쇄 인쇄 2014년 2월 7일
초판 9쇄 발행 2022년 5월 3일

편집 권은숙, 서정아
일러스트 김진용
디자인 김나경

다락원 경기도 파주시 문발로 211
내용문의: (02)736-2031 내선 503
구입문의: (02)736-2031 내선 250~252
Fax: (02)732-2037
출판등록 1977년 9월 16일 제406-2008-000007호

값 13,000원

ISBN 978-89-277-0712-7 54740
978-89-277-0710-3 54740 (set)

http://www.darakwon.co.kr

• 다락원 홈페이지를 방문하시면 상세한 출판정보와 함께 동영상강좌, MP3자료 등 다양한 어학 정보를 얻으실 수 있습니다.

내신 및 시 • 도 교육청 영어듣기평가 완벽 대비

Listening 올리고

Level 2

중학영어듣기 모의고사

DARAKWON

Structure & Features | 구성과 특징

Listening Test

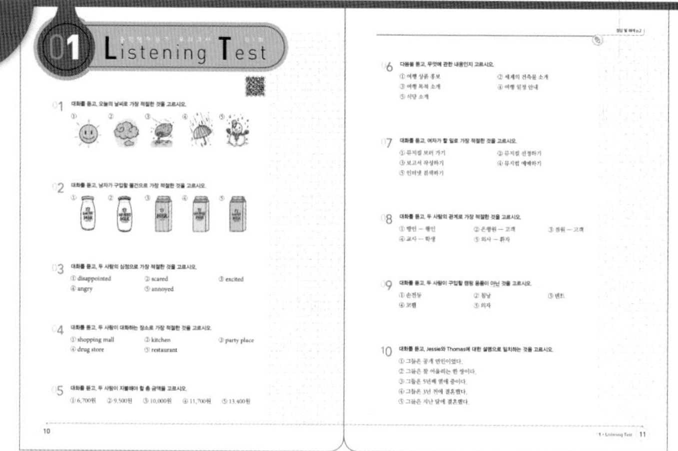

전국 16개 시·도 교육청 주관 영어듣기능력평가 및 내신 교과서 반영!

최신 기출 유형을 철저히 분석, 반영하여 실제 시험과 유사하게 구성한 모의고사로 실전 감각을 키울 수 있습니다. 또한 영어 교과서의 주요 표현 및 소재들을 활용하여 내신까지 효과적으로 대비할 수 있습니다.

Further Study

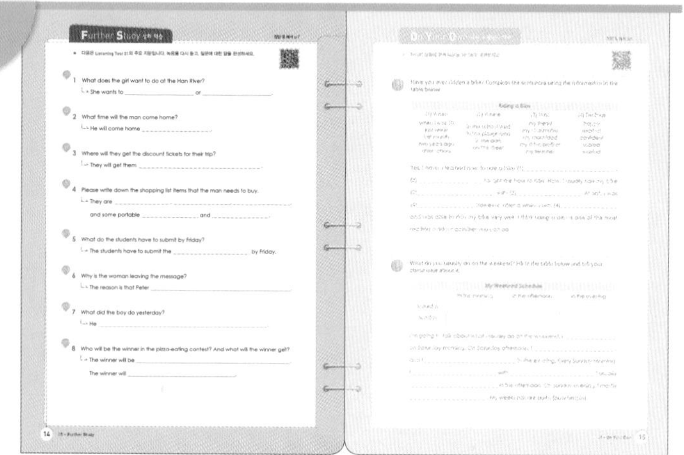

주요 지문 심화학습으로 내신 서술형 완벽 대비!

Listening Test의 주요 지문만을 모아 서술형 문제로 다시 풀어볼 수 있도록 구성하였습니다. 보다 심화된 듣기 문제로 내신 서술형 평가에 철저히 대비하고, 듣기 실력을 강화할 수 있습니다.

On Your Own

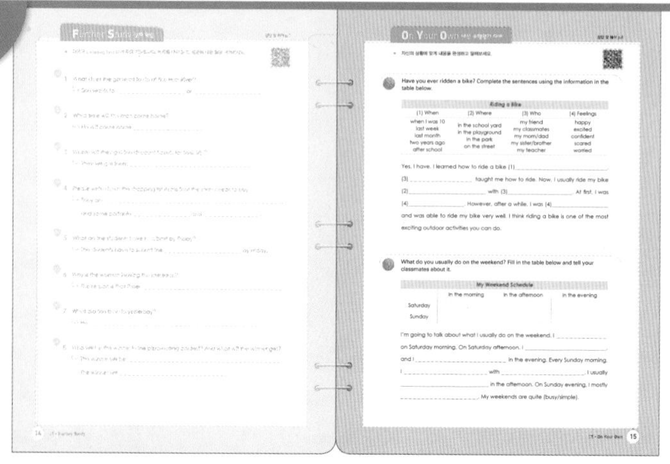

내신 말하기 수행평가 대비까지 한 번에!

Listening Test 및 기출 문제에서 출제된 주제와 소재를 응용한 다양한 연습 문제를 통해 별도로 준비하기 어려운 내신 말하기 수행평가까지 한 번에 대비할 수 있습니다.

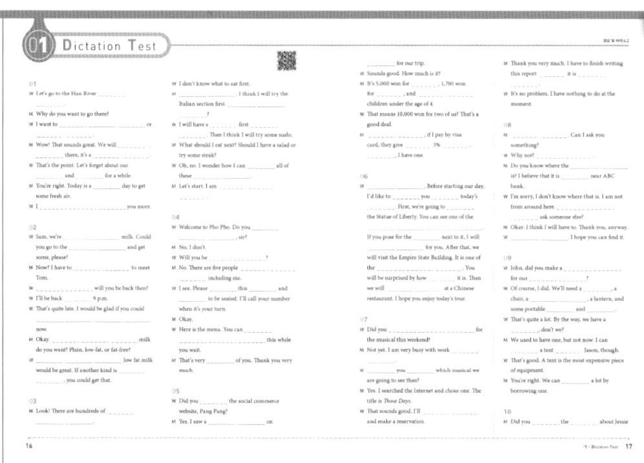

Dictation Test

전 지문 받아쓰기로 꼼꼼한 마무리 학습!

매회 전 지문 받아쓰기를 수록하여 놓친 부분을 빠짐없이 확인할 수 있습니다. 문제의 핵심이 되는 키워드, 중요 표현, 연음 등을 확인하며, 복습은 물론 자신의 취약점을 다시 한 번 확인할 수 있습니다.

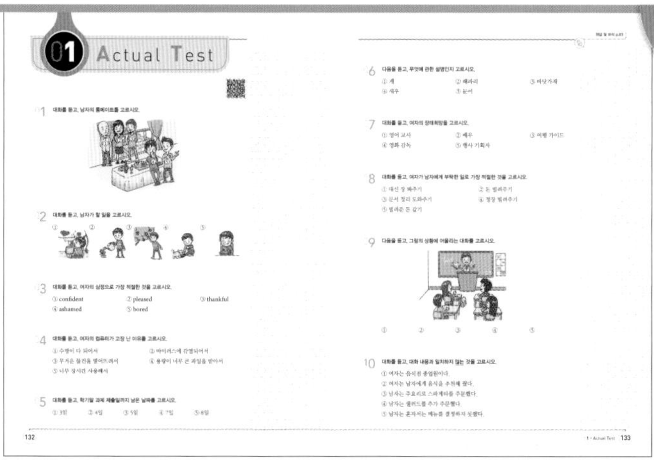

Actual Test

실전 모의고사로 최종 실력 점검!

실제 시험과 가장 유사한 모의고사로서 자신의 실력을 최종 점검해볼 수 있습니다. 시험에 자주 나오는 유형과 표현들을 100% 반영한 영어듣기능력평가 완벽 대비 모의고사입니다.

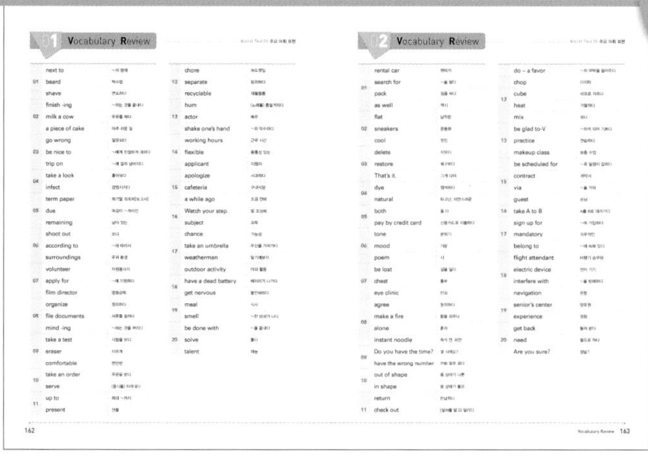

Vocabulary Review

중요 어휘 및 표현을 한눈에!

본문에 나오는 주요 어휘와 표현을 각 모의고사 회별로 한눈에 정리하여 단어 학습을 보다 효율적으로 할 수 있습니다.

Contents I 목차

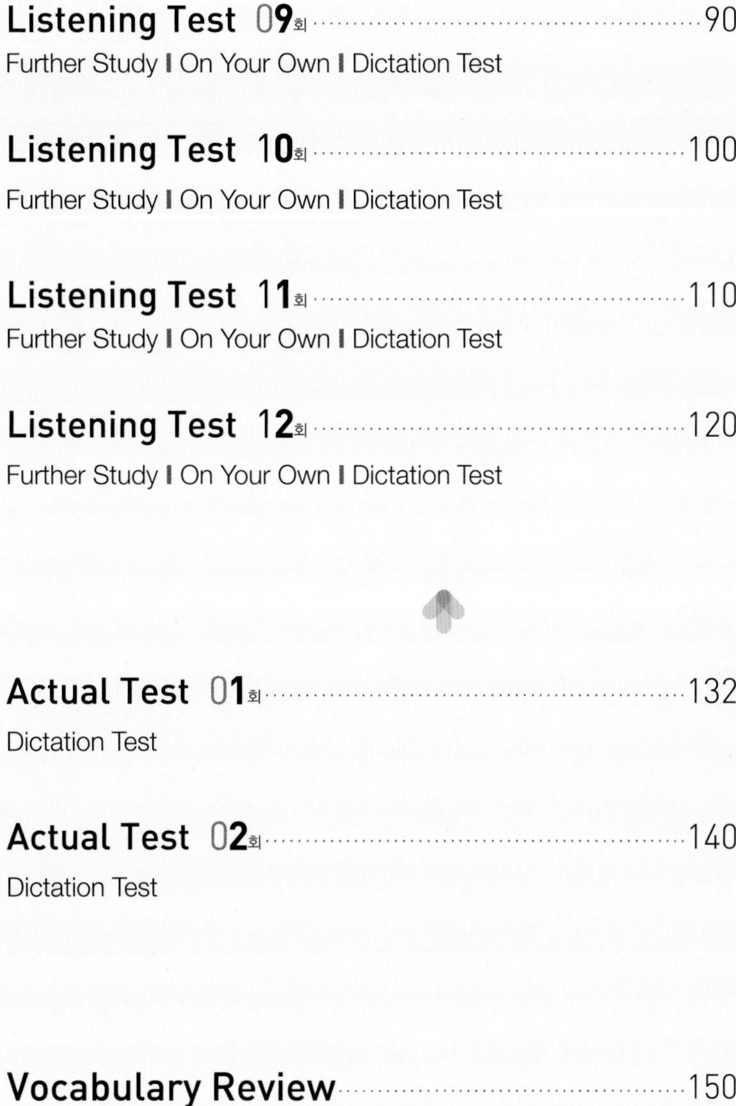

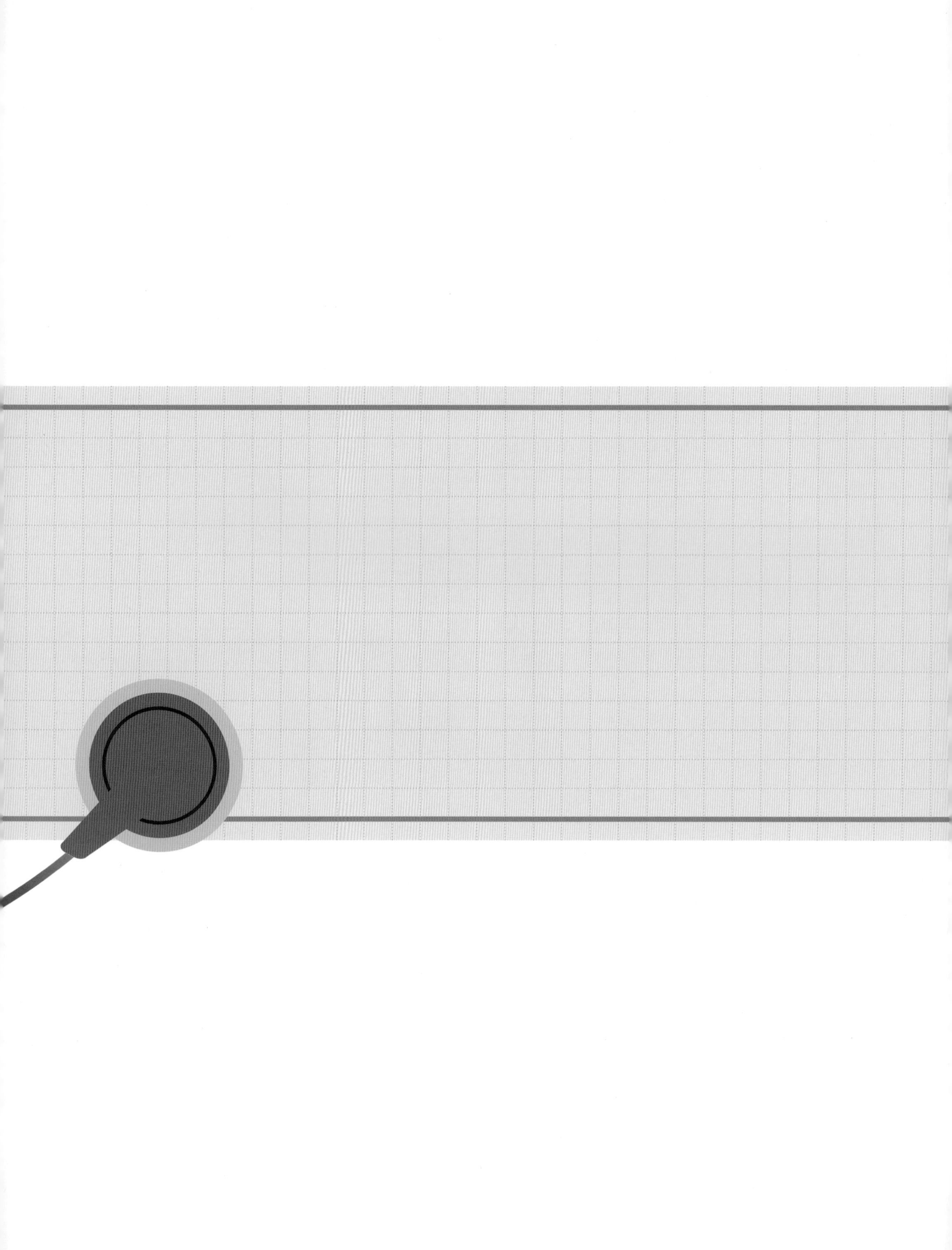

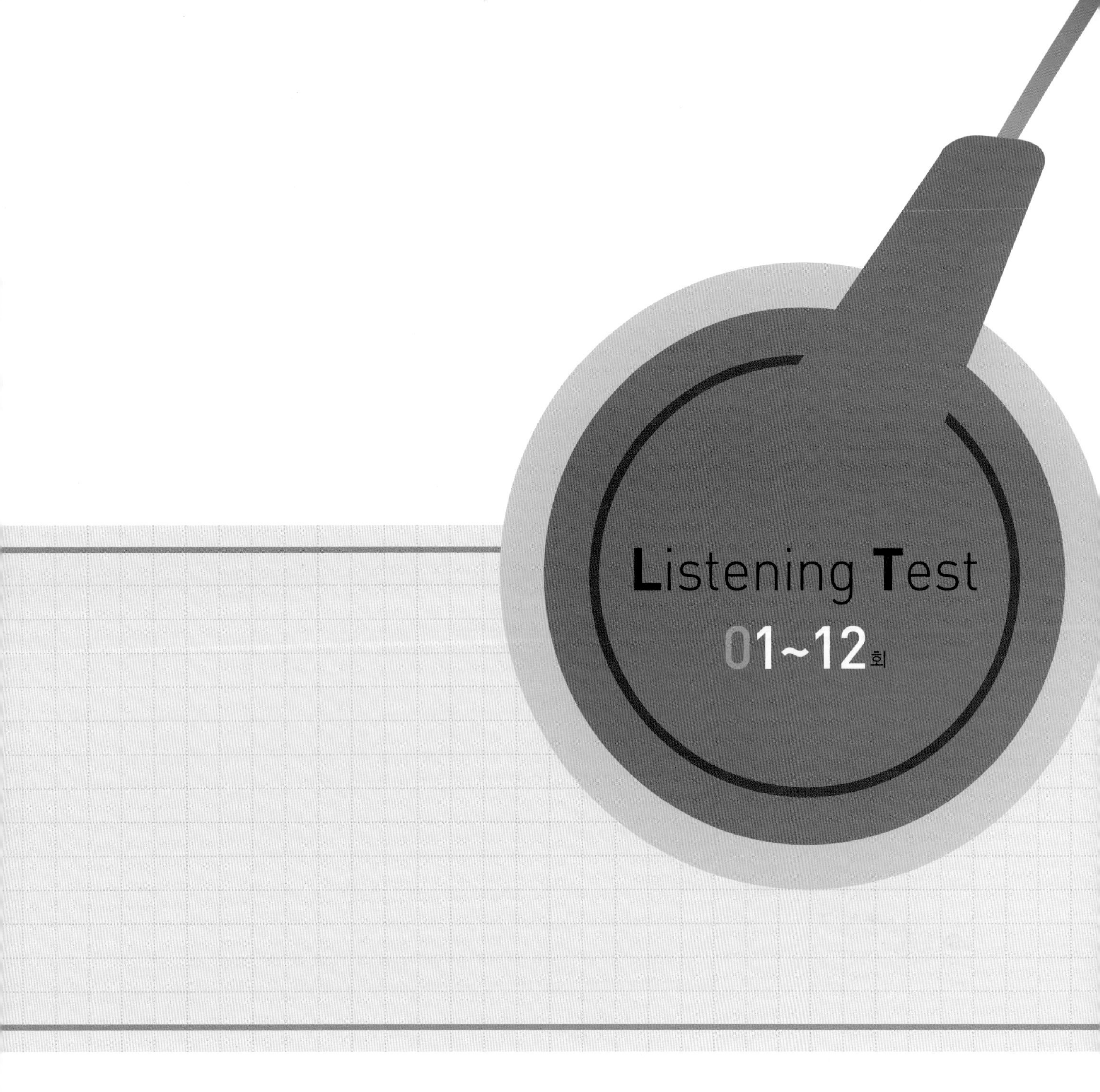
Listening Test
01~12회

01 중학영어듣기 모의고사 01회 Listening Test

01 대화를 듣고, 오늘의 날씨로 가장 적절한 것을 고르시오.

① 
② 
③ 
④ 
⑤ 

02 대화를 듣고, 남자가 구입할 물건으로 가장 적절한 것을 고르시오.

① 

② 

③ 

④ 

⑤ 

03 대화를 듣고, 두 사람의 심정으로 가장 적절한 것을 고르시오.

① disappointed ② scared ③ excited
④ angry ⑤ annoyed

04 대화를 듣고, 두 사람이 대화하는 장소로 가장 적절한 것을 고르시오.

① shopping mall ② kitchen ③ party place
④ drug store ⑤ restaurant

05 대화를 듣고, 두 사람이 지불해야 할 총 금액을 고르시오.

① 6,700원 ② 9,500원 ③ 10,000원 ④ 11,700원 ⑤ 13,400원

06 다음을 듣고, 무엇에 관한 내용인지 고르시오.

① 여행 상품 홍보
② 세계의 건축물 소개
③ 여행 목적 소개
④ 여행 일정 안내
⑤ 식당 소개

07 대화를 듣고, 여자가 할 일로 가장 적절한 것을 고르시오.

① 뮤지컬 보러 가기
② 뮤지컬 선정하기
③ 보고서 작성하기
④ 뮤지컬 예매하기
⑤ 인터넷 검색하기

08 대화를 듣고, 두 사람의 관계로 가장 적절한 것을 고르시오.

① 행인 — 행인
② 은행원 — 고객
③ 점원 — 고객
④ 교사 — 학생
⑤ 의사 — 환자

09 대화를 듣고, 두 사람이 구입할 캠핑 용품이 아닌 것을 고르시오.

① 손전등
② 침낭
③ 텐트
④ 코펠
⑤ 의자

10 대화를 듣고, Jessie와 Thomas에 대한 설명으로 일치하는 것을 고르시오.

① 그들은 공개 연인이었다.
② 그들은 잘 어울리는 한 쌍이다.
③ 그들은 5년째 열애 중이다.
④ 그들은 3년 전에 결혼했다.
⑤ 그들은 지난 달에 결혼했다.

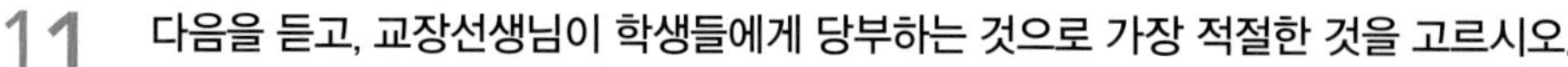

11 다음을 듣고, 교장선생님이 학생들에게 당부하는 것으로 가장 적절한 것을 고르시오.

① 부모님께 가정통신문 보여드리기
② 담임선생님과 면담하기
③ 부모님께 사인 받기
④ 견학에 반드시 참여하기
⑤ 담임선생님께 사인 받기

12 대화를 듣고, 남자가 건강을 유지하는 방법으로 언급되지 않은 것을 고르시오.

① 조깅하기
② 채소 많이 먹기
③ 정기 건강검진 받기
④ 영양제 섭취하기
⑤ 충분한 육류 섭취하기

13 다음을 듣고, 여자가 메시지를 남긴 이유로 가장 적절한 것을 고르시오.

① 보고서 작성 준비를 하기 위해
② 변경된 전화번호를 알려주기 위해
③ 보고서 함께 쓸 것을 제안하기 위해
④ 보고서 주제를 알려주기 위해
⑤ 정보수집 완료를 알려주기 위해

14 다음을 듣고, 표의 내용과 일치하지 않는 것을 고르시오.

Sue's Weekend Schedule

	Morning	Afternoon	Evening
Saturday	clean my room	see a movie	do my homework
Sunday	go to church	take a nap	go out to eat

① ② ③ ④ ⑤

15 대화를 듣고, 두 사람이 오늘 할 일로 가장 적절한 것을 고르시오.

① 바다에서 수영하기
② 실내 수영장 가기
③ 병원 가기
④ 모래성 만들기
⑤ 게 잡기

16 다음을 듣고, 두 사람의 대화가 어색한 것을 고르시오.

① ② ③ ④ ⑤

17 다음을 듣고, 토마토 축제에 관한 내용과 일치하지 않는 것을 고르시오.

① 토마토 축제에서는 다양한 활동들을 할 수 있다.
② 토마토 축제는 아이들만 참가할 수 있다.
③ 7세에서 10세 사이의 어린이는 토마토 따기 시합을 할 수 있다.
④ 아이들은 부모님과 함께 피자를 만들어 먹을 수 있다.
⑤ 피자 먹기 대회는 어른들만 참가할 수 있다.

18 다음을 듣고, 태호가 수빈이에게 할 말로 가장 적절한 것을 고르시오.

① Please be on time.
② I like playing tennis a lot.
③ What time did you go to bed?
④ I'm so sorry for being late.
⑤ Why don't we play tennis now?

[19-20] 대화를 듣고, 남자의 마지막 말에 이어질 여자의 응답으로 가장 적절한 것을 고르시오.

19

① Wow, I envy you.
② I want to buy you a cell phone.
③ I'd like to have a new cell phone.
④ Your birthday party was so much fun.
⑤ My parents can't afford to buy me everything.

20

① Help yourself.
② Okay. See you then.
③ Setting the table is not easy.
④ I'm going to the grocery store.
⑤ Grocery shopping is so much fun.

Further Study 심화 학습

정답 및 해석 p.7

● 다음은 **Listening Test 01**의 주요 지문입니다. 녹음을 다시 듣고, 질문에 대한 답을 완성하세요.

Q1
1 What does the girl want to do at the Han River?

↳ She wants to ______________________ or ______________________.

Q2
2 What time will the man come home?

↳ He will come home ______________________.

Q5
3 Where will they get the discount tickets for their trip?

↳ They will get them ____.

Q9
4 Please write down the shopping list items that the man needs to buy.

↳ They are __________________, __________________, __________________,

and some portable __________________ and __________________.

Q11
5 What do the students have to submit by Friday?

↳ The students have to submit the _________________________ by Friday.

Q13
6 Why is the woman leaving the message?

↳ The reason is that Peter ____.

Q15
7 What did the boy do yesterday?

↳ He ____.

Q17
8 Who will be the winner in the pizza-eating contest? And what will the winner get?

↳ The winner will be ____.

The winner will ___________________________________.

정답 및 해석 p.8

● 자신의 상황에 맞게 내용을 완성하고 말해보세요.

Have you ever ridden a bike? Complete the sentences using the information in the table below.

Riding a Bike			
(1) When	(2) Where	(3) Who	(4) Feelings
when I was 10 last week last month two years ago after school	in the school yard in the playground in the park on the street	my friend my classmates my mom/dad my sister/brother my teacher	happy excited confident scared worried

Yes, I have. I learned how to ride a bike (1)____________________.
(3)________________ taught me how to ride. Now, I usually ride my bike
(2)___________________ with (3)________________. At first, I was
(4)________________. However, after a while, I was (4)________________
and was able to ride my bike very well. I think riding a bike is one of the most exciting outdoor activities you can do.

What do you usually do on the weekend? Fill in the table below and tell your classmates about it.

My Weekend Schedule			
	In the morning	In the afternoon	In the evening
Saturday			
Sunday			

I'm going to talk about what I usually do on the weekend. I ________________
on Saturday morning. On Saturday afternoon, I ____________________,
and I ______________________ in the evening. Every Sunday morning,
I ____________________ with ____________________. I usually
_____________________ in the afternoon. On Sunday evening, I mostly
___________________. My weekends are quite (busy/simple).

01 Dictation Test

01

W Let's go to the Han River __________ __________.

M Why do you want to go there?

W I want to __________ __________ __________ or __________ __________.

M Wow! That sounds great. We will __________ __________ there, it's a __________ __________.

W That's the point. Let's forget about our __________ and __________ for a while.

M You're right. Today is a __________ day to get some fresh air.

W I __________ __________ __________ you more.

02

W Sam, we're __________ __________ milk. Could you go to the __________ __________ and get some, please?

M Now? I have to __________ __________ to meet Tom.

W __________ __________ will you be back then?

M I'll be back __________ 9 p.m.

W That's quite late. I would be glad if you could __________ __________ __________ __________ now.

M Okay. __________ __________ __________ milk do you want? Plain, low-fat, or fat-free?

W __________ __________ __________ low fat milk would be great. If another kind is __________ __________, you could get that.

03

M Look! There are hundreds of __________ __________ __________.

W I don't know what to eat first.

M __________ __________. I think I will try the Italian section first. __________ __________ __________?

W I will have a __________ first __________ __________. Then I think I will try some sushi.

M What should I eat next? Should I have a salad or try some steak?

W Oh, no. I wonder how I can __________ all of these __________ __________.

M Let's start. I am __________ __________ __________.

04

W Welcome to Pho Pho. Do you __________ __________ __________, sir?

M No, I don't.

W Will you be __________ __________?

M No. There are five people __________ __________ __________ including me.

W I see. Please __________ this __________ and __________ to be seated. I'll call your number when it's your turn.

M Okay.

W Here is the menu. You can __________ __________ __________ __________ this while you wait.

M That's very __________ of you. Thank you very much.

05

W Did you __________ the social commerce website, Pang Pang?

M Yes. I saw a __________ __________ on

__________ for our trip.

W Sounds good. How much is it?

M It's 5,000 won for __________, 1,700 won for __________, and __________ __________ children under the age of 4.

W That means 10,000 won for two of us? That's a good deal.

M __________ __________, if I pay by visa card, they give __________ 5% __________. __________, I have one.

06

W __________ __________. Before starting our day, I'd like to __________ you __________ today's __________. First, we're going to __________ the Statue of Liberty. You can see one of the __________ __________ __________ __________. If you pose for the __________ next to it, I will __________ __________ for you. After that, we will visit the Empire State Building. It is one of the __________ __________ __________. You will be surprised by how __________ it is. Then we will __________ __________ at a Chinese restaurant. I hope you enjoy today's tour.

07

W Did you __________ __________ __________ for the musical this weekend?

M Not yet. I am very busy with work __________ __________.

W __________ you __________ which musical we are going to see then?

M Yes. I searched the Internet and chose one. The title is *Those Days*.

W That sounds good. I'll __________ __________ and make a reservation.

M Thank you very much. I have to finish writing this report __________ it is __________ __________.

W It's no problem. I have nothing to do at the moment.

08

M __________ __________. Can I ask you something?

W Why not? __________ __________.

M Do you know where the __________ __________ is? I believe that it is __________ near ABC bank.

W I'm sorry, I don't know where that is. I am not from around here. __________ __________ __________ ask someone else?

M Okay. I think I will have to. Thank you, anyway.

W __________ __________. I hope you can find it.

09

W John, did you make a __________ __________ for our __________ __________?

M Of course, I did. We'll need a __________, a chair, a __________ __________, a lantern, and some portable __________ and __________.

W That's quite a lot. By the way, we have a __________, don't we?

M We used to have one, but not now. I can __________ a tent __________ Jason, though.

W That's good. A tent is the most expensive piece of equipment.

M You're right. We can __________ a lot by borrowing one.

10

M Did you __________ the __________ about Jessie

and Thomas?

W No. __________ __________ to them?

M They are going to get married next month. They __________ __________ __________ for three years.

W For three years? Wow! How could they __________ __________ __________ such a long time?

M I know! Anyway, they __________ __________ __________.

W You're right.

11

M Dear students. This is Michael Hanks, your __________. We are going to __________ __________ __________ __________ __________ to Gyeongbokgung in __________. We have already sent a school newsletter to your parents about the trip. Please get your __________ __________ by Friday and __________ your permission slip to your __________ __________. Without your parent's signature, you won't be able to go on the trip. If you'd like to join, please talk to your parents and __________ the slip __________ to your teacher __________ __________. Thank you.

12

W Hey, Steve. I heard that you were __________ __________ __________. Are you okay now?

M Yes. I feel __________ __________ than before.

W It's good to hear that. Are there any special things that you do to __________ __________?

M Well, I __________ every morning. I __________ __________ __________ and also __________ __________ __________. I also have regular __________.

W I see. Do you take vitamins and other __________ __________?

M Of course I do. They're one of the basic steps to __________ __________ __________.

13

[Beep]

W Hello, Peter. I'm leaving this __________ because you're not __________ your phone. We have to __________ on a topic and start __________ __________ for the __________ __________. Since we have to work as a pair, I'd like to __________ some __________ with you. As soon as you get this message, please call me on my cell phone. My number is 010-0000-7979. I'm __________ __________ __________ hearing from you soon. Bye.

14

① W I'm going to __________ my room on __________ __________.

② W I'm going to __________ __________ __________ on __________ morning.

③ W I'm going to __________ __________ __________ on Saturday evening.

④ W I'm going to __________ __________ __________ on Sunday __________.

⑤ W I'm going to __________ __________ __________ __________ on Sunday __________.

15

W What do you want to do, Sean?

M __________ __________ __________, mom.

W Sweetie, I'm sorry, but __________ __________.

It's __________ __________ __________ swim in the sea. You might __________ __________ __________.

M I see. Maybe we can go to an indoor swimming pool sometime. Shall we try to catch some __________ __________ this time then?

W That sounds good. But how about __________ a __________ __________?

M I already made one yesterday with dad.

W Okay. Let's do what you mentioned a __________ __________.

16

① M Do you know where I can find some __________ __________?

W Yes. I will __________ you where they are.

② M I like this __________ __________ __________ a lot.

W Are you sure you want to buy it?

③ M Do you __________ __________ __________ finding a book?

W No, I like this book very much.

④ M Where is the nearest __________ __________?

W I am sorry. I'm a stranger here, too.

⑤ M __________ __________ at ten o'clock.

W Sure, why not?

17

W __________ __________ the Tomato Festival. This is a __________ __________ for tomato lovers. We have various activities __________ __________ __________ you. For children between __________ and __________, there will be a tomato-picking contest. After that, children can __________ __________ __________ and eat it with their parents. We are also having a pizza-eating contest after that. The __________ in the contest are __________ __________ __________, though. The person who eats the most pizza will __________ some __________ __________.

18

M Subin and Taeho like __________ __________. __________ __________ __________, they play tennis in the park together. Today, Taeho got up late and came to the park late. Subin was __________ __________ him for 30 minutes. In this situation, what would Taeho say to Subin?

19

M Hey, __________ this __________. I got a new cell phone.

W __________ __________! Did your parents get it for you?

M Yeah. You know it was my __________ yesterday.

W Do they always buy you the things you want?

M Yes. They __________ to get them for me.

W Wow, I envy you.

20

[Telephone rings.]

W Hello. __________ __________, honey. Where are you now?

M I am __________ __________ __________ home. Do you want me to __________ anything?

W No. I finished doing all of the __________ __________ this afternoon.

M Then __________ __________?

W I just want to know when you'll be there so that I can __________ __________ __________.

M I think I'll be there __________ 20 minutes.

W Okay. See you then.

Listening Test

중학영어듣기 모의고사 02회

01 대화를 듣고, 남자가 찾고 있는 물건이 있는 장소를 고르시오.

02 대화를 듣고, 대화에 등장하는 인물을 고르시오.

① 
② 
③ 
④ 
⑤ 

03 대화를 듣고, 남자의 심정으로 가장 적절한 것을 고르시오.

① anxious ② upset ③ frustrated
④ pleasant ⑤ excited

04 대화를 듣고, 두 사람이 대화하는 장소로 가장 적절한 것을 고르시오.

① post office ② store ③ fitness center
④ restaurant ⑤ bank

05 대화를 듣고, 남자가 지불해야 할 금액을 고르시오.

① $15.25 ② $15.15 ③ $17.40 ④ $17.75 ⑤ $17.85

06 다음을 듣고, 이어질 내용으로 가장 적절한 것을 고르시오.

① 펜팔의 장점
② 펜팔 소개하기
③ 펜팔의 정의
④ 펜팔 찾는 방법
⑤ 펜팔의 기원

07 대화를 듣고, 남자가 할 일로 가장 적절한 것을 고르시오.

① 안경 구입하기
② 책 옮겨주기
③ 문제 풀기
④ 책 구입하기
⑤ 공부하러 가기

08 대화를 듣고, 두 사람의 관계로 가장 적절한 것을 고르시오.

① 아빠 — 딸
② 코치 — 운동선수
③ 사장 — 사원
④ 은행직원 — 고객
⑤ 교수 — 학생

09 대화를 듣고, 남자의 아침식사 메뉴가 아닌 것을 고르시오.

① 토스트
② 딸기잼
③ 버터
④ 소시지
⑤ 우유

10 대화를 듣고, 대화 내용과 일치하지 않는 것을 고르시오.

① 남자는 토요일에 자주 하이킹을 한다.
② 남자는 매일 조깅을 한다.
③ 남자는 탁구를 잘 친다.
④ 여자는 탁구를 칠 때 서브를 강하게 하는 편이다.
⑤ 남자는 여자와 함께 탁구를 치고 싶어 한다.

11 대화를 듣고, 여자가 남자에게 부탁한 일로 가장 적절한 것을 고르시오.

① 자리 맡아주기
② 자리 옮겨 앉아주기
③ 이사 도와주기
④ 남자친구와 인사하기
⑤ 의자 골라주기

12 대화를 듣고, 여자가 숙면하기 위한 방법으로 언급하지 않은 것을 고르시오.

① 차 마시기
② 낮잠 안 자기
③ 밤 늦게 TV 안 보기
④ 따뜻한 우유 마시기
⑤ 운동하기

13 대화를 듣고, 사람들이 남자를 보고 웃은 이유를 고르시오.

① 학교에 지각해서
② 남자가 창피해 해서
③ 신발이 벗겨져서
④ 서두르다 넘어져서
⑤ 신발을 잘못 신어서

14 다음을 듣고, 내용과 일치하지 않는 것을 고르시오.

Join Our Dance Club

- When to meet?
  ① Every Saturday afternoon at the ABC Center
- What are the advantages?
  ② Learn how to dance
  ③ Stay healthy and slim
  ④ Make new friends
- Who can Join?
  ⑤ Anyone who is interested in dancing

15 대화를 듣고, 남자가 할 일로 가장 적절한 것을 고르시오.

① 기말 보고서 쓰기
② 보고서 주제 정하기
③ 설문지 응답하기
④ 설문지 문항 만들기
⑤ 음료수 사러 가기

16 다음을 듣고, 두 사람의 대화가 어색한 것을 고르시오.

① ② ③ ④ ⑤

17 대화를 듣고, 여자에 대한 내용과 일치하지 않는 것을 고르시오.

① 뉴욕에서 태어났다.
② 현재 로스앤젤레스에서 산다.
③ 남자와 잘 아는 사이이다.
④ 딸 하나 아들 하나가 있다.
⑤ 놀이공원에 와 있다.

18 다음을 듣고, Peter가 Jessica에게 할 말로 가장 적절한 것을 고르시오.

① I am proud of your efforts.
② I don't want you to have a job.
③ Setting goals is very important.
④ I didn't know you are interested in music.
⑤ I can't believe you have grown up so much.

[19-20] 대화를 듣고, 남자의 마지막 말에 이어질 여자의 응답으로 가장 적절한 것을 고르시오.

19

① Have a nice day.
② Please leave a message.
③ Thank you for calling me.
④ You have the wrong number.
⑤ Please tell him to call me back.

20

① Please join me.
② Let's have a talk.
③ I'm happy to join you.
④ Sounds interesting. I'll join you.
⑤ What are you going to do this weekend?

Further Study 심화 학습

정답 및 해석 p.14

● 다음은 **Listening Test 02**의 주요 지문입니다. 녹음을 다시 듣고, 질문에 대한 답을 완성하세요.

Q3
1 Why didn't the woman come to school yesterday?

↳ The reason was that she had ____________________ so ____________________ was ____________________ her a lot.

Q4
2 How much does the man want to deposit?

↳ He wants to deposit ____________________.

Q5
3 Where does the man want to send the parcel?

↳ He wants to send it ____________________.

Q8
4 What things does the man consider in order to decide on grades?

↳ He considers ____________________, ____________________, ____________________, and ____________________.

Q11
5 Why did the woman ask the man to move over one seat?

↳ The reason was that she wants to ____________________ her ____________________.

Q12
6 Please write down 4 tips to sleep well at night.

↳ ① Do not drink ____________________ or ____________________ in the ____________________.

② Do not ____________________ during the day.

③ Drink ____________________ before ____________________.

④ Do some ____________________.

Q15
7 What did the woman ask Jaeil to help her with?

↳ She asked him to help her with ____________________.

Q20
8 What is the man planning to do on Sunday?

↳ He is planning to ____________________.

정답 및 해석 p.14

- 자신의 상황에 맞게 내용을 완성하고 말해보세요.

Ask a classmate the following questions about himself or herself. Then, introduce him or her to the class.

About My Classmate	
(1) What is your name?	
(2) What do you like to do?	
(3) Where do you like to spend time?	
(4) What sports do you like to play?	
(5) How often do you play it?	
(6) What would you like to be?	
(7) Why do you want that job?	

My classmate's name is (1)________________. When (he/she) has spare time, (he/she) likes to (2)__________________________. (He/She) likes to spend time (3)_____________________. (His/Her) favorite sport is (4)_______________. (He/She) plays it with his friends (5)_______________________. (He/She) would like to be (6)_______________ because (7)_____________________________________.

What do you want to be when you grow up? Fill in the table below and tell your classmates about it.

I Want to Be a(n) ...	
(1) What do you want to be?	
(2) What does he/she usually do?	
(3) Where does he/she work?	
(4) Why do you want to be a(n) ...?	
(5) Do you know anyone who is a(n) ...?	

I want to be a (1)________________. A(n) (1)________________ (2)_____________ ________________________________. A(n) (1)________________ usually works (3)_____________________________________. The reasons why I want to be a(n) (1)________________ are that (4)____ ________________________. (5)______________________ is my role model. I think (his/her) passion for (his/her) work is very impressive.

02 Dictation Test

01

M Mom, have you ________ my watch?

W No. Why do you ask?

M Because I ________ ________ it ________.

W Did you look on your ________?

M Yes, but it wasn't there.

W Did you look in your ________ ________? It seems that you sometimes ________ it ________.

M No, not yet. It ________ ________, either. Oh, mom I ________ ________. It's ________ the ________ and the ________ on the desk.

02

W Have you ________ the new science teacher?

M No, not yet. But I heard he is really ________ with the students.

W I've already met him and he was ________ ________ and ________.

M Is he ________?

W Hmm. He's very ________ and ________ with a shiny ________ ________

M Oh, that's ________. He must have a ________ sense of humor.

03

M ________ ________ you ________ to school yesterday?

W My stomach was ________ ________ a lot.

M Did it ________ any ________?

W Well, I'm ________ feeling a bit ________ ________ ________.

M Did you take some medicine?

W Yes, I did. I went to see a doctor and he told me that I had ________ ________ ________.

M I hope you feel better soon.

04

W How's it going?

M I'm good.

W ________ can I ________ ________?

M I'd like to ________ this ________ for ________ dollars, please.

W Do you ________ an account ________ ________?

M No, I don't.

W Then you ________ ________ an account ________. What sort of account would you like to open?

05

W Next! What can I do for you?

M I'd like to ________ this ________ to the United States ________ ________ ________.

W What is in the parcel?

M ________ some ________.

W Okay, let me see ________ ________ it ________. It's about ________kgs. That will be ________ dollars and ________ cents.

M I'd like to ________ my parcel.

W Then it will ________ an additional ________ dollars and ________ cents.

06

M There is a ________ ________ in writing to a ________ ________ who lives ________

__________. The culture, holidays and even the climate may be __________ __________ your own. It is __________ to __________ about __________ __________ from someone your own age. Also, you will be __________ a __________ __________ at the same time. How can you find a pen pal? Follow these directions carefully.

07

M You __________ a little __________ today.

W Oh, that's __________ __________ my new glasses. Do you think they look __________ __________ __________?

M Absolutely yes. You look even __________ in them.

W That's very __________ of you. __________ __________ __________, would you __________ me a __________?

M Of course. What is it?

W Can you __________ __________ __________ these books to the __________?

M No problem.

08

W I was wondering __________ __________ __________ on our __________.

M I consider many things: __________ __________, __________, __________, and __________.

W How do you __________ our scores?

M The mid-term test and the final-term test are __________ percent of your grade; assignments, attendance, and class participation total the remaining __________ percent.

W Will you let us __________ if we have a __________ __________?

M Of course, I will be letting you know what you need to work on.

09

M Good morning, Mom. That smells really good. It's making me __________.

W Breakfast is __________. Can you take the __________ out of the refrigerator and put it __________ __________ __________?

M Sure, I can. May I pour some milk into my glass?

W Yes. Here are some __________ and __________. Do you need some __________?

M That sounds good. And I need the __________ and __________ __________.

W I'm sorry but we've __________ __________ __________ strawberry jam.

10

W Luke, what kind of sports do you do in your __________ __________?

M I __________ __________ with my family __________ __________ when the weather is __________. And I jog __________ __________ __________.

W Good. I like table tennis. Do you play table tennis?

M Yes. I'm really __________ __________ playing it. I have a __________ __________.

W Really? Me, too!

M Why don't we play it tomorrow then?

11

W Excuse me. Is this __________ __________?

M __________. What did you say?

W Oh. Is anyone going to __________ __________ this seat?

M I don't think so. I think you can take it if you want.

W Could you ________ ________ ________ ________, so my boyfriend and I can ________ ________?

M No problem.

12

M Helen, do you ________ ________?

W Yes. Why?

M I ________ ________ ________ ________ these days. Can you give me some ________ ________ how to ________ ________ at night?

W Why don't you try not ________ ________ or ________ in the evening? Also, don't ________ ________ ________ during the day.

M Sounds helpful. ________ ________?

W I think watching TV ________ ________ ________ is not very good, either. I heard that drinking ________ ________ before going to bed, or ________ ________ ________ is also helpful.

M Thank you very much.

13

W Oh, Tony. Look! You are wearing ________ ________.

M Oh, no! People were ________ ________ me ________ ________ ________ to school, but I didn't know why.

W Didn't anyone tell you?

M No. I was very ________. Now I know why they were laughing.

W Were you ________ ________ ________?

M Yes. I woke up late. So...

W I see. You should be ________ ________ next time.

14

W Do you ________ ________? Do you want to learn ________ ________ ________? Why don't you visit our club and ________ us? Dancing ________ ________ makes you happy ________ ________ healthy and slim. You can make new friends, too. We meet at 10 o'clock ________ ________ ________ at the ABC Center ________ ________. Anyone who ________ ________ ________ dancing is welcome to come along. ________ come and join us.

15

W Jaeil, do you ________ ________?

M Yes. ________ ________?

W Can you help me with my ________ ________?

M Sure. What can I do for you?

W Please answer these ________ ________. It will take about ________ ________.

M Okay. Give me the survey.

W Thank you very much. I will ________ you ________ ________ ________ to thank you.

16

① M What are you going to do ________ ________?

W I am going to ________ ________ ________ with my friend.

② M I don't think I did very well on my

__________ __________.

W __________ __________. You can do better next time.

③ M What do you want to be when you __________ __________?

W I want to swim __________ __________ __________.

④ M Did you __________ your __________ __________?

W Not yet.

⑤ M What's your __________ __________?

W I like __________ best.

17

M Hey, Lisa. __________ __________ __________ __________?

W I'm doing great. What about you, David?

M I'm good, too. Where are you living now?

W I'm __________ __________ Los Angeles. I __________ __________ live in New York.

M I see. __________ __________ __________?

W Yes. I have one __________ and one __________.

M It's good to see you here in this __________ __________ after so long.

18

M Peter is __________ __________ his daughter, Jessica. He asks her what she __________ __________ __________ when she grows up. She says she has __________ __________. She is not interested in __________. __________ __________ __________, what will Peter most probably say to his daughter?

19

[Telephone rings.]

W Hello, __________ __________ __________ __________ Dr. Han, please?

M Sorry, but he is not here. He is __________ __________ __________ now.

W Do you know when he is __________ __________?

M __________ around 4 o'clock this afternoon. __________ __________ please?

W This is Hanna from Seoul. May I __________ __________ __________?

M Sure. Go ahead.

W Please tell him to call me back.

20

M Do you have any plans for __________ __________?

W No. I'm free. Why?

M I'm planning to __________ __________ __________ __________. Would you like to join me?

W A nursing home? What would I have to do there?

M You could chat with __________ __________. They will be very happy to talk to you.

W Sounds interesting. I'll join you.

03 Listening Test

중학영어듣기 모의고사 03회

01 대화를 듣고, 남자의 애완동물을 고르시오.

① 

② 

③ 

④ 

⑤ 

02 대화를 듣고, 여자가 가려고 하는 장소를 고르시오.

03 대화를 듣고, 여자의 심정 변화로 가장 적절한 것을 고르시오.

① sorry → worried
② happy → angry
③ scared → mad
④ sorry → pleasant
⑤ upset → relieved

04 대화를 듣고, 두 사람이 대화하는 장소로 가장 적절한 것을 고르시오.

① restaurant
② pharmacy
③ hospital
④ department store
⑤ theater

05 대화를 듣고, 안경을 쓰지 않은 여학생은 몇 명인지 고르시오.

① 5명
② 6명
③ 7명
④ 8명
⑤ 12명

06 다음을 듣고, 무엇에 관한 내용인지 고르시오.

① 세제 광고
② 세탁비 안내
③ 빨래 방법 소개
④ 세탁 서비스 광고
⑤ 웹사이트 만드는 법 소개

07 대화를 듣고, 두 사람이 대화를 마친 후 할 일로 가장 적절한 것을 고르시오.

① 손 씻기
② 머핀 사기
③ 머핀 맛 보기
④ 장보러 가기
⑤ 요리책 보기

08 대화를 듣고, 두 사람의 관계로 가장 적절한 것을 고르시오.

① 약사 — 환자
② 승무원 — 승객
③ 선생님 — 학생
④ 의사 — 환자
⑤ 택시 기사 — 승객

09 대화를 듣고, 과학 시간에 배운 내용으로 언급되지 않은 것을 고르시오.

① 뿌리
② 가지
③ 줄기
④ 잎
⑤ 꽃

10 대화를 듣고, 대화 내용과 일치하지 않는 것을 고르시오.

① 남자는 일찍 자고 일찍 일어난다.
② 남자는 밤에 영어 단어를 암기한다.
③ 여자는 늦게 잔다.
④ 여자는 자주 지각한다.
⑤ 남자는 여자에게 일찍 자라고 충고한다.

11 대화를 듣고, 남자가 할 일로 가장 적절한 것을 고르시오.

① 일본 여행 가기
② 뉴스 녹화하기
③ 부상자 치료하기
④ 돈을 기부하기
⑤ 문자 보내기

12 다음을 듣고, 무엇에 대한 사용법인지 고르시오.

① 세탁기
② 식기세척기
③ 냉장고
④ 전자레인지
⑤ 오븐

13 대화를 듣고, 여자가 운동을 시작하려는 이유로 가장 적절한 것을 고르시오.

① 건강 유지를 위해
② 헬스클럽이 새로 생겨서
③ 친구들의 권유로
④ 살을 빼기 위해
⑤ 운동선수가 되기 위해

14 대화를 듣고, 여자의 생일파티 날짜를 고르시오.

October						
Sun	Mon	Tue	Wed	Thu	Fri	Sat
		1	2	3	4	5
6	7	8	9	10	11	12
13	14	15	16	17	18	19
20	21	22	23	24	25	26
27	28	29	30	31	11/1	11/2

① 10월 5일
② 10월 12일
③ 10월 19일
④ 10월 26일
⑤ 11월 2일

15 대화를 듣고, 두 사람이 함께 할 일로 가장 적절한 것을 고르시오.

① 도서관 가기
② 반성문 쓰기
③ 편지 쓰기
④ 책 읽기
⑤ 선생님과 면담하기

16 다음을 듣고, 두 사람의 대화가 어색한 것을 고르시오.

① ② ③ ④ ⑤

17 대화를 듣고, 상황을 가장 잘 표현한 속담을 고르시오.

① 이미 엎질러진 물이다.
② 보는 것이 믿는 것이다.
③ 로마에 가면 로마의 법을 따라라.
④ 구슬이 서 말이라도 꿰어야 보배다.
⑤ 어려울 때의 친구가 진정한 친구다.

18 다음을 듣고, Becky가 Steve에게 할 말로 가장 적절한 것을 고르시오.

① It would be a great help.
② I love Italian food.
③ Why don't you make a reservation?
④ I'm really sorry. I can't meet you today.
⑤ What are you going to do during vacation?

[19-20] 대화를 듣고, 여자의 마지막 말에 이어질 남자의 응답으로 가장 적절한 것을 고르시오.

19 ① Let me explain.
② Don't worry. Be happy!
③ I'm sorry but I can't.
④ My favorite subject is math.
⑤ Don't mention it. What are friends for?

20 ① I'd love to. Let's go now.
② How often do you read books?
③ Where is the science fiction section?
④ I spend my spare time reading books.
⑤ I'm sorry. I'm not familiar with this area.

Further Study 심화 학습

● 다음은 **Listening Test 03**의 주요 지문입니다. 녹음을 다시 듣고, 질문에 대한 답을 완성하세요.

Q1
1 What kind of pet does the woman have?

↳ She has a ________________. Its color is ________________________.

It has ________________ hair and a ________________ tail.

Q3
2 Why does the man apologize to the woman?

↳ The reason is that his ____________________________ several pages out of the woman's ________________.

Q5
3 How many students have cell phones?

↳ ________________ students have cell phones.

Q9
4 Describe the structure of a plant.

↳ A plant consists of ______________, ______________ and ______________.

Q12
5 What is the first step to use the machine?

↳ ______________ the dirty ______________, ______________, and ______________ inside the ______________.

Q14
6 Why did Terra call George?

↳ The reason was that she wants to ______________ him to ________________________.

Q19
7 What is the woman's problem?

↳ She has to ______________ some ____________________________ by ______________, but ________________________.

Q20
8 What does the woman usually do in her free time?

↳ She usually ____________________________ in her free time.

정답 및 해석 p.21

● 자신의 상황에 맞게 내용을 완성하고 말해보세요.

Let's do a class survey using the questions in the table below. Write numbers in each box and tell your classmates about it.

About My Class		
Questions	Boys	Girls
How many students are there?		
How many students wear glasses?		
How many students have cell phones?		
How many students are wearing caps?		
How many students have ______________?		

There are __________ students in my class: __________ boys and __________ girls. __________ boys and __________ girls wear glasses. On the other hand, there are __________ students without glasses. __________ students have cell phones but __________ boys and __________ girls don't have one. Today, __________ students are wearing caps and there are __________ students who have ______________: __________ boys and __________ girls.

B

What do you usually do in your free time? Fill in the table below and tell your classmates about it.

My Free Time	
(1) What do you do?	
(2) When did you start to do it?	
(3) Why do you like to do it?	
(4) How do you like it?	

I'm going to talk about what I usually do in my free time. I usually (1)__________ ______________ in my free time. I first started to do it when (2)__________ ______________. I like to do it because (3)______________________.

I think (1)______________________ is (4)______________________ ______________.

03 Dictation Test

01

M Do you have a ________?

W Yes, I have a ________. Her name is Mittens.

M ________ does she ________ ________?

W She's ________ and ________. She has a ________ ________ and her hair is ________. How about you? Do you have a pet?

M Yes. I have a ________ ________ ________ is Rover.

W What does Rover look like?

M He has ________ ________ hair and a ________ tail. He's a little bit ________ but he's very active.

02

W Excuse me. Could you tell me ________ ________ ________ to Mega Box?

M Of course. Go straight for ________ blocks. You'll see AK Plaza on the ________. At that corner, ________ ________.

W Oh, wait. I walk ________ blocks and ________ ________ at AK Plaza?

M Yes. Then go ________ ________ and the theater is just ________ ________ ________. It's ________ ________ a bank.

W Okay, I go ________ ________ and the theater is just ________ ________ ________, right?

M That's ________. Enjoy the movie!

W Thanks a lot.

03

M I have to say I'm ________.

W Why? What's ________?

M My little sister ________ ________ ________ out of the ________ which ________ ________ me yesterday.

W Oh my God! What should I do? I ________ ________ without that ________.

M I can't tell you ________ ________ I am. However, as soon as I borrowed your notes, I ________ ________ of them.

04

W How can I help you?

M I think I have a ________ ________. I took some ________ but it ________ ________ at all.

W ________ ________ to be the ________?

M I have a ________ ________, and a ________ ________. Also, I can't stop ________.

W Let me see your throat.

M ________ does it ________?

W You have the ________ but it is ________ ________ ________. I'll ________ you some medicine.

05

M Let's do a class ________!

W That sounds good. Then, we have to ________ the ________ of the students first. Is there anyone ________?

M No one. We are all here so there are ________ students.

W There are ________ ________ and ________ ________, including us.

M How many students ________ ________?

W ________ ________ and ________ ________.

M How many students have a ________ ________?

W ________ except for ________.

06

W Laundry can often make you ________ and take up a lot of your ________ ________. Are you a person who ________ ________ ________? Here is good news for you. We ________ home or office pick-up services for your laundry. As we ________, ________ and ________ it separately, your laundry is not ________ with anyone else's. Also, you can ________ ________ ________ the ________ ________ ________! Please visit our website www. laundryking.co.kr. Cheap rates! Next day delivery!

07

M I want to ________ mom ________. Do you have any ________ ________?

W Why don't we make some ________ ________ for her? She likes ________ things.

M Oh, that's a good idea. But I don't know ________ ________ ________ ________. Can you help me?

W Sure. Let me check ________ we have ________ ________ ________ we need or not. [pause] Perfect. We have everything.

M Then, what should I ________ ________?

W First of all, we should ________ ________ ________.

08

M Excuse me. I am feeling a little ________.

W Oh, I see. Why don't you put ________ ________ ________ a little? Any better?

M I ________ a bit ________. Thanks.

W My pleasure. Do you ________ anything ________ ________?

M Do you have any ________ ________?

W Yes, I'll be right back. Please ________ ________ and take ________ ________.

M Thank you so much.

09

W Hi, Mike. Is it all right if I ________ ________ ________ you?

M Sure, Jennifer. I'm ________ today's lesson from science class.

W That's why you always get the ________ ________. Can I ________ you?

M Why not? We learned about the ________ of ________; the ________, ________ and the ________.

W The function of ________ was mentioned, too.

M That's right. Also, ________ like ________ and ________ are actually ________.

10

W ________ ________ do you ________ ________ ________?

M I go to bed around ________. I like to wake up ________ and ________ English words.

W What time do you get up then?

M I usually get up at ________.

W That's ________ ________. I like studying ________ ________ ________ and sleeping ________.

M That's why you're __________ __________ to class. You'd __________ go to bed __________ so you're not late again.

11

M Did you __________ the __________? A __________ __________ several cities in Japan last night.

W My goodness. Really?

M Some __________ were __________ and many people are either __________ or __________.

W That's terrible. Is there anything we can do to __________ __________ the people there?

M I heard that we can __________ __________ over the phone.

W Do you have the number?

M Yes. I will __________ it to you.

12

M First, __________ the dirty __________, __________, and __________ inside the machine. Second, put a __________ __________ of __________ into the machine. Third, __________ the machine __________. __________ __________ __________, you will hear a sound that lets you know __________ __________ __________. Then, __________ the clean dishes, pans, and glasses __________ __________ the machine.

13

W Sam, do you think I should __________ __________ __________?

M __________ __________ will be good for your __________. Why do you ask?

W Well... I am __________ __________ little by little. And all of my friends are __________. I think I'm the __________ __________ who is fat.

M Don't think like that. You __________ __________ as you are.

W Really? Thank you, Sam.

14

[Telephone rings.]

W Hello. __________ __________ __________ __________ George?

M Speaking. __________ __________?

W Hi, George. This is Terra. I'd like to __________ you to my __________ __________. Can you come?

M When is it?

W It's the __________ __________ of this __________.

M Oh, it's this Saturday! I can come. Please tell me the __________ and the __________.

W Thank you. It will be in my __________ at 2.

15

W __________ __________ __________ __________ here alone?

M I'm writing a __________ of __________.

W A letter of apology?

M Yes. My teacher told me to do it because I didn't do my __________. I had a __________ __________ __________ the right book to use.

W Oh, no. __________ __________ to the library together after this. I'll help you finish your homework.

M Really? Thank you.

W __________ __________. I'll wait for you.

16

① M When did you __________ __________ Atlanta?

W Last month.

② M __________ __________ is the TBC Bank from here?

W It's about __________ __________ __________ from here.

③ M How long __________ __________ __________ in Chicago?

W It's not long.

④ M Do you have __________ __________?

W Yes. I have a pet dog.

⑤ M __________ __________ do you ride your bike?

W Every day.

17

W Brian, can you __________ your shoes __________ before __________ __________ my house, please?

M __________, it's no problem.

W Koreans do not __________ their __________. We always take off.

M Yeah, some Westerners __________ __________ __________, but some __________.

W __________ __________ __________? Do you __________ __________ your shoes inside?

M I usually do not, but this time I will. Haha.

18

W Becky and Steve have been __________ __________ they were 7. Steve was overseas __________ and came back __________ __________ for a __________. Becky has arranged to have __________ with Steve this evening at an Italian __________ to greet him. __________, something __________ has __________ __________ at Becky's home, so she won't be able to have dinner with him. In this situation, what would Becky say to Steve?

19

M You __________ __________ __________. __________ __________ with you?

W I have to __________ these __________ __________ by tomorrow but I can't. Can you help me?

M Sure. __________ __________ __________.

W Do you think you can solve them?

M Fortunately, I can. Do you want me to explain now?

W Yes, please. I don't know __________ __________ __________ you.

M <u>Don't mention it. What are friends for?</u>

20

M Jessica, what do you usually do __________ __________ __________ __________?

W I usually __________ __________.

M What kinds of books do you like best?

W Well, I like all kinds of books, but __________ __________ is my __________.

M I __________ __________ science fiction, too. I usually read science fiction at least __________ __________ __________.

W It's nice to hear that. Why don't we go to the __________ and get some science fiction books together?

M <u>I'd love to. Let's go now.</u>

중학영어듣기 모의고사 04회 Listening Test

01 대화를 듣고, 여자의 언니를 고르시오.

①  ②   ③  ④  ⑤ 

02 대화를 듣고, 여자가 주문한 음식이 아닌 것을 고르시오.

①  ②  ③  ④  ⑤ 

03 대화를 듣고, 여자의 성격으로 가장 적절한 것을 고르시오.

① helpful ② energetic ③ negative
④ shy ⑤ selfish

04 대화를 듣고, 두 사람이 대화하는 장소로 가장 적절한 것을 고르시오.

① hotel ② hospital ③ train station
④ pharmacy ⑤ grocery store

05 대화를 듣고, 남자가 지불할 금액을 고르시오.

① $13.5 ② $15 ③ $45 ④ $50 ⑤ $60

06 다음을 듣고, 남자가 설명하려고 하는 것이 무엇인지 고르시오.

① 요리사의 고충
② 살 빼는 방법
③ 건강한 식단 준비
④ 다양한 요리법
⑤ 먹거리 안전 문제

07 대화를 듣고, 남자가 할 일로 가장 적절한 것을 고르시오.

① 녹화 파일 빌려주기
② 축구 중계방송 시청하기
③ 여자와 축구 경기장 가기
④ 비디오 테이프 구입하기
⑤ 이라크에 대해 공부하기

08 대화를 듣고, 두 사람의 관계로 가장 적절한 것을 고르시오.

① 가정교사 — 학생
② 선생님 — 학생
③ 선생님 — 선생님
④ 아빠 — 딸
⑤ 학생 — 학생

09 대화를 듣고, 여자가 제시한 집에 대해 언급되지 않은 것을 고르시오.

① 방 개수
② 위치
③ 월세
④ 전기세
⑤ 주차비

10 대화를 듣고, 대화 내용과 일치하지 않는 것을 고르시오.

① 여자가 탈 기차는 오전 11시에 출발한다.
② 여자는 10시 15분까지 기차역에 도착하면 된다고 생각한다.
③ 여자는 이미 기차표를 구매했다.
④ 여자의 집에서 기차역까지는 차로 30분 정도 걸린다.
⑤ 그들은 9시 50분에 집에서 출발할 것이다.

11 대화를 듣고, 여자가 남자에게 부탁한 일로 가장 적절한 것을 고르시오.

① 빨간 드레스 사주기
② 옷 골라주기
③ 흰색 치마 사주기
④ 탈의실 위치 알려주기
⑤ 차 태워주기

12 대화를 듣고, 여자가 공부하는 방법으로 언급되지 않은 것을 고르시오.

① 예습하기
② 복습하기
③ 일일 공부 계획 적기
④ 오답 노트 만들기
⑤ 반복하여 외우기

13 대화를 듣고, 남자가 여자에게 화가 난 이유로 가장 적절한 것을 고르시오.

① 약속 시간에 늦어서
② 말을 하지 않아서
③ 혼자 있는 걸 방해해서
④ 기다려 주지 않아서
⑤ 약속을 취소해서

14 대화를 듣고, 내용과 일치하지 않는 것을 고르시오.

	Girl	Boy
① Romance	♥	
② Thriller	♥	♥
③ Horror		♥
④ Comedy	♥	
⑤ Action	♥	♥

15 대화를 듣고, 남자의 조언으로 언급되지 않은 것을 고르시오.

① 약 먹기
② 물 많이 마시기
③ 휴식 취하기
④ 가벼운 운동 하기
⑤ 따뜻한 레몬차 마시기

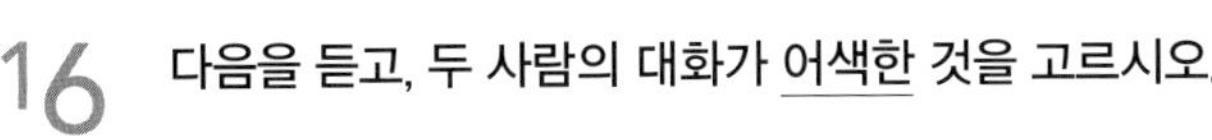

16 다음을 듣고, 두 사람의 대화가 어색한 것을 고르시오.

① ② ③ ④ ⑤

17 대화를 듣고, 대화 내용과 일치하지 않는 것을 고르시오.

① 방학 계획에 대하여 이야기하고 있다.
② 남자는 방학 동안 가족과 함께 여행을 갈 것이다.
③ 남자는 3개국 정도를 방문할 예정이다.
④ 남자는 약 2주 동안 여행을 다닐 예정이다.
⑤ 여자는 남자와 함께 유럽 여행을 갈 것이다.

18 다음을 듣고, 상황을 가장 잘 표현한 속담을 고르시오.

① No pain, no gain.
② Don't cry over the spilt milk.
③ Two heads are better than one.
④ Don't judge a book by its cover.
⑤ Don't put all your eggs in one basket.

[19-20] 대화를 듣고, 여자의 마지막 말에 이어질 남자의 응답으로 가장 적절한 것을 고르시오.

19
① Thanks. I'll tell her.
② I wish you good luck.
③ I'm sorry to hear that.
④ Are you kidding? Let me see.
⑤ Do you know where the hospital is?

20
① Don't mention it.
② Don't say that again.
③ Can I open the window?
④ I didn't know you like hot weather.
⑤ Where is the customer service center?

Further Study 심화 학습

정답 및 해석 p.28

● 다음은 **Listening Test 04**의 주요 지문입니다. 녹음을 다시 듣고, 질문에 대한 답을 완성하세요.

Q1
1 In her family photo, what does the woman look like?

↳ She has ________________, ________________ hair and wears ________________.

Q3
2 How many days do they have before the mid-term exams?

↳ They have ________________ days before the exams.

Q8
3 What is the man going to help the woman with?

↳ He is going to help her with her ________________ about the English infinitive form which is ______________________ for ______________________________.

Q10
4 What time is the woman expected to arrive at the station if there is no traffic jam?

↳ She is expected to arrive there ____________________________.

Q12
5 Why did the man say "Congratulations!" to the woman?

↳ The reason was that she is the _________________________________ again.

Q14
6 What kinds of movies do the woman and the man like?

↳ The woman likes ________________, ________________, and ________________ movies. The man likes ________________, ________________, and ________________ movies.

Q17
7 What is the man going to do during vacation?

↳ He is going to ____________________________ with ____________________________.

Q18
8 Why did the woman say the first impression of her homeroom teacher was scary?

↳ The reason was that he looked ____________________________ and ________________.

정답 및 해석 p.28

● 자신의 상황에 맞게 내용을 완성하고 말해보세요.

Imagine you are in another country for a vacation. Fill in the table below and complete the postcard.

My Vacation	
Where you are	
Describe the weather	
Describe the food	
What you did today	
What you are going to do	

Hi, there!

I'm having a wonderful time in ______________. The weather is ______________ ______________________________________. Also, the food is ______________ ____________________. Today I ______________________________________ ____. Tomorrow I'm going to ____. See you soon!

Talk about your favorite teacher. Fill in the table below and tell your classmates about it.

My Favorite Teacher	
(1) His/Her name	
(2) What he/she looks like	
(3) The subject he/she teaches	
(4) Your first impressions of him/her	
(5) Why you like him/her	

I'm going to talk about my favorite teacher. The name of my favorite teacher is (1)______________. (He/She) is (2)______________ and ______________. (He/She) is (2)______________, too. (He/She) teaches (3)______________. (His/Her) first impressions were (4)______________________________ and ______________________. I like (him/her) very much because (he/she) (5)____.

04 Dictation Test

01

W Here is my old ________ ________.

M Oh, I like it. Tell me about it.

W This is my whole family: my ________, my ________ ________, my ________ ________ and me.

M Which one are you?

W I am the one who has ________, ________ hair and ________.

M Then, who is this person that is ________ and has ________ and ________ ________?

W That's my ________ sister.

02

M May I take your ________?

W I'd like to have a ________ ________, a ________ ________, and ________ ________.

M Would you like anything to ________?

W I'll have an ________ ________, please.

M What would you like for ________?

W What do you have?

M We have apple ________, chocolate ________, and ________ and ________ ice cream.

W I'll have ________ ice cream, please.

03

W You look ________. Are you all right?

M I ________ ________ for the mid-term exams ________.

W Don't worry too much about it. You still have ________ ________ before the ________.

M But ________ ________ is ________ ________ to cover ________ subject. I don't understand math at all.

W I am almost ready for the math test. Do you ________ ________ ________?

M Really? Thank you very much.

04

M How may I help you?

W Can you ________ ________ ________?

M Yes, one moment, please.

W Okay. [pause]

M Your prescription's ________. You should take one of ________ ________ ________ ________ ________.

W Then, do I have to take them ________ ________ ________ ________?

M Exactly. ________ ________ a meal!

W Okay, I ________. How much is it?

05

W Hello, sir. May I help you?

M I'm ________ ________ a ________ for my mother.

W ________ do you ________ ________ this? It is made of ________.

M That looks ________ ________. How much is it?

W It ________ only ________ dollars.

M It's a little ________. Is it possible to get a ________?

W How about a ________ percent discount? That's the ________ that I can do.

M That's okay. I'll ________ ________.

06

M Do you _________ about having _________ _________? You know that _________ the _________ foods will help you _________ _________ and _________. Since most of you live _________, you need to prepare your own meals _________ _________. Therefore, you _________ _________ the best _________ to prepare _________ _________. Today, I am going to show you how to _________ _________ _________ and _________ ways to prepare food.

07

W Hi, Andrew. Did you have a _________ night's _________?

M No, I didn't. I really _________ _________ as I woke up _________ _________ this morning.

W _________ did you get up early?

M I _________ the _________ _________.

W You mean the game with Iraq? How was it?

M It was so _________. Do you want to see it? I _________ it.

W Really? I'd _________ _________ _________ it. Thank you.

08

M I'm happy that we're finally taking a _________.

W It's too hot here. I need something _________ _________ _________.

M Me, too. By the way, _________ was the class?

W The English infinitive form is _________ to _________. I can't do the homework about it.

M I think I'm pretty _________ _________ it. Can I _________ _________ with _________ _________?

W That would be _________. Why don't we do our _________ _________ _________?

M Okay. Let's study together _________ _________.

09

W Hello, _________ can I _________ _________ you?

M I'm looking for a _________-_________ apartment _________ _________.

W I have one. It is located right _________ the street. _________ do you need it?

M As soon as possible. Can you tell me more about the apartment you have available?

W The _________ _________ is $400. There are enough _________ _________ for every resident without _________ _________.

M Sounds good. Can I take a look at it now?

10

M What time does your _________ _________?

W It leaves at _________ in the _________.

M When do you have to be at the station?

W Just _________ _________ _________. I already _________ my ticket.

M Without heavy traffic, it takes about _________ _________ to get to the station.

W Hmm, thirty minutes…

M But it is better to be _________ than to be _________. So, why don't we leave the house at _________ _________?

W Yes, Dad.

11

M Melanie, why are you _________ _________ _________?

W Steve, I ________ ________ which one ________ ________.

M Why don't you just ________ the one ________ that you like more?

W I like this red dress and that white skirt.

M Hmm... ________ ________ ________ them both ________?

W Okay. Please tell me which one suits me better.

M All right. Go to the ________ ________ and try them.

12

M ________! You are the ________ ________ in school again.

W Thanks.

M Do you have any ________ ________ for studying?

W Well, I always ________ and ________. I also write down each day's ________ ________ in my diary.

M Anything else?

W I make a note of the ________ I ________ ________ in tests.

M Wow. I will try to ________ your ________.

13

W Aren't you going to say a ________ ________?

M There's ________ ________ ________.

W Are you ________?

M I can't say no but I'll be okay soon. Just ________ ________ ________ for a while.

W Come on. Please…

M Listen. You are never ________ ________. You always make me wait for you. I'm ________ ________ ________ ________.

W I'm very sorry. I won't be late again.

14

M ________ ________ choose a movie to ________ together ________?

W Sure. What kinds of movies do you like? I like action, ________ and ________ movies.

M I like ________ movies, too. I also like both ________ and ________ movies.

W Good. We ________ one ________ ________. Let me check if there are any action movies running now.

M If possible I'd like to see after 6 p.m.

W Okay.

15

M ________ ________ ________?

W I have a terrible headache. I can't stand it.

M Do you also ________ ________ ________?

W Yes, but it is very ________.

M Well, I think you have ________ ________ ________. It is going around.

W What should I do, then?

M ________ this ________, drink a lot of ________ and ________ lots of ________. Drinking warm ________ ________ would be helpful, too.

W OK. Thank you.

16

① W What do you think of this ________?

M It ________ ________ and ________.

② W ________ ________ do you play the piano?

M Every day.

③ W ________ ________ ________ do you have to write down?

M About 7 pages.

④ W How was your ________?

M I'm going to see a concert on the weekend.

⑤ W How may I help you?

M No. I'm just ________ ________.

17

W Are you ________ ________ this vacation?

M I'm planning to ________ ________ ________ ________ my ________.

W Really? Fantastic! What countries are you going to?

M We are ________ ________ ________ France, Switzerland, and Italy.

W Wow. ________ ________ are you going to be away?

M For about two weeks.

W ________ ________! I wish I could go with you.

18

W I want to talk about my ________ ________. ________, my ________ ________ ________ ________ was quite ________. He looked really ________ and ________. My classmates and I were ________. However, as time passed, we found out that he has a ________ ________ and is ________ ________ ________. All of the students in my class like him very much. So do I.

19

M Hi, Amy. Where are you going?

W I'm ________ ________ ________ to the hospital.

M Why? Are you sick?

W No, not me. My grandmother is ________ ________ ________.

M Oh, no. ________ ________ ________ ________?

W She ________ ________ the tiles in the bathroom this morning and she ________ her ________ ________.

M I'm sorry to hear that.

20

M Oh, no! I ________ ________. It's so hot in here.

W Why don't you ________ ________ the ________ ________? Here is the ________ ________.

M Unfortunately, it's ________ ________ ________. I have been meaning to fix it but I have been too busy ________.

W What should we do?

M ________ ________ ________ if I opened the window?

W Pardon?

M Can I open the window?

중학영어듣기 모의고사 05회 Listening Test

01 대화를 듣고, 그림에서 Mike를 고르시오.

02 대화를 듣고, 남자가 사려고 하는 것을 고르시오.

03 대화를 듣고, 남자의 심정으로 가장 적절한 것을 고르시오.

① hopeful ② excited ③ embarrassed
④ lonely ⑤ envious

04 대화를 듣고, 두 사람이 대화하는 장소로 가장 적절한 것을 고르시오.

① airplane ② airport ③ taxi
④ bus ⑤ subway

05 대화를 듣고, 남자가 받게 될 1달러짜리 지폐가 몇 장인지 고르시오.

① 5장 ② 7장 ③ 10장 ④ 15장 ⑤ 20장

06 **다음을 듣고, 무엇에 관한 설명인지 고르시오.**

① 좋은 첫인상을 남기는 방법
② 자기 소개에 필요한 내용
③ 말을 잘하는 방법
④ 자기 소개의 중요성
⑤ 친구를 사귀는 방법

07 **대화를 듣고, 여자가 할 일로 가장 적절한 것을 고르시오.**

① 머리 자르기
② 남자와 함께 영화 보러 가기
③ 남자와 함께 미용실 가기
④ 남자와 함께 곰인형 사러 가기
⑤ 여동생의 머리 손질해주기

08 **대화를 듣고, 두 사람의 관계로 가장 적절한 것을 고르시오.**

① 엄마 — 아들
② 아빠 — 딸
③ 선생님 — 학부모
④ 사장 — 직원
⑤ 교장선생님 — 선생님

09 **대화를 듣고, 여자가 좋아하는 과일로 언급되지 않은 것을 고르시오.**

① 체리
② 수박
③ 씨 없는 포도
④ 오렌지
⑤ 자몽

10 **대화를 듣고, 대화 내용과 일치하지 않는 것을 고르시오.**

① 여자는 비 오는 날에 침대에 누워 TV 보는 것을 좋아한다.
② 남자는 비 오는 날 산책하면 외로움을 느낀다.
③ 남자는 야외에서 빗방울 소리를 듣는 것을 좋아한다.
④ 남자는 비에 조금 젖는 것은 크게 개의치 않는다.
⑤ 여자는 비 오는 날 밖에 나가는 것을 좋아하지 않는다.

11 대화를 듣고, 여자가 남자에게 부탁한 일로 가장 적절한 것을 고르시오.

① 사진 찍어주기
② 소풍 같이 가기
③ 블로그에 사진 올려주기
④ 휴대전화로 사진 보내주기
⑤ 컴퓨터 고쳐주기

12 대화를 듣고, 남자가 환불을 받기 위해 해야 할 일을 고르시오.

① 홈페이지에서 취소하기
② 서점 방문하기
③ 환불 요청 이메일 보내기
④ 책을 보내주기
⑤ 영수증 사진 전송하기

13 대화를 듣고, 여자가 기뻐하는 이유를 고르시오.

① 바닷가에 가게 되어서
② 날씨가 좋아서
③ 아이스 커피가 맛있어서
④ 예쁜 컵을 갖게 되어서
⑤ 남자가 행복해 해서

14 다음을 듣고, 안내문의 내용과 일치하지 않는 것을 고르시오.

Deli House Restaurant

Open daily from 11 a.m. to 10 p.m.
Enjoy our fresh seafood buffet
23 Main Street, Los Angeles
☎ 310-231-3456

① ② ③ ④ ⑤

15 대화를 듣고, 두 사람이 환경보호를 위해 가장 먼저 할 수 있는 일을 고르시오.

① 재활용 하기
② 전등 끄기
③ 분리수거 하기
④ 지하철 타기
⑤ 버스 타기

16 다음을 듣고, 두 사람의 대화가 어색한 것을 고르시오.

① ② ③ ④ ⑤

17 대화를 듣고, 여자에 대한 설명으로 일치하지 않는 것을 고르시오.

① 교환학생 프로그램에 대해 알아보고 있다.
② 영국에 교환학생으로 가고 싶어 했다.
③ 뉴질랜드로 가는 것은 비싸서 포기했다.
④ 어디로 교환학생으로 갈지 아직 못 정했다.
⑤ 삼촌이 뉴질랜드에서 살고 있다.

18 다음을 듣고, Nikko가 지현이에게 할 말로 가장 적절한 것을 고르시오.

① Let's split the bill.
② Do you tip in Korea?
③ How much is the food?
④ I don't know what else to say but thank you.
⑤ I have really enjoyed the sightseeing and the food today.

[19-20] 대화를 듣고, 남자의 마지막 말에 이어질 여자의 응답으로 가장 적절한 것을 고르시오.

19
① I want to go to China.
② How was your trip to Europe?
③ I don't know why you are so excited.
④ Let's check our schedule to see when we can go.
⑤ I am writing a letter to send to a radio program.

20
① It's 2:15 right now.
② I like jogging in the park.
③ I usually go to bed around 10 o'clock.
④ I stayed up until 1 o'clock in the morning.
⑤ I bought a new bed and it's very comfortable.

Further Study 심화 학습

정답 및 해석 p.35

● 다음은 Listening Test 05의 주요 지문입니다. 녹음을 다시 듣고, 질문에 대한 답을 완성하세요.

Q3
1 Where is the woman planning to go? And how long is she going for?

↳ She is planning to go to ______________ for ______________ days and ______________ nights.

Q5
2 How does the woman break the hundred-dollar bill finally?

↳ She breaks it into ______________ twenties, ______________ tens, ______________ fives and ______________ ones.

Q8
3 How did the boy break the vase on his teacher's desk?

↳ He did it by mistake because he ______________________ a desk leg and ______________________.

Q10
4 What does the man like to do on a rainy day?

↳ He likes to __________________________________ in the rain.

Q11
5 Where did the man upload the pictures?

↳ He ______________ them to ____________________________.

Q13
6 What does the man want to do at the beach?

↳ He wants to ______________ on the ______________ and drink a cup of ______________________.

Q17
7 What is the woman looking at?

↳ She is looking at a ____.

Q19
8 How did the man win two tickets to Europe?

↳ He entered a ______________ on a __________________________________ and he was chosen as the ______________.

정답 및 해석 p.35

- 자신의 상황에 맞게 내용을 완성하고 말해보세요.

Write about your favorite song. Fill in the table below and tell your classmates about it.

My Favorite Song	
(1) The title of the song	
(2) The singer of the song	
(3) The theme of the song	
(4) Reasons you like the song	

The song I like most is (1)____________________. It is sung by (2)____________. The song is about the fact that (3)____.

I like this song because (4)____.

B

If you have a chance to study abroad, which country would you like to go to? Fill in the table below and tell your classmates about it.

If I Had a Chance to Study Abroad...	
(1) Which country would you like to go?	
(2) Why do you want to go there?	
(3) What language do they speak?	
(4) Can you speak the language?	
(5) Does anyone you know live there?	

If I had a chance to study abroad, I would like to go to (1)__________. The reasons why I would like to study there are that I could (2)__________________, __________________, and __________________. People in the country speak (3)__________. I can speak (4)__________________. Actually, (5)____________________________________. I wish I could go to (1)__________ and study there one day.

05 Dictation Test

01

W Hey, look at Joe! He's __________ again.

M Well, as his mom is __________ at the moment, he has to __________ __________ __________ his little brothers. He must be really __________.

W Sam is __________, too. He is __________.

M Look at Mike. He's __________ about the __________ on the __________.

W Yeah, because Jessica is __________ a __________ __________ who looks like Jimmy.

M It sure looks like Jimmy.

02

M Excuse me, can you help me? I want to buy a __________ for my __________ old __________.

W How about this __________ __________ __________? It is really popular with kids.

M Hmm. What about this __________?

W It's nice but he might be __________ __________ for it.

M Oh, I see.

W Then, how about that __________ __________ that the __________ __________ over there is __________ with?

M That would be great. My nephew will love it. I'll take that one.

03

W Our family is planning to go to __________ during the summer vacation.

M That sounds __________. How long are you going for?

W My parents want to go for __________ days and __________ nights.

M I __________ I __________ __________ __________ a __________ like you.

W I __________ you do something fun, too.

M Will you __________ __________ back a souvenir?

W Of course I will.

04

M Good evening. __________ would you like to go?

W Can you __________ __________ to Kimpo Airport?

M Sure. Are you going to __________ a __________?

W Yes. It's a __________ o'clock flight. I have to be there by __________ o'clock. So can you drive __________ __________ __________ __________?

M Oh, we are in a __________ __________ now, but I will __________ __________ __________.

W Thank you.

05

W How can I help you?

M Can you __________ a __________ -dollar bill for me?

W Of course. __________ do you want it?

M Can I get __________ twenties, __________ tens, and __________ __________ in ones?

W I am afraid that I don't have __________ one-dollar bills. Are __________ fives fine with you?

M That's __________ __________.

W Here you go.

06

M How you __________ __________ to others is __________. First impressions can __________ either a __________ or __________ __________ of you. Here are two pieces of advice for __________ a __________ __________ __________. First, always begin with a __________. Second, try to speak an __________ __________ in the conversation. No one likes a person who talks by himself or herself the __________ __________.

07

W Your hair is getting __________ __________.

M I know. My little sister says I look like a __________ with __________ __________.

W I agree with her. Why don't you __________ __________ __________?

M Okay, then how about I get it cut like Won Bin's in the movie *The Man from Nowhere*?

W Wow! I think that hairstyle would __________ __________ you.

M Do you want to __________ __________ with me?

W __________. __________ __________ right now!

08

W I received a phone call from __________ __________ today.

M Oh, no. __________ did she __________?

W She said __________ __________ a vase on her desk. Is it true?

M Yes, but I didn't do it __________ __________.

W What happened then?

M When I passed by Dave's desk, I __________ one of its legs and __________ __________, breaking the vase.

W Weren't you hurt? You need to be __________ __________.

09

M What is your __________ __________, Kelly?

W I love all kinds of fruit.

M So do I. But which fruit do you like the __________?

W Well, I like __________ very much.

M __________ __________ types of fruit do you like?

W I love __________, __________, and __________ __________. What about you?

M I __________ __________ __________ apples and watermelons.

10

M __________ do you like to do on __________ __________?

W I like to __________ __________ __________ and __________ __________ all day. I feel __________ on rainy days. How about you?

M I like to __________ __________ __________ in the rain. It makes me __________ __________.

W Don't you get __________?

M __________ __________. However, it is __________ __________ to listen to the sound of raindrops outside. Why don't you __________ __________ sometime?

W __________ __________!

11

W I heard that you __________ __________ when we __________ __________ the __________.

M Yes. I __________ most of them to my __________.

W My __________ was __________ last week, so it's hard for me to __________ the __________.

M I see. Why don't you get it fixed then?

W I will, but could you __________ some of the __________ to my __________ __________, please?

M Sure.

W Thank you. I can't wait to see them.

12

[Telephone rings.]

W Hello, Bonnie Books. __________ __________ I help you?

M Hello. I ordered a book from your __________, and I __________ it today.

W Uh-huh.

M However, you sent me the __________ one.

W Oh, I'm sorry. Do you want your __________ __________ or would you like to __________ it?

M I'd like to __________ __________ __________.

W Okay. Send us the book and we will give you your money back. __________ __________ the __________.

13

M What a __________ day!

W I wish that I were at the beach.

M __________ on the beach and __________ a cup of __________ __________ would be __________.

W How about going to the beach this __________? Are you busy?

M I have __________ __________ yet. Are you __________?

W Yes. We haven't gone on a trip for __________ __________.

M Yeah, you're __________. Let's go.

W I am so happy.

14

① W The restaurant __________ at 11 in the evening.

② W The restaurant __________ at 11 in the morning.

③ W The restaurant is a __________ __________.

④ W The restaurant is at 23 Main Street, Los Angeles.

⑤ W People can __________ the restaurant at 310-231-3456.

15

W What do you think we can do to __________ our __________ __________?

M Well. There are many things we can do.

W Like what? __________ __________?

M That would be one thing. We should __________ __________ lights when we leave rooms. We should also __________ __________, __________ and __________.

W Anything else?

M We can __________ __________ __________ or __________ instead of cars.

W Oh, we can do the first before we leave.

16

① M When's your __________?
W It's on June 8th.

② M __________ are you __________?
W I'm from Jeju Island.

③ M Can I __________ this __________?
W Sure, go ahead.

④ M What do you want to be when you

__________ __________?

W I want to be a __________ __________.

⑤ M What's your __________ __________?

W I hate __________.

17

M Are you looking at the student __________ __________?

W Yeah. It's hard to __________ where to go.

M Weren't you __________ __________ Britain?

W I was. But it's too __________ there, so I __________ __________ __________ on going there.

M Which __________ are in your mind then?

W I might go to New Zealand, because my uncle lives there.

M That's good.

W Yeah, I think I can __________ __________ __________ __________ him if I go there.

18

M Nikko is visiting Jihyun, one of her Korean friends, in Seoul. Jihyun has taken her to __________ __________ __________. They've visited places like the Han River, N Seoul Tower, 63 Building, and Yeouido Park. Now they are at a __________ __________ located in Gwanghwamun. They've __________ __________ a nice dinner, and they are about to leave. Nikko is __________ whether she has to __________ __________ __________ for the waiter on the table or not. In this situation, what would she say to Jihyun?

19

M Hooray! I __________ __________ this.

W What is it? Why are you so __________?

M I __________ a __________ on a __________ __________ last month. __________, they chose me as the __________.

W Really?

M YES! And I won two __________ to Europe. That means we can go to Europe __________ __________.

W Let's check our schedule to see when we can go.

20

M Honey, the sun is __________ __________ in the sky. It's time to __________ __________.

W I am so __________. Can I __________ __________ __________ for 20 more minutes?

M Didn't you say that you will __________ __________ in the park this week?

W No, not today. I will start next week.

M __________ __________ did you go to bed __________ __________?

W I stayed up until 1 o'clock in the morning.

06 중학영어듣기 모의고사 06회 Listening Test

01 대화를 듣고, Minnie를 찾은 장소를 고르시오.

①  ②  ③  ④  ⑤ 

02 대화를 듣고, 여자가 가고자 하는 곳을 고르시오.

03 대화를 듣고, 남자의 성격으로 가장 적절한 것을 고르시오.

① generous ② rude ③ selfish
④ strict ⑤ careful

04 대화를 듣고, 두 사람이 대화하는 장소로 가장 적절한 것을 고르시오.

① toy shop ② convenience store ③ library
④ community center ⑤ museum

05 대화를 듣고, 오늘 날짜를 고르시오.

① 4월 23일 ② 5월 3일 ③ 5월 13일
④ 8월 14일 ⑤ 8월 24일

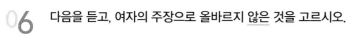

정답 및 해석 p.36

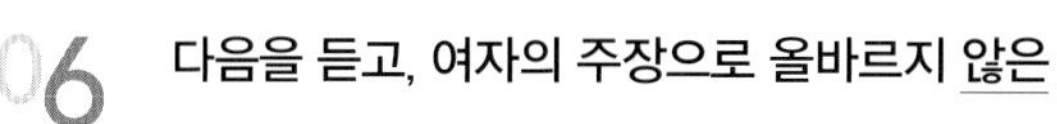

06 **다음을 듣고, 여자의 주장으로 올바르지 않은 것을 고르시오.**

① 자원을 아껴 써야 한다.
② 사용한 물자를 재활용해야 한다.
③ 자원 낭비는 환경 오염을 일으킨다.
④ 자원의 양은 한정되어 있다.
⑤ 병이나 캔을 사용하지 않아야 한다.

07 **대화를 듣고, 여자가 주말에 할 일로 가장 적절한 것을 고르시오.**

① 남자와 영화 보러 가기
② 남자와 도서관에 가기
③ 집에서 책 읽기
④ 남자의 집 방문하기
⑤ 친구들과 외출하기

08 **대화를 듣고, 두 사람의 관계로 가장 적절한 것을 고르시오.**

① 의사 — 간호사
② 간호사 — 환자
③ 교수 — 학생
④ 변호사 — 의뢰인
⑤ 여행사 직원 — 손님

09 **대화를 듣고, 남자가 사고 싶어하는 것과 그 이유를 고르시오.**

① 카메라 — 유행이 지나서
② 휴대전화 — 통화 품질이 떨어져서
③ 카메라 — 성능이 떨어져서
④ 휴대전화 — 사진을 더 잘 찍기 위해서
⑤ 카메라 — 고장이 나서

10 **대화를 듣고, 대화 내용과 일치하지 않는 것을 고르시오.**

① 남자는 버스에서 필통을 잃어버렸다.
② 남자는 수업 시간에 지각했다.
③ 여자는 남자에게 연필을 빌려줬다.
④ 남자는 여자와 교과서를 같이 볼 것이다.
⑤ 남자의 가방에는 아무것도 없다.

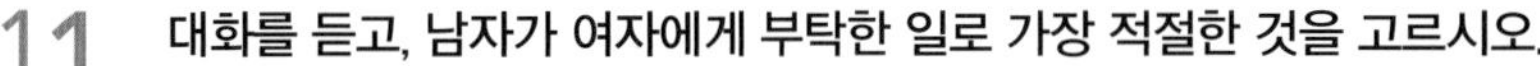

11 대화를 듣고, 남자가 여자에게 부탁한 일로 가장 적절한 것을 고르시오.

① 호텔 객실 예약
② 체크인 시간 확인
③ 퇴실 시간 연장
④ 호텔 위치 안내
⑤ 비행기 시간 변경

12 다음을 듣고, 무엇에 대한 사용법인지 고르시오.

① 토스터
② 전자레인지
③ 가스레인지
④ 전기 밥솥
⑤ 냉장고

13 대화를 듣고, 남자가 화가 난 이유를 고르시오.

① 노트북 컴퓨터를 잃어버려서
② 노트북 컴퓨터의 데이터가 손상돼서
③ 컴퓨터 수리비가 비싸서
④ 친구와 말다툼을 해서
⑤ 리포트 과제가 너무 많아서

14 다음을 듣고, 내용과 일치하지 않는 것을 고르시오.

Grand Opening!
Waves Fitness Center

① Opening Date	: August 20th
② Location	: 2nd floor, Guro Station
③ Business Hours	: 6 a.m. to 11 p.m.
④ Special Offer	: Free locker
	: Free workout clothes and towels
⑤ Membership Fee	: 35,000 won per month

15 대화를 듣고, 두 사람이 방과 후 할 일로 가장 적절한 것을 고르시오.

① 핼러윈 복장 사러 가기
② 핼러윈 파티 참석하기
③ 도서관 가기
④ 숙제 하기
⑤ 핼러윈 파티 계획하기

16 다음을 듣고, 두 사람의 대화가 어색한 것을 고르시오.

① ② ③ ④ ⑤

17 대화를 듣고, 대화 내용과 일치하지 않는 것을 고르시오.

① 여자는 여행책자를 보고 있다.
② 남자는 라스베이거스에 가본 적이 없다.
③ 여자는 라스베이거스가 멋진 도시라고 생각한다.
④ 두 사람은 휴가 때 라스베이거스를 방문할 것이다.
⑤ 두 사람은 여행 경비에 대해선 관심이 없다.

18 다음을 듣고, Cathy가 이웃에게 할 말로 가장 적절한 것을 고르시오.

① Why don't you listen to me?
② I have an important meeting. Wish me luck.
③ Your music is too loud. Please turn it down.
④ Please wake me up at 7 o'clock in the morning.
⑤ I like this music. What's the name of the song?

[19-20] 대화를 듣고, 남자의 마지막 말에 이어질 여자의 응답으로 가장 적절한 것을 고르시오.

19
① I'm not very good at math.
② I hope you will like math one day.
③ Why do you want to be a math teacher?
④ Solving math questions is very difficult for me.
⑤ Come on. Let's do our math homework together.

20
① All right. Go away.
② Okay, never mind. I'll take care of it.
③ I'm sorry. I have to go to the gym now.
④ I love working out, too. Can I join you sometime?
⑤ Well, if you take a good rest, you will feel much better.

정답 및 해석 p.42

- 다음은 **Listening Test 06**의 주요 지문입니다. 녹음을 다시 듣고, 질문에 대한 답을 완성하세요.

Q2
1 Where does the woman want to go?
↳ She wants to go to the ______________________________.

Q3
2 What is the man going to buy the woman and why?
↳ He is going to buy her __________ because she didn't ______________ ____________.

Q7
3 What does the woman usually do when she goes out with her friends?
↳ She usually _________________________ and sometimes __________ ________________ with her friends.

Q8
4 When is the man supposed to see the doctor?
↳ He is supposed to see the doctor this _____________________________.

Q12
5 What happens if you put metal inside the home appliance?
↳ It will cause ____________ and might start ______________________.

Q15
6 Where and when are the man and the woman going to meet?
↳ They are going to meet at ___________________________ in _______ ____________.

Q19
7 What does the woman want to be when she grows up and why?
↳ She wants to be __________________ because _________________ ________ releases __________________.

Q20
8 Why is the man walking so slow?
↳ The reason is that ______________________.

정답 및 해석 p.42

● 자신의 상황에 맞게 내용을 완성하고 말해보세요.

Complete the conversation using the directions in the table below.

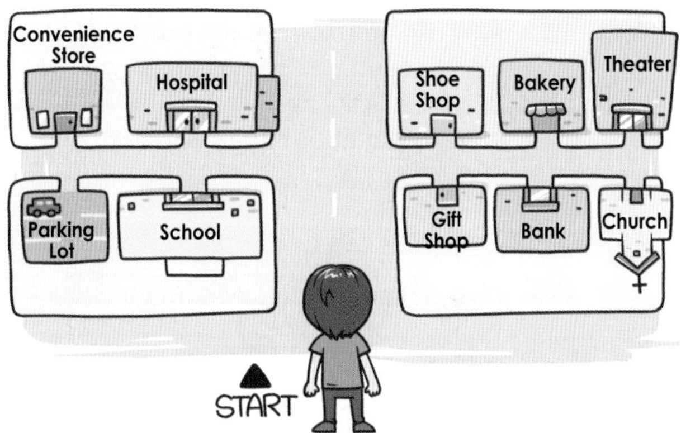

Directions
(1) Go straight for one/two block(s). (2) Turn right/left. (3) on your right/left (4) across from, next to

M: Excuse me. How can I get to the nearest ____________?

W: (1)____________________ and (2)____________________.

You will see it (3)______________. It's (4)____________________.

You can't miss it.

Please make an invitation card for your birthday. Fill in the card below and tell your classmates about it.

YOU ARE INVITED

You are invited to my ________th Birthday Party!
Please come and celebrate with me!!!

(1) Date: ____________________
(2) Time: ____________________
(3) Theme (color): ____________________
(4) Place: ____________________
(5) Contact No.: ____________________

I would like to invite you to my ____________th birthday party. It will be on (1)________________ at (2)________________. The theme color is (3)____________, so if you have anything in (3)____________, please wear or carry it with you. The place will be at (4)____________________. You can contact me on (5)____________________. Please come and enjoy! I will be looking forward to seeing you.

06 Dictation Test

01

M Mom! I can't find Minnie _________. She isn't in the _________ _________, and in the _________.

W What about the _________ _________? You know she likes to _________ there.

M No, she's _________ there, _________.

W Don't worry too much. I'm sure she's somewhere.

M What if she's _________? What should I do?

W Oh, look! There she is. She's _________ _________ _________!

02

W Excuse me, sir. Can you tell me where the _________ _________ _________ is?

M Sure. Go down _________ block and _________ _________.

W _________ block _________ and _________ _________?

M Yes, you will find it _________ _________ _________. It's the _________ building from the corner. You _________ _________ it.

W Thank you for helping me.

M Not at all.

03

M It's already 1 o'clock. Let's _________ _________ for lunch.

W Can I _________ some money from you? I _________ _________ my _________ to work today.

M You don't need to. I'll _________ _________ _________.

W Are you sure? You are so _________.

M And I look handsome, too?

W Of course, you do. So, _________ are you _________ _________?

M What about Sue's Kitchen?

04

W May I help you?

M I _________ _________ the _________ that I want to read.

W Did you check the database?

M Yes, it said the book was _________ _________ _________ but it was _________ _________.

W Maybe we have _________ it. We'll get a _________ copy of it soon. Do you want me to _________ _________ _________ _________?

M Yes, please. Thanks a lot.

05

W _________ is your _________?

M Mine is on _________ the _________. How about yours?

W My birthday is on _________ the _________.

M Oh, there are _________ _________ left until _________ _________. Are you planning to _________ _________ _________?

W Yes, I am. Would you like to _________ _________ my birthday party?

M That would be great. Thank you _________ _________ _________.

06

W Our earth has a _________ amount of _________. If we _________ _________ but just ________ our resources, there will be ________ materials that our grandchildren ________ ________. Also, wasting resources can ________ the environment, so we have to ________ the materials we have used. When we recycle cans, bottles, and paper, we are ________ resources ________ ________ ________.

07

M Do you like to ________ ________?

W Yes. I like to go out with my friends. What about you?

M I love to ________ ________, reading ________ or ________ ________. Where do you usually go out?

W We usually ________ ________ ________ ________. Sometimes we go to the ________ to read books.

M Would you like to ________ ________ ________ ________ this Saturday, then? I have lots of interesting ________ and ________.

W That would be great.

08

[Telephone rings.]

W Hello. Dr. Kim's office.

M I'd like to make an ________ for an ________ ________, please.

W Have you ________ the doctor ________?

M No, I haven't.

W Can I have ________ ________ please, sir?

M ________ ________ Mike Park.

W All right. How about this ________ ________ at 2?

09

M I need a ________ ________ ________, mom.

W Why? Is yours ________? I just bought it for you a few months ago.

M A few months? No. It has been almost ________ ________. I can't take ________ with it very well.

W I bought you a cell phone, ________ a ________. There is ________ ________ with ________ calls, and sending ________ ________, right?

M But mom, please.

W My answer is no.

10

W Why were you ________ for class?

M I ________ the bus. Oh, I ________ to bring my pencil case. Can you ________ ________ ________ ________?

W Of course. Here you are.

M I didn't bring my ________, either. Can you ________ ________ with me?

W Sure. Then ________ did you bring in your bag today?

M ________. Something is ________ with me today.

11

W ________ ________. May I help you?

M What is the ________ time here?

W It's ________ o'clock. I mean ________.

M I see. Is it possible to ________ the checkout time? My ________ is at 7 p.m.

W Sure. When do you want to check out then?

M ________ ________, at 3 o'clock, please.

12

M This is a very ________ ________ ________ that almost every household has. This will warm up ________ not only ________ but also ________. What you have to do is open the door, place some food on the ________, close the door, ________ the timing ________, and press the start button. You should use a ________ ________ and should not put ________ inside this appliance. Metal will cause ________ and might start a ________.

13

W Are you okay? You ________ ________.

M My friend ________ ________ on my laptop computer.

W My goodness. Did you take it to the ________ ________?

M Yes. But the ________ said that he can't ________ my ________. Even worse, I didn't back my data up.

W I'm so ________ to hear that.

M Now I have to ________ ________ my final report.

14

W Waves Fitness Center opening on August 28th. We ________ ________ ________ the second floor of Guro ________. Our ________ ________ are ________ 6 in the morning ________ 11 at night. We ________ you a free ________, ________ ________ and ________. Our ________ ________ is 35,000 won per month. Please come and join us. We will ________ ________ ________ ________ seeing you!

15

W Would you like to ________ ________ with me ________ ________?

M Sure. What do you want to buy?

W I want to buy a ________ for the Halloween ________.

M Oh, I have to buy one, too. I ________ ________ about that. Thanks for ________ me.

W You're welcome. I'm so ________ ________ the party.

M ________ ________. Let's meet at the school ________ in 10 minutes. I have to ________ ________ the library quickly.

W Okay.

16

① W How do you like this ________?

M It's so ________.

② W Where are you going?

M I'm ________ ________ ________ to a meeting.

③ W Would you like to ________ ________ on the weekend?

M Of course I would.

④ W When's your ________?

M It's on ________ 28th.

⑤ W Are you ________?

M No, I have a ________.

17

W ________ ________ ________ ________ ________ Las Vegas?

M No, I haven't. Why?

W I'm looking at a __________ __________ and the city looks __________.

M Yeah, I saw it on TV. If I have a __________, I really want to go.

W Why don't we __________ __________ __________ to go there during this vacation? They offer a __________ __________ for the __________ __________ reservations.

M Sounds great. Let's do that.

18

M It's 3 o'clock __________ __________ __________. Cathy is __________ __________ __________ trying to go to sleep. However, she hears __________ __________ coming from next door. She is trying to __________ the noise, but she can't. She has an __________ __________ tomorrow, so she needs to __________ __________ right away. She has no more __________, and wants the __________ to know that she is annoyed. In this situation, what would Cathy most likely say to the neighbor?

19

M What do you want to be when you __________ __________?

W I want to be a __________ __________. __________ math problems helps to __________ my __________.

M Really? That sounds __________. Doesn't it give you more stress when you can't answer them?

W __________ __________ __________. I enjoy using __________ for finding answers very much.

M Really? That sounds strange. I __________ math.

W I hope you will like math one day.

20

M I started __________ __________ this morning. I feel like I'm __________ already.

W Haha. Already? But why are you walking so slow?

M __________, my __________ __________ all over. I think I worked out __________ __________.

W Oh, no. You shouldn't do that. __________ since today was your first day.

M I'm __________ it now. I don't know what I am __________ to do.

W Well, if you take a good rest, you will feel much better.

중학영어듣기 모의고사 07회

Listening Test

01 다음을 듣고, 지금 날씨로 가장 적절한 것을 고르시오.

① 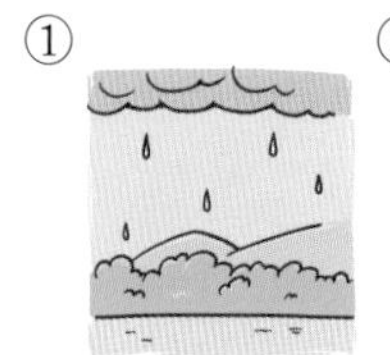 ②  ③  ④  ⑤ 

02 대화를 듣고, 남자가 사려고 하는 넥타이를 고르시오.

①  ②  ③  ④   ⑤ 

03 대화를 듣고, 남자가 놀라워하는 이유로 가장 적절한 것을 고르시오.

① 호주는 크리스마스가 여름이어서
② 호주는 크리스마스를 기념하지 않아서
③ 여자가 크리스마스를 보내는 방식이 독특해서
④ 한국과 호주의 계절이 매우 비슷해서
⑤ 여자의 고향이 호주라고 해서

04 대화를 듣고, 여자의 직업으로 가장 적절한 것을 고르시오.

① 입국 심사관 ② 경찰 ③ 승무원
④ 여행사 직원 ⑤ 사업가

05 대화를 듣고, 남자가 구입할 장미가 몇 송이인지 고르시오.

① 2송이 ② 11송이 ③ 12송이 ④ 24송이 ⑤ 36송이

06 다음을 듣고, 남자의 주장으로 알맞은 것을 고르시오.

① 애완동물에게 먹이를 잘 줘야 한다.
② 애완동물의 청결에 관심을 가져야 한다.
③ 애완동물을 기르는 것은 신중하게 결정해야 한다.
④ 애완동물에 너무 빠지는 것은 좋지 않다.
⑤ 자신의 기호에 따라 애완동물을 결정해야 한다.

07 대화를 듣고, 여자가 일요일에 한 일을 고르시오.

① 영어 교과서 찾기
② 아버지와 세차하기
③ 영어 숙제 하기
④ 조부모님 댁 방문하기
⑤ 하루 종일 공부하기

08 대화를 듣고, 두 사람의 관계로 가장 적절한 것을 고르시오.

① 아파트 관리인 — 입주민
② 택배 직원 — 고객
③ 백화점 직원 — 고객
④ 통신사 직원 — 고객
⑤ 사장 — 직원

09 다음을 듣고, 그림의 상황에 어울리는 대화를 고르시오.

① ② ③ ④ ⑤

10 대화를 듣고, 대화 내용과 일치하는 것을 고르시오.

① 여자는 현재 캐나다에서 살고 있다.
② 여자는 3주간의 해외여행을 다녀왔다.
③ 여자는 나이아가라 폭포를 보지 못한 것을 아쉬워한다.
④ 여자는 캐나다의 풍경에 깊은 인상을 받았다.
⑤ 여자는 기후가 맞지 않아 여행이 즐겁지 못했다.

11 대화를 듣고, 남자가 여자에게 부탁한 일로 가장 적절한 것을 고르시오.

① 생일 파티에 초대해 주기
② 소설책 추천해 주기
③ 소설책 빌려주기
④ 생일 파티 함께 준비하기
⑤ 음식 맛 보기

12 다음을 듣고, 상담원과 연결을 원할 때 눌러야 하는 것을 고르시오.

① 1번 ② 2번 ③ 3번 ④ # ⑤ 0번

13 대화를 듣고, 남자가 책을 빌려줄 수 없는 이유를 고르시오.

① 책을 가져오지 않아서
② 친구가 잃어버려서
③ 지금 사용해야 해서
④ 다른 친구에게 빌려줘서
⑤ 낙서를 많이 해 놓아서

14 다음을 듣고, 내용과 일치하지 <u>않는</u> 것을 고르시오.

Clearance Sale!!

① Hello Mart
② From May 1st to May 7th
③ Up to 18% off
④ Store hours: 10 a.m. to midnight
⑤ No reward points available during this period

15 대화를 듣고, 두 사람이 내일 할 일을 고르시오.

① 축구 경기 보러 가기
② 이사하기
③ 축구 경기 표 예매하기
④ 이사할 집 알아보기
⑤ 축구 경기 표 팔기

16 다음을 듣고, 두 사람의 대화가 어색한 것을 고르시오.

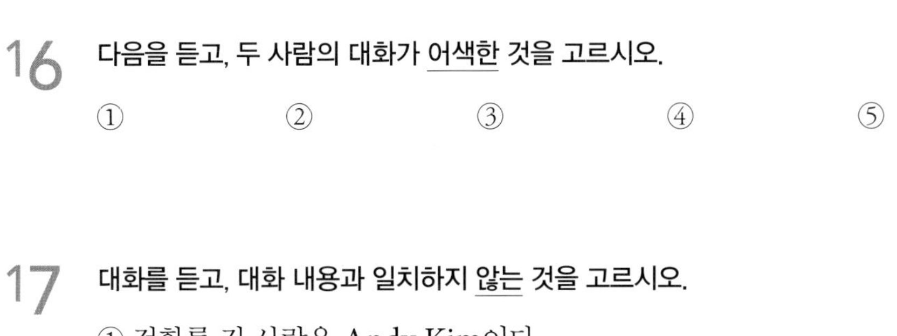

① ② ③ ④ ⑤

17 대화를 듣고, 대화 내용과 일치하지 않는 것을 고르시오.

① 전화를 건 사람은 Andy Kim이다.
② 남자는 Dr. Wilson과 통화를 원한다.
③ 남자가 찾는 사람은 현재 자리에 없다.
④ 남자의 원래 약속 시간은 오늘 오후 5시이다.
⑤ 남자는 여자와의 약속을 취소하고 싶어한다.

18 다음을 듣고, 선생님이 Tony에게 할 말로 가장 적절한 것을 고르시오.

① How was the lecture?
② Please take this medicine.
③ You always have to tell the truth.
④ Why don't you go to the hospital?
⑤ You can't get good grades if you don't make an effort.

[19-20] 대화를 듣고, 남자의 마지막 말에 이어질 여자의 응답으로 가장 적절한 것을 고르시오.

19
① Please explain the course again.
② Let's sign up for Dr. Michael's class.
③ I didn't do well on the pop quiz.
④ Okay. Oh, he is coming now.
⑤ This is the second time I've taken Dr. Michael's class.

20
① I didn't bring my umbrella.
② I think so. I will go there again next holiday.
③ Because of the car accident, the traffic was heavy.
④ I had a wonderful time on Jeju Island.
⑤ Since the rain is heavy, you'd better stay at the hotel.

Further Study 심화 학습

정답 및 해석 p.48

● 다음은 **Listening Test 07**의 주요 지문입니다. 녹음을 다시 듣고, 질문에 대한 답을 완성하세요.

Q2
1 What color suit and shirt will the man be wearing?
↳ He will be wearing a ________________ suit with a ________________ shirt.

Q4
2 What does the woman ask the man to show her?
↳ She asks him to show her ________________ and ________________.

Q7
3 Why didn't the woman do her English homework?
↳ The reason was that she ________________ her ________________.

Q8
4 Where does the woman ask the man to leave her package?
↳ She asks him to leave it ________________ at her apartment building.

Q11
5 What kind of books does the man's mom like?
↳ She likes ________________.

Q14
6 What time does the store open and close?
↳ It opens ________________ and closes ________________.

Q15
7 What is the woman supposed to do tomorrow?
↳ She is supposed to ________________.

Q18
8 Why is the teacher going to give Tony a lecture?
↳ The reason is that Tony ________________.

정답 및 해석 p.48

● 자신의 상황에 맞게 내용을 완성하고 말해보세요.

A Imagine you are a weather reporter. Complete the sentences choosing the words from the table.

Today's Weather Report	
(1) cold / chilly / mild / hot	(2) sunshine / clouds / winds / fog
(3) clear skies / rain / snow / storm	(4) more snow / less rain / less snow...

Today will be (1)_______________ with temperatures around _______________ degrees. We expect some (2)_______________ this afternoon. Tonight we will see (3)_______________ and a low of _______________ degrees. Tomorrow we're expecting (4)_______________ and a high of _______________ degrees. From the Korean Weather Center, I'm _______________.

B What is the most memorable trip of your life? Fill in the table below and tell your classmates about it.

The Most Memorable Trip of My Life	
(1) Where and when did you go?	
(2) Who did you go with?	
(3) How long did you stay there?	
(4) What did you do there?	
(5) Why was that trip memorable?	① ②
(6) Would you like to visit again?	

I'm going to talk about what is the most memorable trip of my life. I went to (1)______________________________. I went there with (2)_______________ for (3)_______________. We (4)____. It was the most memorable trip of my life because ①______________________________. Also, ②____. That is why this trip is the most memorable trip of my life and I (6)______________________________.

07 Dictation Test

01

W Good morning, Juliet Smith here with your weekend weather report. __________ __________, it is __________ degrees and __________. We're expecting the __________ __________ to last until late afternoon. However, from __________, we'll see __________ and a low of __________ degrees. __________ you can expect __________ __________ throughout __________ __________. Now, stay tuned for sports.

02

W What can I do for you?

M I'd like to buy a __________ for __________ __________ __________.

W What __________ suit will you be __________?

M A __________ suit with a __________ shirt.

W Then what about this __________ silk tie? Or this __________ one?

M I __________ the __________ tie __________ the __________ one. I think it will go well with my black suit.

03

M What are the __________ like in your __________, Judy?

W You know I __________ __________ Australia. The seasons in Australia are __________ __________ __________ in Korea, so we have Christmas __________ __________ __________.

M Oh, that is very __________. Do you __________ Christmas?

W __________, we celebrate it exactly __________ __________ __________ other people, only with __________ __________.

M That's __________. Christmas in summer!

04

W Hello. Could you show me your __________ and __________ __________, please?

M Sure. Here you go.

W What is the __________ of your __________?

M I am here __________ __________.

W __________ __________ are you planning to __________ __________?

M I'll be staying at Grand Hotel for two weeks.

W Okay, enjoy your stay!

05

M I'd like to buy __________ __________ for a close friend.

W Do you have __________ __________ in mind?

M Not really. I just want something very __________.

W What about a __________ __________? We have some very nice roses today.

M That __________ __________. Can you wrap __________ dozen roses for me, please?

W Yes, of course. Would you like a __________ to __________ a __________ on as well?

06

M Do you want a __________ that you can __________ __________ __________? Before you __________ to raise a pet, think about what it will mean to you to __________ __________ __________ __________. Remember that a pet __________ __________ without you. You have to ________ it and ________ its cage. If you are ________ that you can take good care of an animal, then it is time ________ ________ ________ ________.

07

W What did you do ________ ________?

M On Saturday, I ________ all day. Then, yesterday I helped my father ________ ________ ________. What about you?

W I visited my ________ on Saturday. On Sunday, I ________ to do my English homework but ________ ________ my textbook. I was looking for it all day.

M Really? I found an ________ English book in my ________. Is this ________?

W Oh, it's ________. Thank you so much.

08

[Telephone rings.]

M Hello, may I speak to Mina Kim, please?

W ________. Who's ________?

M I'm ________ a ________ to your address but there is ________ home right now.

W I'm sorry I'm ________ ________. Can you leave the package in the ________ ________ at my apartment building?

M Yes, I can. If there is ________ ________, please ________ ________ at this number.

W Thanks, I appreciate your consideration.

09

① W What's ________ with you?

M I have a ________.

② W May I ________ your ________?

M Yes. I want to have spaghetti.

③ W For ________ or ________ ________?

M To go, please.

④ W ________ is in the ________?

M Some toy robots.

⑤ W These boxes are too ________ for me to ________.

M Can I ________ you ________ ________?

10

M I heard you took a ________ to Canada.

W Yes, I did.

M ________ did you ________ it?

W I ________ it. I had a ________ ________ there.

M ________ did you go in Canada?

W I visited many ________ ________ such as Niagara Falls and Banff National Park.

M ________ ________ did you ________ there?

W ________ ________ ________. I'm missing the beautiful scenery of Canada.

11

W Hey, Joe. What's up?

M Hi, Kaitlin. I'm ________ ________ a book for my mom. Today is her ________.

W I see. Does she like to read?

M Yes. She ________ likes ________ ________.

W Really? I like them, too. She has the ________ ________ in books ________ me.

M That's good. Can you ________ one for me, then?

W Sure, ________ ________?

12

W Thank you for ________ Eagle Airlines. If you would like to ________ ________ ________, please press one. If you would like to ________ your ________, please press two. If you would like to ________ your ________, please press three. If you would like to talk to a ________, please press ________. To ________ this message, please press the ________ ________.

13

W Hey, Han. Can you ________ me your ________ book ________ ________ ________?

M I'm sorry I can't.

W Please. I forgot to ________ mine, and I have a class ________ ________ ________.

M I can't lend it to you because I don't have it.

W Why?

M I already lent it to Jessie. She asked me for it ________ ________ you came.

W Oh, I'm sorry.

14

M Hello Mart is going to have a ________ ________. The sale will be on from May 1st to May 7th. All items will be ________ ________ and there will be ________ of ________ ________ 80%. The store will ________ at 10 a.m. and ________ at ________. Please note that no ________ ________ are ________ during this ________. Please come and enjoy shopping at the store.

15

W Hi, Josh. I got two tickets for a ________ ________. Will you go with me?

M When is it?

W ________ at ________.

M Tomorrow? Don't you ________ that you are ________ to be helping me ________ ________, then?

W Oh, I'm so sorry. I will help you.

M How about the tickets? Will you ________ them?

W No, I will give them to my ________ or ________.

16

① W Are you ________ ________ ________?

M Yes. I will have ________ ________, please.

② W How was your ________ ________?

M It wasn't easy.

③ W Does this bus go to Dongdaemun?

M Yes. You can ________ ________ ________.

④ W Why are you so ________?

M I'll have a ________ ________ tomorrow.

⑤ W How is your new school?

M It's ________ good.

17

[Telephone rings.]

M Hello. May I speak to Dr. Wilson, please?

W I'm sorry. ________ ________ ________ yet. Who's ________ ________ ________?

M This is Andy Kim. I am supposed to meet him at 5 o'clock this ________, but...

W Do you mean you ________ ________?

M I'm so sorry, but yes.

W Okay. I will __________ __________ __________.
May I have your __________?

M My number is 010-1243-1244. Thank you.

18

W Tony was __________ __________ this morning. He said he __________ __________ the hospital because he had a __________. However, when the teacher called his mom, she said Tony just __________ __________ __________. Tony's teacher is really angry because Tony always __________ __________ __________ for being late. Tony's teacher thinks she has to __________ Tony __________ his __________ __________.
In this situation, what would the teacher most likely say to Tony?

19

M Please __________ __________ __________.
The class will start __________ __________ __________.

W Okay. I'm so __________ to take Dr. Michael's class.

M Me, too. Is this your first time to take his class? He is __________ __________ the __________ __________ in this school.

W I heard that. Is he __________? Does he give many __________ __________?

M Not really. Let's __________ carefully when he __________ the course, though.

W Okay. Oh, he is coming now.

20

M __________ __________ __________ __________ to Jeju Island?

W I didn't enjoy it that much.

M __________? What happened?

W I mostly stayed at the hotel __________ __________ a __________. The __________ __________ and the __________ were quite __________.

M Oh, that's too bad. It's good that you came back without having an __________, though.

W I think so. I will go there again next holiday.

08 Listening Test

중학영어듣기 모의고사 08회

 대화를 듣고, 여자가 입고 있는 옷을 고르시오.

①  ②  ③  ④  ⑤ 

 대화를 듣고, 여자가 구입할 채소로 가장 적절한 것을 고르시오.

① 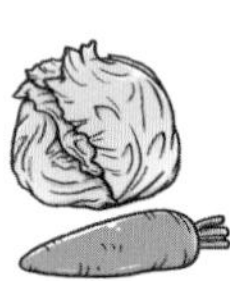 ②  ③  ④  ⑤ 

03 대화를 듣고, 여자의 심정으로 가장 적절한 것을 고르시오.

① interested ② proud ③ regretful
④ relieved ⑤ annoyed

04 대화를 듣고, 두 사람이 대화하는 장소로 가장 적절한 것을 고르시오.

① hospital ② fire station
③ grocery store ④ drugstore
⑤ electronics store

05 대화를 듣고, 남자가 받은 거스름돈을 고르시오.

① $5.50 ② $5.85 ③ $6.15 ④ $6.50 ⑤ $6.85

06 **다음을 듣고, 남자의 주장으로 알맞은 것을 고르시오.**

① 온라인 쇼핑은 물건을 싸게 구입하는 데 도움이 된다.
② 아이디와 비밀번호를 만들 때는 숫자와 철자만 사용해야 한다.
③ 비밀번호를 복잡하게 만들어야 한다.
④ 개인정보를 타인에게 공개하는 것은 위험하다.
⑤ 비밀번호에 특수문자만 사용하면 개인 정보는 보호된다.

07 **대화를 듣고, 여자가 대화를 하기 전 한 일을 고르시오.**

① 화장실 청소하기　② 변기에 장난감 버리기
③ 변기에 음식물 버리기　④ 샤워하기
⑤ 요리하기

08 **대화를 듣고, 남자의 장래희망을 고르시오.**

① 의사　② 과학 교사　③ 역사가
④ 변호사　⑤ 예술가

09 **다음을 듣고, 그림의 상황에 어울리는 대화를 고르시오.**

①　②　③　④　⑤

10 **대화를 듣고, 대화 내용과 일치하지 않는 것을 고르시오.**

① 여자는 혼자 집안일 하는 것을 싫어한다.
② 여자는 설거지와 빨래를 할 것이다.
③ 남자는 진공청소기로 청소할 것이다.
④ 여자는 남자가 훌륭한 남편이라고 생각한다.
⑤ 두 사람은 청소가 끝나면 함께 저녁식사를 준비할 것이다.

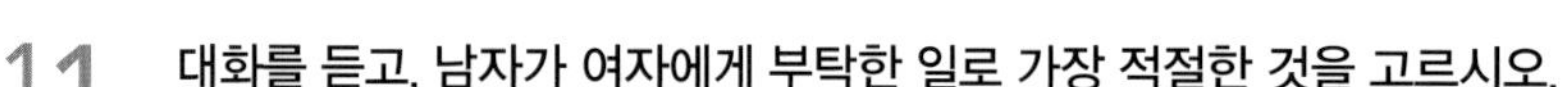

11 대화를 듣고, 남자가 여자에게 부탁한 일로 가장 적절한 것을 고르시오.

① 출산 예정일 계산해 주기
② 아기 돌 잔치에 참석하기
③ 산부인과 추천해 주기
④ 산모와 아기 돌봐주기
⑤ 신생아 용품 추천해 주기

12 대화를 듣고, 면접을 잘 보는 방법으로 언급되지 않은 것을 고르시오.

① 면접 질문을 뽑아보기
② 거울 앞에서 연습하기
③ 연습한 것을 녹음해서 들어보기
④ 정장 입고 가기
⑤ 큰 목소리로 대답하기

13 대화를 듣고, 남자가 졸린 이유로 가장 적절한 것을 고르시오.

① 건강이 나빠서
② 아침 일찍 일어나서
③ 밤늦게까지 공부해서
④ 밤늦게까지 인터넷 소설을 읽어서
⑤ 불면증으로 잠을 못 자서

14 다음을 듣고, 표의 내용과 일치하지 않는 것을 고르시오.

Name	Age	Height (cm)
Brandon	13	154
Adam	15	167
Evan	18	178

① ② ③ ④ ⑤

15 대화를 듣고, 여자가 할 수 있는 음식이 아닌 것을 고르시오.

① 김밥
② 불고기
③ 갈비
④ 김치
⑤ 잡채

16 다음을 듣고, 두 사람의 대화가 어색한 것을 고르시오.

① ② ③ ④ ⑤

17 대화를 듣고, 남자에 대한 설명으로 일치하지 않는 것을 고르시오.

① 수학 성적이 좋지 않다.
② 여자의 위로를 고마워한다.
③ 부모님이 화내실 것에 대해 걱정한다.
④ 여자와 함께 수학 공부를 하고 싶어한다.
⑤ 다음 시험에 더 열심히 노력할 것이다.

18 다음을 듣고, Mina가 남자에게 할 말로 가장 적절한 것을 고르시오.

① Excuse me, sir. How much is the wallet?
② I like your wallet. Where did you buy it?
③ Do you know where I can find wallets for men?
④ This is for you. Happy birthday!
⑤ Excuse me, sir. You dropped your wallet.

[19-20] 대화를 듣고, 남자의 마지막 말에 이어질 여자의 응답으로 가장 적절한 것을 고르시오.

19
① Yeah, it was fantastic!
② Don't worry. I believe in you.
③ Please take a picture for me.
④ I've never been to Paris. I envy you.
⑤ The bridge closes at 7 in the evening.

20
① What's your shoe size?
② I'd love to, but I'm broke.
③ Let's go shopping together.
④ When is your brother's birthday?
⑤ Please say "Happy birthday" to your brother.

Further Study 심화 학습

정답 및 해석 p.55

● 다음은 **Listening Test 08**의 주요 지문입니다. 녹음을 다시 듣고, 질문에 대한 답을 완성하세요.

Q1
1 What is the man wearing?

↳ He is wearing a ____________________ and ____________________.

Q4
2 What are the symptoms that the man has?

↳ He __________________________________ or ________________.

Q5
3 What is included in Happy Meal Set A?

↳ ________________, ________________ and ________________ are included.

Q6
4 How can we make a safe password?

↳ We have to make a password with ______________, ______________ and ______________________________.

Q12
5 What is the man going to do tomorrow?

↳ He is going to have a __________________________.

Q15
6 When is the housewarming party?

↳ It is __________________________.

Q18
7 Who is Mina walking with?

↳ She is walking with ______________________________.

Q20
8 What is Ava doing?

↳ She is ____.

정답 및 해석 p.55

● 자신의 상황에 맞게 내용을 완성하고 말해보세요.

What is your favorite painting? Fill in the table below and tell your classmates about it.

My Favorite Painting			
(1) Title	(2) Painter	(3) Description	(4) Reasons I like

My favorite painting is (1)____________________ by (2)____________________.

The painting describes (3)____.

In the picture, (3)____

__________________________. I love this painting because (4)________________

____.

B

What is your favorite food? Write down the steps to make it and tell your classmates about it.

My Favorite Food	
(1) Name of the food	
(2) Ingredients	
(3) How to make	① ② ③ ④

I'm going to talk about my favorite food. My favorite food is (1)________________.

The ingredients are (2)____________________________, and ________________.

I will tell you how to make it. First, ①____________________________________.

Second, ②____. Third,

③____. Lastly, ④__________________

________________________________. Please try to cook it. It will be a lot of fun!

08 Dictation Test

01

W Are you __________ to play the __________?

M Yes. What do we do?

W First, we look at each other's __________. Then, we __________ __________ __________ __________ and list what we __________.

M Okay, that's easy. I'm ready.

W What do you remember?

M You're __________ a __________ blouse and __________ __________. Now it's your turn.

W You're wearing a __________ __________ and __________ __________.

02

M Hi. May I help you?

W Yes, please. What vegetables are __________ __________?

M Everything is good, but the __________ and the __________ are __________ __________.

W The lettuce looks great. I'll take __________ __________ of lettuce, please.

M How about __________? They just __________ in __________ __________.

W Okay, I'll take __________. That's __________ for today. Thank you.

03

W Here is a __________ for you.

M Let me see. Mom, I __________ __________. This is an __________ __________ from Stanford University.

W Are you __________?

M Yes, Stanford University accepted me!

W Oh, congratulations! I'm __________ __________ for you.

M You know it is __________ __________ __________. I'm very __________ that my dream __________ __________ __________.

04

M Excuse me.

W Yes, sir. How can I help you?

M I have a __________ __________. I __________ __________ very well or __________. I need __________ __________.

W Why don't you take __________ __________ __________?

M Oh, I __________ that on TV. __________ is it?

W It __________ really __________.

M Then, I guess I'll try it.

05

W May I take __________ __________?

M Yes, I'd like to have Happy Meal Set A, please.

W The set is a __________ __________, __________ __________ and a __________. Do you want __________ __________?

M No, that's __________.

W Okay, that will be __________ dollars and __________ cents.

M Here is __________ dollars.

W Here is __________ __________. Enjoy your meal!

06

M When you __________ __________, you have to make an ID and a __________. If you choose an __________ password, __________ __________

__________ can __________ be exposed. Therefore, you should select a __________ password to __________ your data. For example, make a password with __________, __________ and __________ __________.

07

W Dad, __________ __________ here quickly!

M Just a minute, Helen.

W Dad! The __________ is __________.

M Oh, my God. What did you do to it?

W I just put __________ __________ __________ in it, but it was a __________ amount.

M Again? I told you __________ __________ __________ that. What a day!

08

M What do you want to __________ __________?

W I'd like to major in __________. How about you?

M I'm __________ in __________ but my parents want me to be a __________.

W So, are you going to let your __________ __________ your major for you?

M No, I want to be a __________ __________ and I plan to explain to them just __________ __________ I want it.

W I am __________ they will __________.

09

① M Do you have your __________ __________?

W Yes, here it is.

② M May I __________ this shirt __________?

W Yes. The __________ __________ is over there.

③ M Can you help me __________ the __________?

W No problem.

④ M How can I help you?

W I'd like to __________ a __________ __________.

⑤ M Excuse me. May I __________ __________?

W I'm sorry but that seat's __________.

10

W I hate to do __________. It never __________.

M Let's do it __________. Many hands make light work.

W Oh, really? Then, I'll __________ the dishes and do the laundry. Can you clean the __________ and do the __________?

M Okay. Let's get started!

W You are the world's __________ __________.

M And you're a good wife. Why don't we go out for __________ after doing all these chores?

W That __________ __________!

11

W __________ __________ __________ __________. How are you doing?

M I'm good. It's __________ to see you.

W Me too. What are you doing here, anyway? Are you __________ __________ __________?

M Yes. My __________ is going to __________ __________ next month.

W __________! Do you need any help?

M Yes. Can you __________ some things to buy for __________ __________ to me?

W Sure.

12

W __________ __________ __________ with you?

M I'm very __________ because I'm going to have __________ __________ __________ tomorrow. Can you give me some __________?

W Why don't you ________ ________ ________ ________ of ________ interview ________ and ________ answering them?

M OK. I will.

W You should stand ________ ________ ________ the mirror while practicing. ________ yourself is a good way, too.

M Oh, I see. ________ ________?

W Well, wearing a ________ will make you look ________ and ________.

M Thank you.

13

W Hello, Albert. ________ ________? Are you sick?

M No, I'm just really ________ right now. I can't ________ ________ anything.

W What did you do ________?

M I read an online ________ called *Good-bye* until late at night. I think I am ________ to the Internet.

W Are you ________? You should stop doing that. It will not only ________ your ________ but also your ________.

M I know. I'm trying.

14

① W Evan is ________ ________ of the three.

② W Adam is ________ ________ Brandon.

③ W Brandon is the smallest ________ ________ ________.

④ W Adam is ________ ________ Evan.

⑤ W Evan is ________ ________ Adam.

15

M I heard that you are a ________ ________.

W ________ ________. But people seem to enjoy my food a lot.

M What kinds of ________ can you cook?

W Well... I can cook gimbab, bulgogi, galbi, and chapchae. But I can't make kimchi yet.

M Wow! When are you going to make some food? ________ ________ ________ try one of those dishes.

W Haha. Please come to my ________ ________ this ________.

M Okay, I will.

16

① W What time did you ________ ________ this morning?

M I ________ ________ ________ at 8 o'clock.

② W How do you go to school?

M ________ ________.

③ W When is the ________ ________?

M This ________ ________.

④ W ________ ________ no see.

M Yes. Nice to see you again.

⑤ W Where did you ________ your bag?

M I think I left it ________ ________ ________.

17

W David, you don't look good. ________ ________ ________ ________ ________?

M I got a C on my ________ ________.

W You can do better next time. ________ ________!

M Thank you. But I'm ________ of my parents seeing my ________ ________. They will be really angry.

W I __________. But if you did your best, they won't be upset.

M I __________ so. I will tell them I will __________ __________ next time.

18

M Mina is walking on the __________ with her __________ __________. __________ she is walking, she sees a man __________ in front of her drop his wallet __________ __________ __________. The man doesn't know that he has dropped it. So she __________ __________ the wallet and wants to __________ it __________ to the man. In this situation, what would Mina most likely say to him?

19

M Wow! __________ __________ this picture. That __________ is so __________.

W I think so too. I took the photo in London and I'd like to go there again.

M Did you see the __________ __________?

W Of course I did. Look at the __________ __________. You can see it opening.

M __________ __________! I __________ __________ my eyes.

W Yeah, it was fantastic!

20

M What are you doing, Ava?

W I'm __________ the web to buy __________ __________ __________ __________.

M A pair of sneakers? Again? You just bought your new pair __________ __________.

W I know. This time they are for my __________ __________. His birthday is __________ __________.

M I see. What a __________ sister! Do you want to buy a pair for your sister, too?

W I'd love to, but I'm broke.

09 중학영어듣기 모의고사 09회 Listening Test

01 대화를 듣고, 남자의 동생을 고르시오.

02 대화를 듣고, 남자가 방학 동안 한 일이 아닌 것을 고르시오.

① 
②  
③ 
④  
⑤ 

03 대화를 듣고, 남자의 심정으로 가장 적절한 것을 고르시오.

① scared ② annoyed ③ nervous
④ comfortable ⑤ satisfied

04 대화를 듣고, 두 사람이 대화하는 장소로 가장 적절한 것을 고르시오.

① dry cleaner's ② clothing shop ③ coffee shop
④ hairdresser's ⑤ bakery

05 대화를 듣고, 남자가 지불할 돈으로 가장 적절한 것을 고르시오.

① $99 ② $198 ③ $270 ④ $297 ⑤ $540

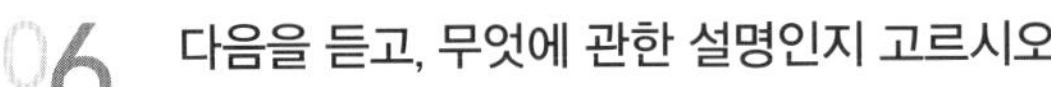

06 다음을 듣고, 무엇에 관한 설명인지 고르시오.

① 컴퓨터 ② 오디오 ③ 휴대전화
④ 사진기 ⑤ TV

07 대화를 듣고, 여자가 Tom을 싫어하는 이유를 고르시오.

① 늘 혼자 있으려고 해서
② 자신에 대한 이야기만 해서
③ 유머감각이 부족해서
④ 말이 너무 많아서
⑤ 타인에 대해 늘 나쁜 말을 해서

08 대화를 듣고, 남자가 할 일을 고르시오.

① 식료품 사오기 ② 불고기 요리하기
③ 잡채 요리하기 ④ Kevin에게 전화하기
⑤ 식탁 차리기

09 다음을 듣고, 그림의 상황에 어울리는 대화를 고르시오.

① ② ③ ④ ⑤

10 대화를 듣고, 대화 내용과 일치하지 않는 것을 고르시오.

① 남자에게는 총 7명의 손자와 손녀가 있다.
② 남자는 손녀에게 줄 인형을 샀다.
③ 여자는 상점 직원이다.
④ 남자는 여자에게 선물 포장을 요청했다.
⑤ 선물 포장에는 분홍색 리본이 사용될 것이다.

11 대화를 듣고, 여자가 남자에게 부탁한 일로 가장 적절한 것을 고르시오.

① 축구장에 같이 가기
② 재방송 시간 알려주기
③ 축구 규칙 설명해주기
④ 달리기 같이 하기
⑤ 축구 중계방송 함께 시청하기

12 대화를 듣고, 복사기 사용 방법으로 언급되지 않은 것을 고르시오.

① 복사기 전원 켜기
② 스캔 대에 책 올려 놓기
③ 복사 수량 선택하기
④ 종이 크기 설정하기
⑤ 시작 버튼 누르기

13 대화를 듣고, 여자가 당황한 이유를 고르시오.

① 예약 번호를 잃어버려서
② 예약을 거부당해서
③ 체크인 시간을 착각해서
④ 빈 객실이 없어서
⑤ 예약이 되어 있지 않아서

14 다음을 듣고, 초대장의 내용과 일치하지 않는 것을 고르시오.

Sandy's Surprise Party

Date: December 2nd, 7:00 p.m.
Place: Jake's Steak House
Contact: Julia, 651-7788-9999

① ② ③ ④ ⑤

15 대화를 듣고, 남자가 가장 먼저 할 일을 고르시오.

① 샌드위치 만들기
② 컴퓨터 작업 끝내기
③ 거실 청소하기
④ 컴퓨터 게임 하기
⑤ 계란 사오기

16 다음을 듣고, 두 사람의 대화가 어색한 것을 고르시오.

① ② ③ ④ ⑤

17 대화를 듣고, 남자가 사려는 노트북 컴퓨터와 설명이 일치하지 않는 것을 고르시오.

① 14인치 LCD 모니터가 있다.
② 무게는 1.1kg이다.
③ 원래 가격은 $190이다.
④ 50% 할인 중이다.
⑤ 색상은 세 가지가 있다.

18 다음을 듣고, Jessica가 남자에게 할 말로 가장 적절한 것을 고르시오.

① I'm sorry. We're closed.
② I wish you had come earlier.
③ Why do you want to see the doctor?
④ Please take a ticket and wait your turn.
⑤ The doctor is not in right now. Please wait a few minutes.

[19-20] 대화를 듣고, 여자의 마지막 말에 이어질 남자의 응답으로 가장 적절한 것을 고르시오.

19
① What time is it now?
② I've already seen that movie.
③ Let's meet at 5 o'clock at BLG cinema.
④ I'm sorry. Let's make it next time.
⑤ I don't know where the movie theater is.

20
① Let's go to the airport.
② That's very nice of you.
③ I don't want to study abroad.
④ Nice! Let's have a welcome home party for him.
⑤ Do you know when Jinho is coming back to Korea?

Further Study 심화 학습

정답 및 해석 p.61

● 다음은 **Listening Test 09**의 주요 지문입니다. 녹음을 다시 듣고, 질문에 대한 답을 완성하세요.

Q2
1 What did the man do during vacation?

↳ He ______________________ with his family in ______________

______________________.

Q5
2 How long will the man be staying at the hotel and with whom will he stay?

↳ He will be staying there for ______________ with ______________.

Q8
3 What does the woman ask the man to do?

↳ She asks him ______________________.

Q10
4 What wrapping paper does the man choose?

↳ He chooses the one with the ______________ on it.

Q12
5 What is the last step of making a photocopy?

↳ The last step of making a photocopy is ______________________

______________________.

Q14
6 When is the party?

↳ It is on ______________________.

Q17
7 What colors are available for the laptop computer?

↳ ______________, ______________, and ______________ are available.

Q19
8 What does the woman ask the man to do this weekend?

↳ She asks the man ______________________.

정답 및 해석 p.61

● 자신의 상황에 맞게 내용을 완성하고 말해보세요.

Introduce a place you visited with your family during summer vacation. Fill in the table below and tell your classmates about it.

The Place I Visited during Summer Vacation		
(1) The place I visited	(2) How I went there (Transportation)	(3) Things I did
		① ② ③ ④

During my summer vacation, I visited (1)______________________ with my family. We got there (2)________________. We ①________________, ②________________________, and ③____________ ________________________ there. We also ④____________________ ______________ and it was the best. We had a great time there.

Suppose you are writing an email to make a reservation for a hotel room. Fill in the table below and tell your classmates about it.

Making a Reservation for a Hotel Room	
(1) When do you want to stay?	
(2) How many days are you going to stay?	
(3) How many people are going to stay?	
(4) Would you like a(n) ocean/city view?	
(5) Would you like a twin/double bed?	
(6) Your name and contact number	

I would like to make a reservation for a hotel room. I'd like to stay there on (1)________________. I want to stay for (2)________________ (days/weeks/months). (3)______________ people are going to stay, including me. If possible, please give me a room with a(n) (4)________________ view. Lastly, I'd like a (5)____________ bed rather than a (5)____________ bed. My name is (6)____________ and my contact number is (6)____________. Thank you.

09 Dictation Test

01

M Look at this old __________. My mom sent it to me.

W Oh, is this you?

M Yes, with my __________ __________ and __________. We would __________ __________ __________ together.

W You were cute. Which one is __________ __________?

M He is wearing a __________ T-shirt and a __________.

W I need __________ __________. Which row is he in?

M He is in the __________ row.

02

W Did you have a __________ __________?

M Yes, I __________ __________ __________ __________ with my family.

W Oh! That sounds interesting. __________ did you travel?

M We went in my father's __________. We __________ in the mountains a lot.

W __________ else did you do on your trip?

M We visited __________ __________, picked plums and __________ in a __________. I had a really exciting time.

03

M I am __________ and __________ of my girlfriend.

W Why? What's __________ with you guys?

M She likes __________ __________ __________ and I hate it. Yesterday she shopped __________ __________ long.

W Most girls like shopping, but she seems a little bit too __________ about it.

M Yes, also she often __________ me to give her __________ gifts.

W I don't think she is the __________ __________ for you.

04

W Good morning. I'd like to have this coat __________.

M Okay, let me look at it. There is a __________ on the __________. Do you know that?

W Yes, it is a __________ __________. Can you __________ it?

M I'll do my __________. Do you want me to __________ it?

W Yes, please. __________ __________ can I get it back?

M It will be ready __________ __________.

05

M Good morning, I would like to __________ a room for __________ __________ and __________.

W Good morning, sir. We have a room available for two people __________ __________.

M Oh, that's fine with me. __________ __________ is the room?

W It is __________ dollars a night plus __________ __________ tax.

M Okay, I'd like to stay for __________ __________.

W Can I have your name and phone number, please?

06

W This is an __________ __________ in our lives. Nowadays this is the __________ __________ to use to __________ with others, as it is __________ to __________ from one place to another. Also, this has __________ __________, such as taking __________, listening to __________, and transferring __________. Besides, parents are __________ to __________ __________ __________ their kids using this.

07

M __________ do you __________ __________ Tom?

W He's __________. I think he is __________.

M Is he? Why do you think that?

W He talks about __________ all the time. He's only __________ in one thing, and that's Tom __________.

M Don't you think he is __________?

W No, I don't. He is a __________ __________.

08

W Dinner will be __________ in ten minutes. Are you hungry?

M Yes, I am. __________ have you __________?

W I have cooked bulgogi, chapchae and some side dishes.

M Oh, they __________ really __________. Is somebody coming to dinner?

W Yes, Kevin is __________ __________ __________ to eat with us and I know he likes those dishes. Would you __________ __________ the __________?

M Of course not. __________ __________ the placemats?

09

① M Mom, I __________ __________.

W Why don't you drink some __________ __________?

② M __________ __________ are you going to?

W My button is __________ __________. Thanks.

③ M Can I have the __________?

W __________. Here it is.

④ M Can I pay for this __________ __________?

W Of course you can.

⑤ M Let's take the __________!

W That is __________ a very good idea. Let's take the __________.

10

M Hello, can you __________ this? The salesclerk said to come over to this counter.

W That's __________, we do it here. This is a pretty doll.

M It is __________ my granddaughter. I have __________ __________. Now, finally I have a granddaughter.

W Congratulations! Which style of __________ __________ would you __________?

M I'll take that one with the __________ on it.

W Good choice. And a __________ ribbon?

M Yes, please.

11

W Did you see the Korea-Japan __________ __________ last night?

M Of course. It was the best match __________ __________ __________.

W I wish I had seen it. Who __________ __________ __________?

M __________, __________ won. Why don't you watch the rerun?

W Oh, can I? Tell me when it is on, please.

M __________ __________ __________. Let me check.

12

W Could you please tell me how to __________ __________ __________ of this book?

M Sure. First, you have to __________ __________ the copy machine and __________ __________ __________ to __________ __________.

W And then?

M Place the book on the __________ __________ after opening the cover. Press the __________ to select the amount of copies.

W Is that all?

M Lastly, __________ the cover and press the __________ __________.

W Thanks.

13

M __________ __________ Western Inn. Can I help you?

W Yes. I have a __________ and I'd like to __________ __________.

M Okay. Please __________ me your name.

W It's Mary Simpson.

M I'm sorry ma'am. I __________ __________ your name __________ the __________ __________.

W Are you sure? I made a reservation a __________ __________. Please __________ it again.

M All right. Please __________ your __________ __________ for me.

14

① M The party is for Sandy.

② M The party is on __________ __________.

③ M The party will be at a restaurant.

④ M The __________ __________ is 651-7788-9999.

⑤ M __________ __________ will be __________ by Sandy.

15

W Sweetie, can you buy me some __________, please? There aren't any in the __________.

M I'm doing work __________ __________ __________ now, though. You also asked me to clean the __________ __________.

W I'm sorry. But I have to __________ __________, so I can't go out.

M Well, if I help you do that, then, can I play __________ __________ tonight?

W Okay. You can play computer games __________ __________ __________ tonight.

M Hooray! I love you, mom.

16

① W Can I __________ __________ now?

M No, you have to __________ __________ your room first.

② W How are you?

M I'm good.

③ W Can you __________ __________?

M Yes. I am Korean.

④ W My mom is __________ __________ __________.

M I'm sorry to hear that.

⑤ W I'm __________.

M Me too. __________ __________ a sandwich.

17

W Welcome to ACE Computer Shop. __________ __________ __________ __________?

M Yes. I'm looking for a __________ __________. Can you __________ one for me?

W Sure. How about this? It has a 14-inch LCD monitor and it only weighs 1.1kg.

M __________ __________ __________ __________?

W It is actually 190 dollars, but I will give you a 15% __________.

M Good. What colors are __________?

W We have __________, __________, and __________ in stock.

18

W Jessica is working as a __________ in a __________ __________. __________, an old man comes into the clinic and tries to go __________ into the __________ __________. He says that he has a __________ __________ and __________ __________ the pain. It seems that he is a walk-in, so he doesn't have an __________. In this situation, what would she most probably say to the man?

19

W Hi, Henry. What are you going to do this __________?

M I have __________ __________ yet. I might __________ __________ __________ and take a good rest. Why?

W I was wondering if you would like to __________ __________ __________ with me. I'd like to see *The Face Reader.*

M Okay. I heard that it is very __________.

W __________! When and where shall we meet?

M Let's meet at 5 o'clock at BLG cinema.

20

W Did you know that Jinho __________ __________ __________ __________ the U.S.?

M Are you __________? When?

W He __________ me __________ last night and said he had just __________ at the __________.

M Really? I will call him. I have really __________ him.

W He said that too. He asked me how you are doing. He also said that he will __________ you __________.

M Nice! Let's have a welcome home party for him.

10 중학영어듣기 모의고사 10회 Listening Test

01 대화를 듣고, 남자가 샌드위치에 넣지 않는 것을 고르시오.

① ② ③ ④ ⑤

02 대화를 듣고, 여자의 방을 고르시오.

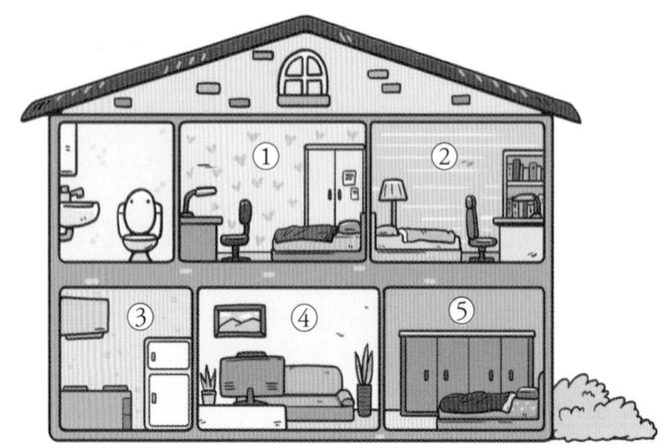

03 대화를 듣고, 여자의 직업으로 가장 적절한 것을 고르시오.

① hotel receptionist ② secretary ③ tour guide
④ police officer ⑤ repairman

04 대화를 듣고, 여자가 야구 하는 것을 꺼리는 이유를 고르시오.

① 야구를 싫어해서 ② 다리가 아파서
③ 땀을 너무 많이 흘려서 ④ 공부 시간을 빼앗겨서
⑤ 야구를 잘 못해서

05 대화를 듣고, 여자가 학교에 도착할 시간으로 알맞은 것을 고르시오.

① 7:10 ② 7:30 ③ 7:40 ④ 8:00 ⑤ 8:10

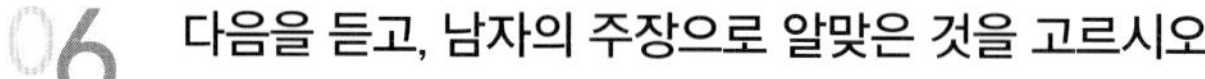

06 다음을 듣고, 남자의 주장으로 알맞은 것을 고르시오.

① 더울 때는 수영장이나 해변을 가는 게 좋다.
② 더운 날씨에 물에 들어가는 것은 위험하다.
③ 수영장에서는 꼭 안전요원을 배치해야 한다
④ 익사사고 예방을 위해 수영을 배워야 한다.
⑤ 물놀이를 할 때는 안전규칙을 숙지하고 따라야 한다.

07 대화를 듣고, 남자가 가본 나라로 언급되지 않은 것을 고르시오.

① 태국 ② 일본 ③ 중국 ④ 영국 ⑤ 미국

08 대화를 듣고, 여자가 어제 저녁에 한 일을 고르시오.

① 친구 집들이 가기
② 중국음식점에서 저녁 먹기
③ 친구와 영화 보기
④ 친구 이사 도와 주기
⑤ 중국음식 배달해서 먹기

09 다음을 듣고, 그림의 상황에 어울리는 대화를 고르시오.

① ② ③ ④ ⑤

10 대화를 듣고, 대화 내용과 일치하는 것을 고르시오.

① 여자는 TV 소리가 너무 작다고 생각한다.
② 여자는 남자와 함께 TV를 보고 있는 중이다.
③ 남자는 청소를 다 끝냈다.
④ 여자는 남자가 TV를 너무 많이 본다고 생각한다.
⑤ 남자는 30분 동안 계속 TV를 보고 있는 중이다.

11 대화를 듣고, 남자가 여자에게 부탁한 일로 가장 적절한 것을 고르시오.

① 팬클럽 가입하기
② 콘서트 같이 가기
③ 선물 전해주기
④ 사진 찍어주기
⑤ 사인 받기

12 다음을 듣고, 무엇에 관한 설명인지 고르시오.

① 핸드드라이어
② 헤어드라이어
③ 종이 타월
④ 자동 수도
⑤ 비데

13 대화를 듣고, 남자가 초록색 벽지를 선호하는 이유를 고르시오.

① 가격이 저렴해서
② 눈이 편안해져서
③ 여자가 좋아해서
④ 하늘색을 싫어하므로
⑤ 정서적으로 좋아서

14 다음을 듣고, 도표의 내용과 일치하지 않는 것을 고르시오.

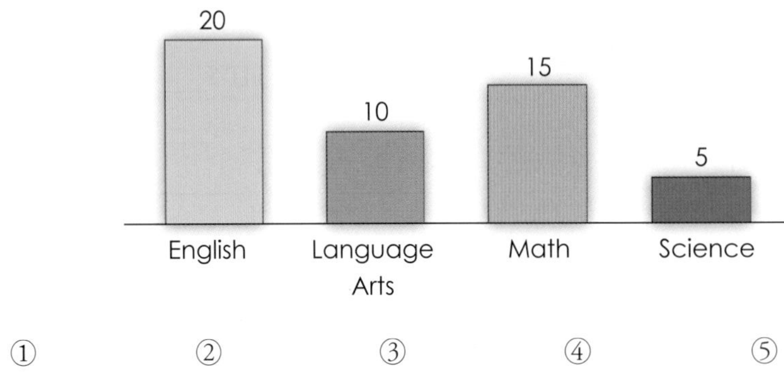

① ② ③ ④ ⑤

15 대화를 듣고, 여자가 남자를 위해 할 일로 알맞은 것을 고르시오.

① 회의에 대신 가기
② 택시 잡아주기
③ 지하철역까지 태워 주기
④ 우산 빌려주기
⑤ 버스정류장까지 태워 주기

16 다음을 듣고, 두 사람의 대화가 어색한 것을 고르시오.

① ② ③ ④ ⑤

17 대화를 듣고, 영수에 대한 내용과 일치하지 않는 것을 고르시오.

① 오늘 학교에 나오지 못했다.
② 교통사고를 당했다.
③ 팔다리가 부러지는 중상을 입었다.
④ 지금 병원으로 이송 중이다.
⑤ 병원에 최소 2주 입원해야 한다.

18 다음을 듣고, Dennis가 Alice에게 할 말로 가장 적절한 것을 고르시오.

① I can't find my notebook.
② Can I borrow your notes?
③ I don't like Social Studies.
④ Please come to class on time.
⑤ I will lend you my notes if you want.

[19-20] 대화를 듣고, 여자의 마지막 말에 이어질 남자의 응답으로 가장 적절한 것을 고르시오.

19
① Which class are you interested in?
② Good. We have only one place left.
③ No problem. I will show you the timetable.
④ I would also like to sign up for the evening class.
⑤ Wow. I didn't know that you are interested in cooking.

20
① It leaves in an hour.
② You're an early bird.
③ It's 18,000 won per person.
④ Why are you going to Busan?
⑤ Can I pay with a credit card?

Further Study 심화 학습

정답 및 해석 p.68

- 다음은 **Listening Test 10**의 주요 지문입니다. 녹음을 다시 듣고, 질문에 대한 답을 완성하세요.

Q2
1 How many people are there in the woman's family?

↳ There are ______________ people in her family: ____________________, ____________________ and ______________.

Q4
2 What does the man advise the woman to do regarding her sweating?

↳ He advises her to _________________________ about her sweating if she thinks that is ______________.

Q5
3 Why does the girl ask the man to go back home?

↳ The reason is that she _________________________________ with all her ______________ in it there.

Q10
4 Why does the woman think the man is wasting his time?

↳ The reason is that he is watching TV, even though he hasn't finished _________ ____.

Q13
5 Why does the man like the color green?

↳ He said green ____.

Q15
6 Why is there a heavy traffic?

↳ The reason is that there is ____________________.

Q17
7 Is Youngsoo hurt bad?

↳ Yes. He ____.

Q18
8 What happened to Alice because of her cold?

↳ She ___________________________________ for three days.

정답 및 해석 p.68

- 자신의 상황에 맞게 내용을 완성하고 말해보세요.

Introduce your favorite book to your classmates. Fill in the table below and complete the sentences.

My Favorite Book				
(1) Title	(2) Writer	(3) Main character	(4) What he/she does	(5) Why I like the book
				① ②

I'd like to introduce my favorite book, (1)__________. It was written by (2)__________. In the story, (3)__________ (4)__________ __________. I like the book because ①__________ __________. Also, ②__________ __________. I think you will all like it, too.

B

What is your favorite color? Fill in the table below and tell your classmates about it.

My Favorite Color	
(1) What is your favorite color?	
(2) Why do you like the color?	
(3) What are 3 typical things in the color?	
(4) What items do you have in the color?	

I like the color (1)__________ because it (2)__________ __________. (3)__________, __________, and __________ are all (1)__________. I have (4)__________, __________, and __________ in (1)__________. What is your favorite color? Do you like the color (1)__________, too? If so, please share your things with me.

10 Dictation Test

01

W Let's have __________ for __________.

M That's a __________ __________, Mom.

W What would you like on your sandwich?

M What is __________?

W We have ham, lettuce, tomato, cheese, tuna, __________, and onion.

M Could I have some __________, __________, __________ and __________?

W __________ __________. Here you go.

02

M __________ __________ __________ are in your house?

W We have __________ bedrooms: one for my __________, one for my __________ __________, and one for __________.

M Tell me about __________ __________.

W It is in the __________ of the __________ floor.

M Is your house a two-story building?

W Yes it is, but it is __________ all that big.

M I envy you. I live in the __________ where I have to __________ a bedroom __________ my brother.

03

W Good afternoon, sir.

M Hello. My name is Michael Lee. __________ __________ made a __________ under my name.

W Ah, yes, Mr. Lee. A __________ room for __________ __________?

M That's __________.

W Here's your __________, Room 514. It is on the __________ __________.

M Where is the __________?

W It's just __________ you. Have a nice evening.

04

M What is your __________ __________?

W My favorite sport is __________.

M Do you prefer __________ or __________ baseball?

W I like __________ it __________ than playing it.

M Why don't you __________ to play it?

W I __________ __________ __________ during __________ and it makes me __________.

M If you think that is __________, why don't you __________ to a __________ about it?

05

W What time is it, daddy?

M It's __________ __________.

W How long does it take __________ __________ __________ __________?

M Why? Did you __________ something?

W Yes. I think I __________ my __________ with all my __________ in it there.

M Well, it'll only take __________ minutes. But it will take __________ __________ minutes to get to your school from home.

W Can we go __________ __________, daddy?

06

M When it becomes __________, everybody likes to be in or around the __________. Going to the __________ __________ or the __________ on a hot day is a great way to __________ the heat. As long as there are __________, most people don't

think much about __________ __________.
However, a lot of people __________ because of __________. So we have to __________ and __________ __________ __________ in water __________ we go swimming.

07

W Are you __________ in __________?

M Yes, I really like it. I've been to lots of places.

W Have you ever traveled __________?

M Yes. I have been to __________, __________ and the __________.

W What about __________?

M Yes, I've been there, __________. It's a place of __________.

W Which country do you __________ that I __________ during this summer vacation?

08

M What did you do __________?

W Oh, a lot. In the __________ I went to a __________ __________ with my friend. It was quite __________.

M Where did you __________ __________?

W I had lunch at my favorite __________ __________.

M Sounds great. What did you do in the __________?

W I went to Erin's __________ __________.

M Wow! What a __________ day you had!

09

① M __________ are you doing?

W I'm doing my __________.

② M Why don't you eat __________ __________?

W No thanks. I'm __________.

③ M Excuse me. __________ can I __________ __________ City Hall?

W I __________ your __________?

④ M Can I __________ the menu?

W Yes, __________ __________ __________.

⑤ M Are you going to __________ all these books?

W Yes. I love __________ __________.

10

W Can you __________ __________ the volume on TV, please?

M Oh, I'm sorry. I didn't know __________ were __________.

W That's fine. Anyway are you all __________ with __________?

M No, I still need to clean the __________ and the __________.

W I think you are watching __________ __________ TV. You're wasting your time.

M Come on. It has been just __________ __________ since I started watching TV. I'm just taking a short rest.

11

W __________ __________. Look! It's Girls' Generation.

M Girls' Generation? __________? __________? I'm __________ __________ __________ __________ them.

W Why don't you go and get their __________, then?

M I'd like to, but I'm __________ __________. Can you do that for me?

W What? Come on. __________ __________.

M Oh, please. I shall __________ __________ your __________.

W Okay. I will try.

12

W In __________ __________, this is __________ near the __________. You use this after washing your hands. If you __________ your __________ __________ the air hole, the hot air will __________ __________ __________ and __________ your wet hands. If you __________ your hands together, they will dry __________ and __________. It also __________ __________ automatically when you __________ __________.

13

W Charles, I'm going to change the __________ __________ in your room.

M Really? I'm happy to hear that. What color do you have __________ __________?

W I'm thinking of __________ __________ or __________. Is there any color you'd like to have?

M Green is my __________ __________. It makes me __________ __________ and __________.

W Green also makes people's __________ __________.

M Please __________ it soon. I am very excited about it.

14

① M Students __________ __________ 20 hours a week.

② M Students __________ Language Arts __________ __________.

③ M Students study Math __________ __________ Language Arts.

④ M Students study Math __________ __________ English.

⑤ M Students study Science __________ __________.

15

M Oh, I'm __________ __________ the __________. I've got to __________ __________ __________.

W I heard on the news that __________ is __________ __________ __________ due to the __________ __________.

M What should I do, then?

W You'd better take __________ __________ like a __________ or the __________.

M I see. By the way, would you drop me off at the subway station? I think that's the __________ __________.

W Okay, I will.

16

① W How was your __________?

M I really __________ __________.

② W Can I __________ your pen?

M Sure. Here it is.

③ W Do you have a __________ __________?

M Yes. I will __________ it for you.

④ W When does the __________ __________?

M I will take __________ __________ 2.

⑤ W What do you want to eat?

M I will have a __________.

17

W Did you __________ __________ Youngsoo?

M No. Why?

W I heard that he had a __________ __________ on the way to school this morning.

M I'm sorry to hear that. Is he __________ __________?

W __________, yes. He __________ his __________ and __________, so he's in the __________ now.

M Oh, no. How long does he have to __________ __________ __________ __________?

W __________ __________ two weeks.

18

W Alice is __________ __________ __________ for three days because of a __________ __________. __________, on the day she __________ __________ to school, she will __________ a Social Studies __________. Dennis feels bad about it, so he wants to offer to __________ his __________ __________ Alice. In this situation, what would Dennis most probably say to Alice?

19

W I'd like to __________ in the __________ __________. Can you show me a __________?

M Sure. Here it is. If you __________ __________ __________, please let me know.

W Okay. Thanks. [pause] Is the __________ class still __________?

M Would you like to take a __________ __________ or an __________ __________?

W I would __________ an evening class.

M Good. We have only one place left.

20

W I'd like to buy __________ to Busan. When is the __________ I can leave?

M __________ __________ __________. There is a bus __________ __________ __________.

W In an hour? Isn't there an __________ one?

M I'm sorry. That's the __________.

W I __________ __________ __________ then I suppose. Please give me two __________ __________. How much are they?

M It's 18,000 won per person.

11 중학영어듣기 모의고사 11회 Listening Test

01 대화를 듣고, 여자가 설명하는 그림을 고르시오.

① ② ③ ④ ⑤

02 대화를 듣고, 상황에 알맞은 표지판을 고르시오.

①  ②  ③  ④  ⑤ 

03 대화를 듣고, 여자의 마지막 말에 대한 남자의 심정으로 가장 적절한 것을 고르시오.

① relieved ② shocked ③ excited
④ bored ⑤ scared

04 대화를 듣고, 여자가 말한 음식점을 남자가 싫어하는 이유를 고르시오.

① 음식 맛이 없어서
② 청결 상태가 좋지 않아서
③ 식당까지의 거리가 멀어서
④ 한국 음식만 좋아하기 때문에
⑤ 과거 오래 기다린 경험 때문에

05 대화를 듣고, 남자가 지불한 금액으로 적절한 것을 고르시오.

① $10 ② $12 ③ $15 ④ $17 ⑤ $30

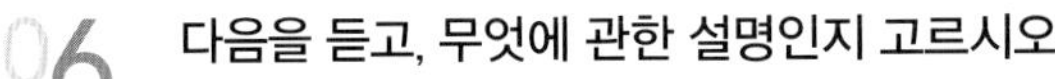

06 다음을 듣고, 무엇에 관한 설명인지 고르시오.

① radio ② printer ③ TV ④ telephone ⑤ camera

07 대화를 듣고, 여자가 대화를 마친 후 가장 먼저 할 일을 고르시오.

① 남자의 동생 자전거를 타기
② 자전거 펌프 가지러 가기
③ 남자의 동생을 태워서 가기
④ 호수로 산책 가기
⑤ 자전거 타이어에 바람 넣기

08 대화를 듣고, 남자가 최종적으로 메모한 내용으로 알맞은 것을 고르시오.

① From: Sumi / Tel. 720-3617 / "Call this afternoon."
② From: Sumi / Tel. 720-3671 / "Call this afternoon."
③ From: Jenny / Tel. 725-3671 / "Call tonight."
④ From: Jenny / Tel. 725-3671 / "Call this afternoon."
⑤ From: Sumi / Tel. 720-3617 / "Call tonight."

09 다음을 듣고, 그림의 상황에 어울리는 대화를 고르시오.

① ② ③ ④ ⑤

10 대화를 듣고, 대화 내용과 일치하지 않는 것을 고르시오.

① 여자는 조용한 지역에서 산다.
② 여자가 사는 동네에는 나무와 공원이 많다.
③ 여자는 5살 때부터 같은 동네에서 살고 있다.
④ 남자는 다음달에 이사 갈 예정이다.
⑤ 남자가 사는 동네에는 상점들이 많다.

11 대화를 듣고, 남자가 여자에게 부탁한 일로 가장 적절한 것을 고르시오.

① 여권 보여주기
② 여행 정보 안내하기
③ 입국 신고서 가져다주기
④ 비행기 편명 알려주기
⑤ 입국 신고서 작성 도와주기

12 대화를 듣고, 독감을 예방하는 가장 좋은 방법으로 언급된 것을 고르시오.

① 운동하기
② 예방주사 맞기
③ 마스크 하기
④ 양치하기
⑤ 손을 자주 씻기

13 대화를 듣고, 여자가 남자를 찾아간 이유를 고르시오.

① 매장 위치를 물어보려고
② 티셔츠 가격을 물어보려고
③ 진열된 가방을 사려고
④ 지갑을 잃어버려서
⑤ 할인쿠폰을 받으려고

14 다음을 듣고, 안내문의 내용과 일치하지 않는 것을 고르시오.

Welcome to Safari World

✓Open	9:00 a.m. to 6:00 p.m. 365 days a year
✓Entrance Fee	$10 – Free for children under the age of 7 – Free for the elderly and the disabled
✓Children's Entrance	Children under the age of 10 must be accompanied by an adult.
✓Warning	Do not scare or feed the animals.

① ② ③ ④ ⑤

15 대화를 듣고, 두 사람이 이번 주말에 할 일을 고르시오.

① 야구 경기 보러 가기
② 야구 경기 표 예매하기
③ 야구 용품 사러 가기
④ 야구 경기 시청하기
⑤ 야구 연습하기

16 다음을 듣고, 두 사람의 대화가 어색한 것을 고르시오.

① ② ③ ④ ⑤

17 대화를 듣고, 대화 내용과 일치하지 않는 것을 고르시오.

① 남자는 자전거에서 떨어졌다.
② 남자는 팔꿈치와 무릎을 다쳤다.
③ 여자는 남자의 부주의함에 화를 냈다.
④ 여자는 시험을 앞두고 있다.
⑤ 여자는 시험 공부를 이미 했다.

18 다음을 듣고, 상황을 가장 잘 표현한 속담을 고르시오.

① Better late than never.
② Many drops make a shower.
③ Two heads are better than one.
④ The early bird catches the worm.
⑤ When in Rome, do as the Romans do.

[19-20] 대화를 듣고, 여자의 마지막 말에 이어질 남자의 응답으로 가장 적절한 것을 고르시오.

19
① I'm so hungry.
② That sounds great!
③ I prefer sunny days.
④ Okay, let's go home.
⑤ I listen to the radio every morning.

20
① Yes, she will get better soon.
② Please say hello to her for me.
③ Let's go to the hospital together.
④ How old is your grandmother?
⑤ No, she's just not feeling very well today.

Further Study 심화 학습

● 다음은 **Listening Test 11**의 주요 지문입니다. 녹음을 다시 듣고, 질문에 대한 답을 완성하세요.

Q3
1 What does their new neighbor do?

↳ He is a ______________________.

Q4
2 Why did they have to wait for a long time at the restaurant and how long did they wait?

↳ They did not ______________ so they had to wait for ____________ to get one.

Q7
3 Why is the woman going to ride the man's brother's bike?

↳ One of the ____________ on her bike is ____________ and they ____________ for it.

Q10
4 How long has the man lived in the current neighborhood?

↳ He has lived there just for ____________, moving there ____________.

Q12
5 Please write down three things that you can do to prevent flu.

↳ ① ______________ / ② ______________ / ③ ______________

Q15
6 Why did Justin call Mary?

↳ The reason was that he wants to ask her to ______________________ ______________________.

Q18
7 What did Hudson do in order to save money?

↳ He didn't ______________________.

Q19
8 What does the woman want to do when the rain stops?

↳ She wants to ______________________.

정답 및 해석 p.75

● 자신의 상황에 맞게 내용을 완성하고 말해보세요.

What kind of house do you want to live in? Complete the sentences referring to the examples and tell your classmates about it.

The House I Want to Live in			
(1) Type of house	(2) Location	(3) Rooms	(4) Other facilities
apartment single-story house two-story house	city country	bedroom, bathroom, kitchen, living room, study, laundry	swimming pool, garden, barbecue

I'd like to introduce my dream house. It is a(n) (1)________________ located in (2)________________. It has (3)________________. Also, it has (3)________________. Most of all, there (is/are) (4)________________ in the backyard. In (4)________________, there (is/are) ________________. I wish I could live in my dream house now.

Suppose you lost something and now you are in a lost-and-found center. Fill in the table below and tell your classmates about it.

Lost-and-Found Center	
(1) What did you lose?	
(2) Where did you lose it?	
(3) When did you lose it?	
(4) What does it look like?	
(5) What color is it?	
(6) Your contact number	

I want to tell you about something that I lost. I lost (1)________________. I think I lost it (2)________________. If my memory is right, I lost it (3)________________. It looks like (4)________________. It is (5)________________. My contact number is (6)________________.

Thank you.

11 Dictation Test

01

M It is time to close the book. Now, what do you remember about the picture?

W First, at the ________ of the picture there are some ________ in the sky.

M What about at the ________ of the picture?

W ________ ________ are flying ________.

M How about the ________? Where is it?

W It is in the ________ ________ corner.

M That's ________. You remembered ________. Good job!

02

W Dad, look at that ________ ________. The man is walking on the ________ of a ________.

M Oh, that is actually a ________. The man is walking across a crosswalk.

W What does the sign mean?

M It means we are ________ up to a ________.

W Are we going to ________ the street?

M Yes, we are. Remember ________ ________ ________ and ________ ________ ________ ________ before we cross.

03

W Do you know ________ ________ yesterday?

M No, what happened?

W I looked out the window and saw our ________ ________ holding a ________ with ________ on his shirt!

M What? He might have killed somebody! Did you ________ the ________?

W Yes! The police came quickly!

M So did they find a ________ ________? Did he ________ someone?

W No! It turned out he was just a ________ artist!

04

M ________ would you like to go for dinner?

W What do you think of that ________ restaurant we went to last month? It's a ________ ________, isn't it?

M I ________ think so. We waited ________ ________ ________ to get the ________ there.

W Of course, we forgot to ________ a table.

M Let's go to a ________ restaurant.

W Okay, if you want.

05

M Good morning ma'am, I'd like ________ tickets for the Picasso exhibition.

W Of course, and if you have a ________ ________, you can get a student ________.

M Here it is.

W That will be ________ ________ per person. Do you need a ________? It only costs an ________ ________ ________ for all of the people in a single group.

M That would be ________. May I ________ by credit card?

W Sure. Thanks, here is your ________.

06

W This is one of the ________ ________ in human history. ________ it was invented,

__________ was the __________ method of __________. Also, people had to go to one another and talk to __________ __________. Thanks to this invention, people no longer had to talk face to face. It has played a __________ __________ in making the world a __________ __________.

07

M Do you want to __________ __________ __________ with me?

W Okay, I'll ride with you. Where are we going?

M Let's go to the lake.

W Sounds good. By the way, do you have a bike __________? One of my tires is __________.

M I don't have one. How about leaving your bike at __________ and __________ my brother's bike?

W That's __________ of you.

08

W May I talk to Jenny, please? It is Sumi here.

M Sorry, she's __________ __________ __________. Would you like to __________ __________ __________?

W Yes, please tell her to call me back __________ __________. My number is 720-__________.

M Okay, let me repeat that: Sumi, 720-3617. Please call __________.

W Actually, it's __________ and I would like her to call me __________ __________.

M I'm sorry.

W That's okay. Thank you.

09

① W Did you __________ the dog?

M I think I did.

② W May I help you?

M Yes, can I __________ this __________ into the library?

③ W Can you help me __________ a __________ for my son?

M Sure. How about this one?

④ W Can you __________ the __________?

M Sure, I can.

⑤ W Thanks for __________ __________ to __________.

M Don't mention it.

10

M What kind of neighborhood do you live in?

W It's a very __________ neighborhood. It has __________ __________ with lots of __________ and __________.

M __________ __________ have you lived there for?

W I've lived there since I was __________ years old. How about yours?

M I live in a very __________ __________. There are lots of __________, __________, and __________.

W Have you lived there for a __________ __________?

M No, I only moved there __________ __________.

11

W Excuse me. Can you __________ me your __________?

M Okay. Here you are.

W What is the __________ of the visit?

M I am taking a __________.

W Did you fill out the immigration __________ __________?

M No, not yet. Can you __________ me __________ with it, please? I don't __________ some of the

English words.

W Okay. But next time, you have to ________ it ________ in the plane.

12

M Did you hear the news that a boy ________ ________ ________ ________ this morning?

W Really? I can't ________ that flu can ________ ________.

M Hard to believe, right? It happens though. We need to ________ our ________ more often.

W Okay. I heard that is the best way to ________ flu. What else can we do, anyway?

M ________ a ________ and ________ your ________ are also helpful.

W I see. Thank you.

13

W Can I ask you something?

M Sure. What is it?

W Someone ________ my ________ ________ ________ my bag while I was choosing a T-shirt on the ________ ________.

M Oh, no. Where was the display stand?

W It was on ________ ________ ________ next to the ________.

M I see.

W Since there is a ________ ________ being offered ________, the area was ________ ________ people.

M I will check the CCTV coverage of that area. I'm so sorry for the ________.

14

① M The zoo ________ ________ 9:00 a.m. ________ 6:00 p.m. ________ ________ ________.

② M The ________ ________ is free for children and the elderly only.

③ M If not ________ ________ an adult, children under the age of 10 may not be admitted.

④ M People should not ________ ________ ________.

⑤ M People are not allowed to ________ ________ ________.

15

[Telephone rings.]

M Hello. Can I talk to Mary?

W Hello, ________ ________. Who's this?

M It's me, Justin. Would you like to go to see a ________ ________ this weekend?

W Really? Were you able to get tickets? I heard that all tickets were ________ ________ ________ ________ ________.

M ________, I got a couple of them. I'm so excited.

W Thanks for asking me. I really wanted to ________ ________ ________.

16

① W Are you ________ ________ late tonight?

M Yes. My mom got angry because I came home late.

② W Where is Steve?

M I saw him ________ ________ ________.

③ W Do you like ________?

M Yes, I do.

④ W What do you think of this __________?

M It's very __________.

⑤ W How was the food?

M I __________ it a lot.

17

W Are you okay? I heard that you __________ __________ your __________.

M Yes. I __________ my __________ and __________. But I'm okay.

W You should be __________ __________ when you're riding your bike next time.

M Thank you for your __________. By the way, are you __________ __________ the test?

W Well. I think so. But I'm going to __________ __________ it one more time.

M You're a __________ student.

18

W There was a boy named Hudson. He wanted to buy a __________ __________ __________, but he didn't have __________ __________ __________ __________ __________. So, __________ __________ to save his money by not buying __________ things. He saved his money for __________ months, and one day he was able to buy a new cell phone. What __________ do you think matches the story?

19

W It's been raining __________ __________ __________. I want to see __________ __________.

M I've got good news for you then. I heard that the rain will stop __________ __________ on the __________ this morning.

W Really? I'm so happy.

M What do you want to do when the __________ __________?

W Shall we __________ __________ __________ __________ tomorrow?

M That sounds great!

20

W What are you doing? Aren't you going to __________ __________ __________ Camilla's birthday party?

M Oh, I'm afraid I __________ __________ the party.

W Why? __________ __________ __________ with you?

M You know my grandmother is 101 years old. She is sick and __________ __________ __________ so I __________ __________ __________ her.

W That's too bad. Does she have a __________ __________?

M No, she's just not feeling very well today.

12 중학영어듣기 모의고사 12회 Listening Test

01 대화를 듣고, 여자가 판매하지 못한 것을 고르시오.

①  ②  ③  ④  ⑤ 

02 대화를 듣고, 여자가 설명하는 것과 일치하지 않는 가구를 고르시오.

03 대화를 듣고, 남자의 직업으로 가장 적절한 것을 고르시오.

① reporter ② firefighter ③ security guard
④ lifeguard ⑤ police officer

04 대화를 듣고, 두 사람의 관계로 가장 적절한 것을 고르시오.

① 약사 — 환자 ② 상사 — 부하 직원 ③ 의사 — 환자
④ 면접관 — 구직자 ⑤ 선생님 — 학생

05 대화를 듣고, 두 사람이 내일 만날 시각을 고르시오.

① 11:30 ② 12:00 ③ 12:30 ④ 1:00 ⑤ 1:30

06 다음을 듣고, 이어질 내용으로 가장 적절한 것을 고르시오.

① 일상소재로 악기 만드는 방법
② 악기 구입 장소
③ 좋은 악기 고르는 방법
④ 밴드에 참여할 수 있는 방법
⑤ 실로폰 연주 방법

07 대화를 듣고, 남자가 학교에 갈 수 없다고 말한 이유를 고르시오.

① 숙제를 하지 않아서
② 병원에 가야 해서
③ 감기에 걸려서
④ 수업 시간에 늦어서
⑤ 잠을 더 자고 싶어서

08 대화를 듣고, 여자가 남자에게 충고한 내용으로 가장 적절한 것을 고르시오.

① 룸메이트를 이해해주어라.
② 룸메이트와 함께 음악을 들어라.
③ 룸메이트에게 먼저 화해하라.
④ 룸메이트에게 자신의 고충을 말하라.
⑤ 룸메이트에게 방을 따로 쓰자고 말하라.

09 다음을 듣고, 설명과 일치하지 않는 그림을 고르시오.

①
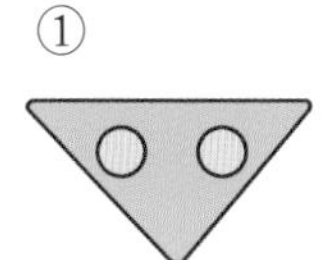
②

③

④

⑤

10 대화를 듣고, 대화 내용과 일치하지 않는 것을 고르시오.

① 남자와 여자는 겨울방학 동안 만나지 못했다.
② 여자는 날씬하고 건강해졌다.
③ 여자는 방학 동안 운동을 열심히 했다.
④ 남자는 방학 동안 공부나 운동을 전혀 안 했다.
⑤ 남자는 내일부터 아침에 조깅을 할 예정이다.

11 대화를 듣고, 여자가 남자에게 부탁한 일로 가장 적절한 것을 고르시오.

① 야시장까지 차로 태워주기
② 야시장 위치 알려주기
③ 야시장에서 물건 사다주기
④ 야시장 함께 가기
⑤ 외출 중 집 봐주기

12 대화를 듣고, 남자가 현재 학교에 가는 방법을 고르시오.

① 스쿨버스
② 자전거
③ 택시
④ 도보
⑤ 지하철

13 대화를 듣고, 남자가 약속을 지킬 수 없는 이유를 고르시오.

① 열이 많이 나서
② 약속이 있는 걸 잊어버려서
③ 병원에 환자가 많아서
④ 여동생을 병원에 데려가야 해서
⑤ 다른 약속이 생겨서

14 다음을 듣고, 시간표의 내용과 일치하지 않는 것을 고르시오.

Sujin's Weekly Class Schedule					
	Mon	Tue	Wed	Thu	Fri
Morning	English	Math	Art	Science	English
Afternoon	Math	History	Social Studies	P.E.	Science
Evening	Language Arts	English	Music	Language Arts	History

① ② ③ ④ ⑤

15 대화를 듣고, 남자가 대화를 마친 후 할 일을 고르시오.

① 가스비 납부
② 거실 청소
③ 편지 쓰기
④ 벌금에 대한 항의
⑤ 우편물 수거

16 다음을 듣고, 두 사람의 대화가 어색한 것을 고르시오.

① ② ③ ④ ⑤

17 대화를 듣고, 대화 내용과 일치하지 않는 것을 고르시오.

① 남자는 애완동물을 키우고 있다.
② 여자는 뱀을 만져본 적이 없다.
③ 남자는 뱀을 잘 만진다.
④ 여자는 뱀에게 물릴까 걱정한다.
⑤ 여자는 애완용 뱀을 사려고 한다.

18 다음을 듣고, 상황을 가장 잘 표현한 속담을 고르시오.

① Strike while the iron is hot.
② Practice makes perfect.
③ The grass is greener on the other side.
④ A bird that flies higher can see farther.
⑤ A problem shared is a problem halved.

[19-20] 대화를 듣고, 여자의 마지막 말에 이어질 남자의 응답으로 가장 적절한 것을 고르시오.

19 ① I'm sorry to hear that.
② Are you ready to order?
③ Yes. She liked it very much.
④ Yes, my mom enjoys cooking a lot.
⑤ No, I don't understand what you are saying.

20 ① Help yourself.
② No, never mind.
③ Yes. Please wrap it for me.
④ That sounds interesting.
⑤ Where is the fitting room?

정답 및 해석 p.82

● 다음은 **Listening Test 12**의 주요 지문입니다. 녹음을 다시 듣고, 질문에 대한 답을 완성하세요.

Q2
1 What furniture does the woman have in her bedroom?

↳ She has ________, ________, ________, ________ and ________. However, she doesn't have a ________ in her bedroom.

Q4
2 What time did the woman arrive at work and why?

↳ She arrived at work at ________, ________ late, and she said the reason was that she had a ________.

Q7
3 What does the boy ask the woman to do?

↳ He asks her to tell his teacher that he was too ________ to ________ ________.

Q8
4 What is the man's problem with his roommate?

↳ His roommate ________ all the time and the man can't ________.

Q11
5 Where are they going to go?

↳ They are going to go to ________.

Q12
6 How did the man go to school when he was in elementary school?

↳ He ________.

Q17
7 What did the woman say when the man asked her to touch his pet snake?

↳ She said it was ________.

Q18
8 Why is Jane disappointed?

↳ The reason is that ________.

정답 및 해석 p.82

● 자신의 상황에 맞게 내용을 완성하고 말해보세요.

Make your own musical instrument and share how to make it with your classmates. Following are given as examples.

My Own Musical Instrument	
(1) What it is	Water Glass Xylophone
(2) Step 1	line up seven or more water glasses that are the same size
(3) Step 2	put some water in the first glass
(4) Step 3	put a little more water in each of the other glasses
(5) Step 4	carefully tap the water glasses with a spoon

I'd like to introduce the way to make your own musical instrument, (1)______________________________. There are several steps to make it. First, (2)______________________________. Second, (3)______________________________. Third, (4)______________________________. Finally, (5)______________________________. Now, you can make beautiful sound with them.

Do you have a pet? If so, describe it. If not, think of an animal you would like to have as a pet. Fill in the table below and tell your classmates about it.

My Pet	
(1) What do you (want to) have as a pet?	
(2) What do you like about it?	
(3) What does it look like?	
(4) Where did/can you get it?	
(5) What do you (want to) do with it?	

I (want to) have a(n) (1)_______________ as a pet. I think it is (2)_______________, _______________, and _______________. It (3)______________________________. Also it (3)______________________________. I got[can get] it (4)______________________________. I (would like to) (5)______________________________, ______________________________, or ______________________________ with it.

12 Dictation Test

01

W We had a __________ __________ last spring.

M Really? What did you __________?

W My brother's old __________, my old __________ and some of my mom's old __________. So many things!

M Did you sell __________ of them?

W No. Things like my mom's old handbag and my old sneakers weren't sold.

M What were the hot selling items, then?

W We sold all of my __________ __________ stuff: his old __________, __________, __________, and even his old __________.

02

M What is __________ __________ like?

W I __________ it with my sister.

M What __________ do you have in your room?

W We each have a bed and a desk, but we __________ a dresser, drawers and a closet.

M Do you have a __________?

W No. Our family computer is in the __________ __________.

M I don't have the computer in my bedroom, either.

03

W Good morning, officer. My car was __________ this morning. I want to __________ a __________.

M All right. __________ __________ of car is it?

W It is a black Kia K5 with a leather interior.

M What is the __________ __________?

W It's 10A 2435. It was __________ in front of my __________.

M Can I see your ID and your car registration please?

W __________ __________ __________.

04

M So you're finally here. You are __________ __________ __________!

W I'm sorry Mr. Park. It will not happen again.

M I hope not. The meeting was at __________ __________. Did you __________?

W I knew what time it was, but I had a __________ __________.

M Whenever you are late, I hear __________ __________ old __________. What should I do?

W I __________ how you feel. I'm really sorry.

M Okay, this is your __________ __________. Don't let it happen again.

05

W Do you have __________ __________ for tomorrow?

M I'm going to visit the National Museum. Do you __________ __________ __________ __________?

W Sure. __________ shall we meet?

M Let's meet in front of our __________ at __________ o'clock.

W Why don't we meet __________ __________ __________ and eat lunch together?

M __________ __________. What do you want to eat for lunch?

06

M It is fun to make __________ __________ from

things you can __________ __________ in your home. You can __________ a comb __________ a harmonica or __________ __________ into a xylophone. Does this sound __________? If so, follow the following __________ and in no time you will be __________ your own instrument!

07

W Frank, wake up. You're going to be __________ __________ __________.

M I don't feel well, mom. I __________ __________ to school today.

W What's wrong?

M I feel __________. I can't stop __________.

W Well, you need to go see a __________ and get a __________ to cure your __________.

M No, mom. I think I'm okay now. But can you tell my teacher that I was __________ __________ that I couldn't do my __________?

W That's __________ you __________ __________ to go to __________. No way!

08

M I have serious problems with my __________.

W Why? Is he __________ to you?

M No. He is quite a __________ guy, but he listens to __________ __________ all the time.

W Have you talked to him about it?

M No, I haven't. I am __________ __________ __________ with him; I just __________ __________ his loud music __________.

W Well, then, why don't you just tell him about __________ __________ __________?

M I'll try, but what if I feel awkward after telling him?

09

① W There is an __________ - __________ triangle with __________ small circles in it.

② W A girl is playing with __________ __________.

③ W There is an __________ eating a carrot with its trunk.

④ W A __________ shaped __________ is on the wall.

⑤ W There is a man __________ __________ __________ in his hand.

10

M It's nice to see you again, Helen.

W Max! I __________ __________ you all winter vacation.

M Wow! You look so __________ and __________.

W Thanks. I've __________ a lot. You look like you gained __________ __________ __________.

M I did. I just __________, __________ and __________ all vacation. I __________ __________ at all.

W __________ are you going to start exercising again?

M I'm going to start __________. I'm planning on __________ in the __________.

W Sounds great. If you need a companion, just ask me.

11

W Do you want to go to the __________ __________ with me?

M When?

W __________ __________. If you are going, I will __________ you __________ at your house.

M That's __________ __________ __________ me. I will pass this time.

W Oh, come on. Let's go. There will be lots of things to enjoy. __________, tomorrow is __________. You can take a rest.

M Alright. __________ __________ __________ __________ before you come to pick me up, though.

12

W How do you go to school?

M I used to walk to school when I was in __________ __________, but now I take a school bus.

W I see. __________ __________ does it take to get there?

M It usually takes __________ __________ __________. It __________ __________ the __________ though.

W Have you ever tried to take __________ __________, like a __________ or the __________?

M Yes, I have. But it takes much longer.

13

[Telephone rings.]

M Hello, Emma. This is Jacob.

W Hi, Jacob. __________ __________?

M I'm sorry to tell you that I can't __________ __________ __________ __________ __________. My sister is sick.

W Why? What's wrong with her?

M She has a __________ __________. I think I will have to take her to the __________.

W That's too bad. Do you want me to go with you?

M I would __________ your __________ if you could do so. Thank you.

14

① M Sujin studies English __________ __________ __________ __________.

② M Sujin has P.E class on __________ afternoon.

③ M Sujin has __________ classes every __________ and __________.

④ M Sujin has __________ class on Wednesday __________.

⑤ M Sujin's __________ __________ classes are __________ in the __________.

15

W Honey, did you __________ __________ __________ in the __________ __________?

M Not yet. Why? Is there an __________ letter?

W In a way, yes.

M What is it?

W It is a notice that says we didn't pay our gas bill last month, so we __________ __________ __________ a __________ __________.

M What?

W Besides, if we don't __________ __________ __________ by today, the gas company will __________ __________ the gas.

M Oh, no. I will do an __________ __________ right away.

16

① W Do you __________ __________ __________?

M Yes, please.

② W How's the __________ today?

M I hate the cold.

③ W Do you know how to __________ __________ __________?

M Of course. I'm a good __________.

④ W __________ __________ __________ play a

computer game?

M I'd love to but I can't.

⑤ W Where are you going?

M I'm going to the __________.

17

W Do you have a pet?

M Yes. I have a __________ __________.

W My goodness! A pet snake? Isn't it __________?

M __________ __________ __________. If you touch its __________, it is very __________ and __________. Would you like to touch it?

W No. No. No. I'm very scared of it. It is __________ to me. I'm also __________ it might __________ me.

M Haha. No, it won't.

18

W Jane __________ __________ __________ on her English test in the __________ __________. Her __________ is quite far __________ __________. She is __________ because her grade is __________ __________ __________ her __________ __________. However, her classmate Brandon failed his midterm exam but got a __________ __________ on the final exam. Jane asked him what his secret was and he said that he just __________ __________ __________. He memorized at least __________ words every day. He told Jane that "No one can beat a __________ __________." What proverb do you think matches this story?

19

W Did you go to the Italian restaurant that I told you about?

M Yes. I had lunch there with my mom __________ __________.

W How was the __________? Was it __________?

M It was __________. I shared __________ __________ and Gorgonzola cheese pizza with my mom. I ate every last bite.

W Did your mom __________ __________ __________, too?

M Yes. She liked it very much.

20

W May I help you?

M I'm looking for a __________ for my mom.

W We have __________ __________ here. What about this __________ __________ one? It is __________ among women.

M I see. How about this __________ one? It quite __________.

W It is also nice. Are you going to __________ it?

M Yes. Please wrap it for me.

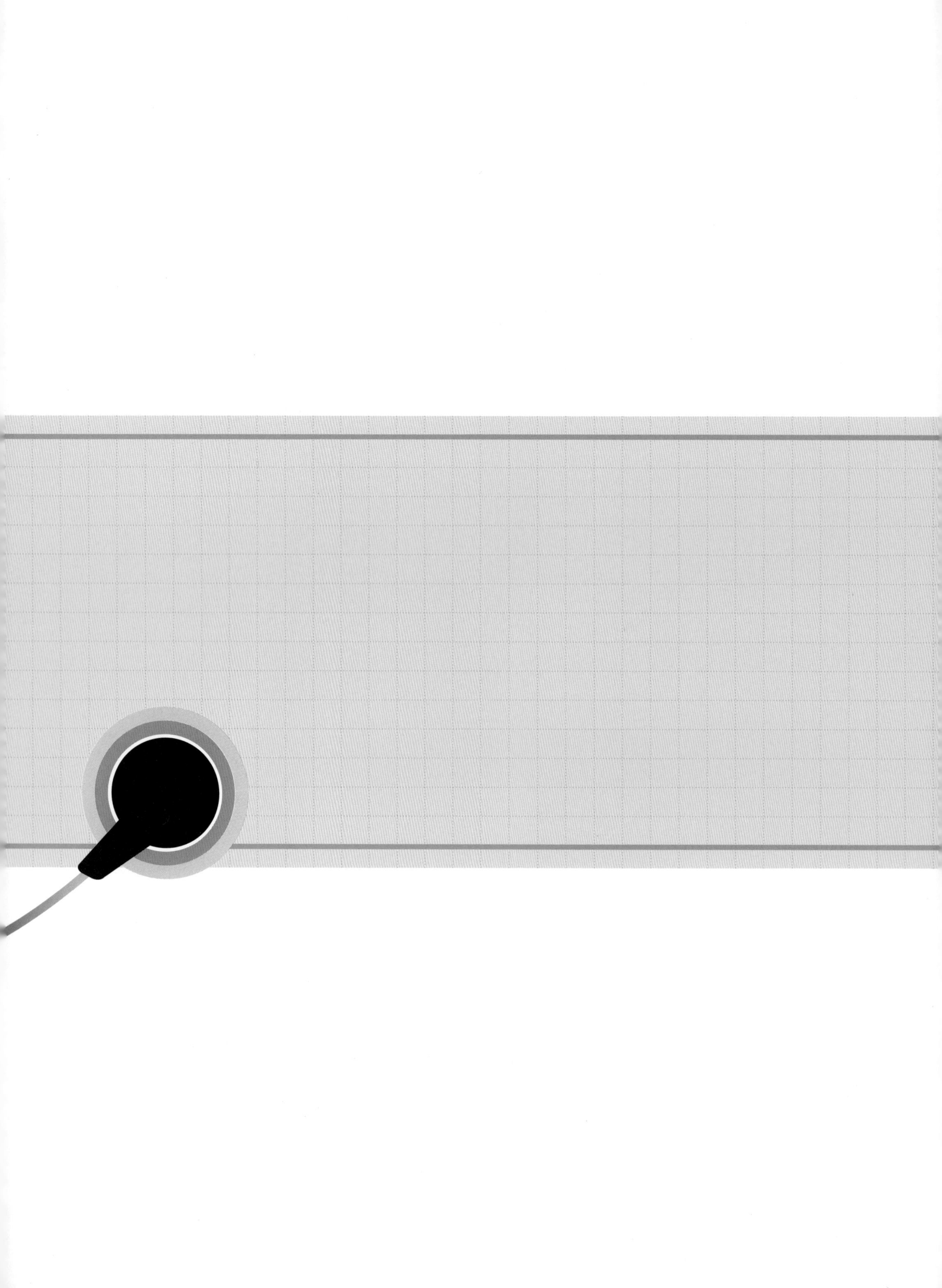

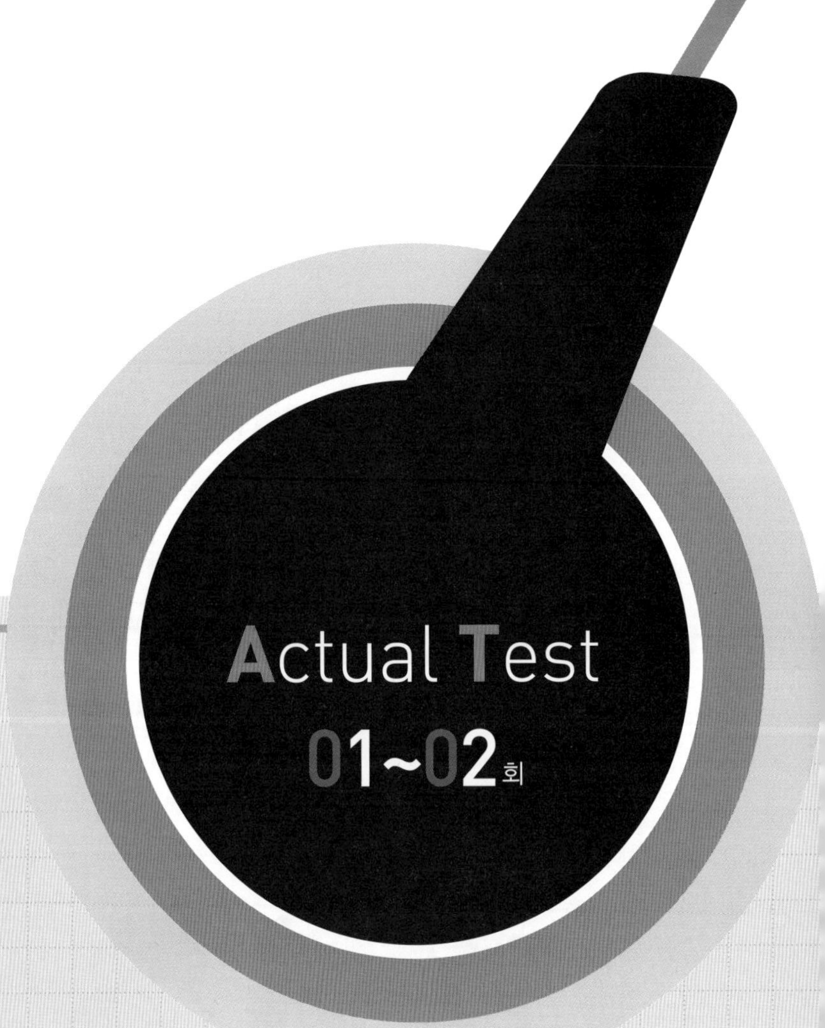
Actual Test
01~02회

01 Actual Test

01 대화를 듣고, 남자의 룸메이트를 고르시오.

02 대화를 듣고, 남자가 할 일을 고르시오.

①  ②  ③  ④  ⑤ 

03 대화를 듣고, 여자의 심정으로 가장 적절한 것을 고르시오.

① confident ② pleased ③ thankful
④ ashamed ⑤ bored

04 대화를 듣고, 여자의 컴퓨터가 고장 난 이유를 고르시오.

① 수명이 다 되어서
② 바이러스에 감염되어서
③ 무거운 물건을 떨어뜨려서
④ 용량이 너무 큰 파일을 받아서
⑤ 너무 장시간 사용해서

05 대화를 듣고, 학기말 과제 제출일까지 남은 날짜를 고르시오.

① 3일 ② 4일 ③ 5일 ④ 7일 ⑤ 8일

06 다음을 듣고, 무엇에 관한 설명인지 고르시오.

① 게 ② 해파리 ③ 바닷가새
④ 새우 ⑤ 문어

07 대화를 듣고, 여자의 장래희망을 고르시오.

① 영어 교사 ② 배우 ③ 여행 가이드
④ 영화 감독 ⑤ 행사 기획자

08 대화를 듣고, 여자가 남자에게 부탁한 일로 가장 적절한 것을 고르시오.

① 대신 장 봐주기 ② 돈 빌려주기
③ 문서 정리 도와주기 ④ 정장 빌려주기
⑤ 빌려준 돈 갚기

09 다음을 듣고, 그림의 상황에 어울리는 대화를 고르시오.

① ② ③ ④ ⑤

10 대화를 듣고, 대화 내용과 일치하지 않는 것을 고르시오.

① 여자는 음식점 종업원이다.
② 여자는 남자에게 음식을 추천해 줬다.
③ 남자는 주요리로 스파게티를 주문했다.
④ 남자는 샐러드를 추가 주문했다.
⑤ 남자는 혼자서는 메뉴를 결정하지 못했다.

11 대화를 듣고, 남자가 여자에게 부탁한 일로 가장 적절한 것을 고르시오.

① 쇼핑 사이트 주소 알려주기
② 세일 기간 알려주기
③ 보석 가게 알려주기
④ 여자친구 선물 골라주기
⑤ 대신 선물 구입해주기

12 대화를 듣고, 남자가 용돈을 모은 방법들로 언급되지 않은 것을 고르시오.

① 빨래
② 방 청소
③ 재활용품 분리 수거
④ 설거지
⑤ 구두 닦기

13 대화를 듣고, 여자가 기분이 좋은 이유를 고르시오.

① 좋은 커피숍을 발견해서
② 좋아하는 배우를 봐서
③ 유명 정치인과 악수를 해서
④ 사진이 잘 나와서
⑤ 재미있는 노래를 배워서

14 다음을 듣고, 내용과 일치하지 않는 것을 고르시오.

ACE Mart Job Opportunities

① **Job Position**: Salesclerk
② **Working Hours**: 8 hours a day (Working times flexible)
③ **Qualifying Conditions**: At least 1 year of experience
④ **Contact**: Robert Wilson ☎ 210-231-3456
⑤ **E-mail**: apply@jobsearch.com

15 대화를 듣고, 여자가 할 일로 가장 적절한 것을 고르시오.

① 구내 식당에서 식사하기
② Kevin에게 문자 보내기
③ 수업 듣기
④ 구내 식당에 전화하기
⑤ Kevin을 찾아가 사과하기

16 다음을 듣고, 두 사람의 대화가 어색한 것을 고르시오.

① ② ③ ④ ⑤

17 대화를 듣고, 대화 내용과 일치하지 않는 것을 고르시오.

① 현재 구름 낀 날씨이다.
② 오늘 밤에 비 올 확률이 있다.
③ 남자는 여자에게 우산을 챙길 것을 권한다.
④ 내일도 비가 올 것이다.
⑤ 여자는 내일 공원에서 자전거를 타려고 한다.

18 다음을 듣고, Lisa가 고려해야 할 속담으로 가장 적절한 것을 고르시오.

① No pain, no gain.
② Look before you leap.
③ Pride will have a fall.
④ No news is good news.
⑤ To sing psalms to a dead horse.

[19-20] 대화를 듣고, 남자의 마지막 말에 이어질 여자의 응답으로 가장 적절한 것을 고르시오.

19
① For here or to go?
② How much is it in total?
③ I hope you like the food.
④ The non-smoking area, please.
⑤ Oh, we will cook it again for you.

20
① Good for you!
② English is so fun.
③ Let's start the homework now.
④ When can you finish doing the homework?
⑤ I think everyone has his or her own talent.

13 Dictation Test

01

M There are lots of people coming to this __________.

W Yes. Is your __________ __________ here, as well?

M __________ __________, he's right over there.

W Which one is he?

M He is standing __________ __________ the __________.

W The guy with the __________?

M No, the one with the __________ __________.

02

W Did you __________ __________ the dog?

M Yes, I did. And I __________ the __________ as well. Do you want me to do __________?

W Sounds good. Can you __________ the __________?

M But mom, I am __________ very __________ __________ it.

W Then, what about __________ some __________?

M Okay. That is a __________ __________ __________. How many apples should I pick?

03

M How was your __________ __________ of work?

W Oh, it was just __________. It was really embarrassing.

M I'm sorry to hear that. Tell me about it.

W The job is __________ and the people there are really __________ __________ __________.

M Sounds good. So what __________ __________?

W When I __________ __________ the welcome meeting, I __________ __________ the doorway. On my first day at work, I __________ __________.

04

W What's wrong with this? It __________ __________.

M Are you having __________?

W Oh, do you know about __________? Can you help me?

M Sure! What is the problem?

W After __________ some files, my computer isn't working at all.

M Let me __________ __________ __________. Well... It looks like your computer is __________ with a __________.

W What shall I do?

05

M Let's have a __________, shall we?

W No. Our term paper is __________ on __________ __________.

M We already finished two pages of it.

W We need a __________ page term paper, though! And today is __________.

M Don't worry about it. We can put lots of __________ __________ __________. They will take up three or four pages.

W We __________ __________ __________. We have to __________ the remaining __________ pages.

06

W This lives in the __________. It doesn't have any __________ and it has a __________ __________.

There are two main ways for it to __________ __________. One is to __________ __________ black ink from its body. The other is for it to __________ __________ __________ according to its __________. It has two eyes and __________ __________. What is it?

07

M The Bucheon Film Festival is __________ __________ volunteers.

W I know, but I __________ __________.

M Why not? You want to be a __________ __________.

W That's right, but I'm __________ __________ __________ at speaking English.

M Come on, your English is __________. It'll also be a __________ __________ to practice it.

W I guess you're right. I'll apply for it __________ __________.

M Good luck to you!

08

W I just got a new job.

M Congratulations! What are you doing at the new company?

W I'm a __________. I __________ and __________ documents.

M Great! I'm so __________ of you.

W Well, I don't have enough __________ __________ __________ to work and __________ __________ until I get paid. Would you __________ __________ me some __________?

M Of course __________. Do you want to __________ __________ __________?

W That would be wonderful. Thanks.

09

① M It is time to __________ __________ __________. Put __________ into your __________.

W What about my pencil and eraser?

② M How many __________ do you want?

W A dozen, please.

③ M __________ __________ do you want to take?

W I want to enroll in the __________ __________.

④ M May I help you?

W I'm looking for comfortable __________ __________.

⑤ M Would you __________ __________ __________?

W Yes, please.

10

W Good afternoon. May I take your order?

M It's __________ to choose. What can you __________?

W Why don't you try __________ __________?

M The meatball spaghetti?

W Yes, we will also serve you a fresh __________ and some corn __________.

M Sounds great! I'll __________ __________.

W OK! I'll be __________ __________ with your meal.

11

W Hey, what's up?

M Oh, I'm just doing some __________ __________. A lot of websites are __________ __________ __________. You can __________ __________ __________ 80% on some items.

W Really? That's a big saving. What are you looking for?

M Well, I'm looking for a __________ __________ for my girlfriend. I think I will get her a necklace.

W I see.

M Can you __________ a nice necklace for me?

W Sure.

12

W Wow! I like your new shoes. They __________ very __________.

M You're right. I had to __________ __________ for several months to get them.

W Really? What did you do?

M I mostly did __________ __________. I did the __________, __________ my room, and __________ my parents' __________.

W They don't sound easy. I don't think I could do those things.

M I wanted the shoes __________ __________. I even __________ the __________.

13

M Chloe, why are you __________ __________?

W Because I __________ __________ today.

M What makes you feel so good?

W I saw my __________ __________ in a __________ __________ this afternoon. When I was walking out, he was walking in.

M Really? Did you __________ his __________?

W Of course I did. I even __________ __________ __________ with him and shook his hand.

M Wow! Good for you!

14

M ACE Mart is __________ __________ __________. The working hours are __________, but you have to work __________ __________ __________ __________ a day. Applicants should have at least 1 year of __________. E-mail your __________ to apply@jobsearch.com. If you have any questions, please call Robert Wilson on 210-231-3456. We look __________ __________ __________ from you.

15

M Do you know that Kevin is __________ __________ __________ you?

W Yes. But __________ __________ I can do.

M Why don't you call him? He has __________ __________ now.

W I tried __________ __________ but he isn't answering my phone calls and __________ __________.

M That's too bad. I think you'd better go see him and __________. I saw him in the __________ a while ago.

W Thank you for your __________.

16

① W Please show me your new bag.
M I know it is very expensive.

② W __________ __________ __________.
M Oh, thank you.

③ W What's up?
M Nothing much. I just feel tired.

④ W Please pass me the __________ and the __________.
M Sure. Here they are.

⑤ W What's your __________ __________?
M I like English best.

17

W It's __________ __________, today. Did you see __________ __________ __________?

M Yes. There is a __________ __________ __________ tonight. You'd better take an __________ with you.

W Thanks. How about __________? Will it rain?

M No, the __________ said that tomorrow will be a perfect day for __________ __________.

W __________! I am going to ride my bike with my __________ in the park then.

M Have fun!

18

W Your best friend Lisa __________ __________. She is waiting for a call from her __________ __________. He was supposed to call her __________ __________ __________, but he hasn't called her yet. Lisa calls her brother's cellular phone, but it is __________ __________. After a while, her brother calls her on his friend's phone and tells her that his phone __________ __________ __________ __________. You think that Lisa cares about her brother too much and gets __________ __________ __________. What proverb do you think Lisa should keep in mind?

19

W Excuse me. __________ __________ __________ to order?

M Yes. We will have __________ __________ __________ and __________ fried rice.

W How about drinks?

M Just water, please. [pause]

W Your __________ is __________. __________ __________ __________.

M Thanks. Wow! It smells so good! My mouth is __________.

W I hope you like the food.

20

W __________ __________ __________ with your homework?

M Yes. I just __________ it. How about you?

W I have three more math __________ to __________. If you don't mind, could you please __________ them to me?

M Sure, I will. __________ __________ me the __________.

W Here they are. I __________ you a lot. I wish I was as __________ __________ __________ as you.

M You're good at English. I envy you.

W I think everyone has his or her own talent.

02 Actual Test

01 대화를 듣고, 남자가 아직 준비하지 않은 것을 고르시오.

02 대화를 듣고, 남자가 신고 있는 신발을 고르시오.

03 대화를 듣고, 여자의 심정으로 가장 적절한 것을 고르시오.

① nervous ② upset ③ sad
④ painful ⑤ confused

04 대화를 듣고, 남자의 직업으로 가장 적절한 것을 고르시오.

① engineer ② editor ③ hairdresser
④ chef ⑤ artist

05 대화를 듣고, 여자가 지불할 금액을 고르시오.

① $17 ② $34 ③ $70 ④ $140 ⑤ $147

06 다음을 듣고, 무엇에 관한 내용인지 고르시오.

① 그림책의 중요성
② 그림책의 종류
③ 그림책에서 그림의 역할
④ 삽화를 그리는 방법
⑤ 그림을 이해하는 방법

07 대화를 듣고, 두 사람이 대화하는 장소로 가장 적절한 것을 고르시오.

① department store
② fitness center
③ airport
④ bus terminal
⑤ hospital

08 대화를 듣고, 여자가 할 일로 가장 적절한 것을 고르시오.

① 라면 끓이기
② 나무 줍기
③ 텐트 치기
④ 불 피우기
⑤ 휴식하기

09 다음을 듣고, 그림의 상황에 어울리는 대화를 고르시오.

① ② ③ ④ ⑤

10 대화를 듣고, 대화 내용과 일치하지 않는 것을 고르시오.

① 여자는 체중이 늘었다.
② 남자는 건강 관리를 잘하고 있다.
③ 남자는 수영을 해서 살을 5킬로 뺐다.
④ 여자는 다음 주부터 에어로빅을 할 계획이다.
⑤ 남자는 여자에게 규칙적으로 운동하라고 충고한다.

11 대화를 듣고, 여자가 남자에게 부탁한 일로 가장 적절한 것을 고르시오.

① 책 반납해주기 ② 강의실 위치 알려주기
③ 책 대여해주기 ④ 보고서 함께 쓰기
⑤ 도서관에 함께 가기

12 대화를 듣고, 김치볶음밥을 만드는 방법으로 언급되지 않은 것을 고르시오.

① 김치를 물에 씻기
② 김치와 햄 다지기
③ 프라이팬에 기름 넣고 달구기
④ 제일 나중에 밥 넣기
⑤ 달구어진 프라이팬에 재료 넣고 섞기

13 대화를 듣고, 여자가 일요일에 오보에 연습을 못하는 이유로 가장 적절한 것을 고르시오.

① 독서실에 가야 해서 ② 쇼핑을 해야 해서
③ 동창회가 있어서 ④ 보충수업이 있어서
⑤ 집에서 시험 공부를 해야 해서

14 다음을 듣고, 원그래프의 내용과 일치하지 않는 것을 고르시오.

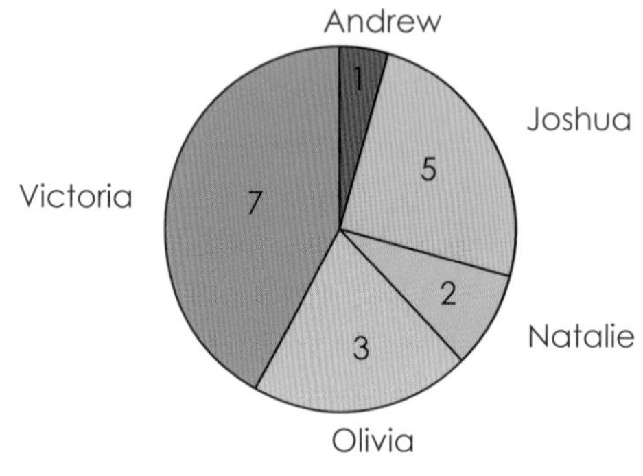

① ② ③ ④ ⑤

15 대화를 듣고, 남자가 해야 할 일이 아닌 것을 고르시오.

① 이메일 확인하기 ② Costner 씨와 회의하기
③ 음료와 다과 준비하기 ④ Herrington 씨와 회의하기
⑤ 계약 업무 진행하기

16 다음을 듣고, 두 사람의 대화가 어색한 것을 고르시오.

① ② ③ ④ ⑤

17 대화를 듣고, 대화 내용과 일치하지 않는 것을 고르시오.

① 여자는 학교 동호회에 대해 잘 모른다.
② 학교에는 15개의 동호회가 있다.
③ 남자는 댄스 동아리에 가입되어 있다.
④ 동호회 가입은 의무사항이다.
⑤ 남자는 여자에게 댄스 동아리 가입을 권유하고 있다.

18 다음을 듣고, Carol이 남자 승객에게 할 말로 가장 적절한 것을 고르시오.

① Excuse me. Please turn it off.
② You've got a nice mp3 player.
③ What is the song you are listening to?
④ Can I borrow your mp3 player, please?
⑤ Can you turn the volume down, please?

[19-20] 대화를 듣고, 여자의 마지막 말에 이어질 남자의 응답으로 가장 적절한 것을 고르시오.

19 ① I'll bring my diary.
② Please try to be quiet in this area.
③ Sounds perfect. We can go right now.
④ She said it will be a good experience for me.
⑤ I don't think so. There's nothing we can do there.

20 ① Stop doing that!
② Actually, I'm from Mexico.
③ Right, it's late. Let's go home now.
④ No problem. I often forget things, too.
⑤ I know. The book is very expensive.

01

W Are you ________ for your ________ to Mexico?

M Yes, but I still have ________ ________ ________ ________ to prepare.

W Have you paid for your ________ ________ yet?

M ________ ________. I'll search for one on the Internet.

W What about ________?

M Yes, I packed them with my clothes, underwear and swimsuit.

W ________ ________ to take your ________ as well!

02

M Do you have a ________ pair of shoes?

W I sure do. They are ________ ________ shoes with white ribbons.

M ________ ________ them for you?

W My grandfather did on my ________. What about you?

M These new ones that I'm ________ ________. All ________ sneakers with ________ ________ on them.

W Oh, you bought them! They ________ ________!

03

W I ________ Julia. I will ________ ________ her!

M What's wrong with her?

W She wanted to ________ ________ ________ so I let her.

M Did she ________ it?

W No, but she ________ all my music files. I tried to restore them but ________ ________.

M Have you ________ to her about it?

W Yes, she just said, "________!" That was it.

04

M Hello, how may I help you?

W My hair is ________ ________ ________. I'd like to have it ________.

M ________ ________ do you want me to cut?

W Maybe two inches off the ends? I want it to ________ ________.

M All right. And would you like to dye your hair?

W No, I want to ________ my ________ ________.

M Okay, I see.

05

W Hello. Can I see that pair of ________ in size 7?

M Yes, we also have ________ ________: red, black, brown, and pink.

W Then, can you show me the ones ________ ________ ________ ________?

M Of course. Here they are.

W ________ ________ are they?

M They are ________ dollars a pair.

W I want to take ________ ________, please. Can I pay by credit card?

06

M In a ________ ________, the pictures help you to ________ the story. They show you ________ the people and the places

__________ __________, and what is happening. The pictures also show the story's __________ or __________. The pictures tell you if a story is __________, __________ or __________. Pictures may help you catch the feeling of poems, too.

07

W Are you __________ __________ something?

M Yes, I'm __________ __________.

W __________ do you want to go?

M I'm supposed to __________ a __________ X-ray.

W The X-ray room is __________ __________, next to the __________ __________.

M Yes, there is the sign. Thank you so much.

08

M This camping trip is __________. It is so __________ to be out here.

W I __________. This was a great idea. Look at the beautiful colors in the sky.

M It's __________ a bit __________ though. I'll __________ some __________ to make a fire.

W Okay, do you __________ my help?

M __________ __________. I can do it __________.

W Then I'm going to __________ __________ __________.

M Sounds perfect!

09

① M Do you have __________ __________?

W Yes, it is 6 o'clock.

② M Can I buy __________ __________ for the 7 o'clock __________?

W I'm sorry we don't have any seats available.

③ M Can I __________ __________ Carl, please?

W I think you have the __________ __________.

④ M I'd like to __________ a car for a week.

W Okay, what kind of car do you want to rent?

⑤ M Good morning, front desk.

W I'd like to __________ __________ this morning, please.

10

M You look like you are gaining some __________.

W Yes, I am. I gained 5kgs. I am really __________ __________ __________.

M I swim three times a week. It helps me __________ __________ __________.

W That's why you __________ so __________. I'm __________ to take an aerobics class from __________ __________.

M It is important to __________ __________ before you exercise. You should also exercise __________.

W Thank you for your __________. I'll keep it in mind.

11

W Edison, where are you going?

M I'm __________ __________ __________ to the library.

W Why? Do you have something to __________?

M No. I'm going to __________ __________ some books for my report.

W I see. Can you do me a __________?

M Sure. What is it?

W Can you please __________ this book for me? __________ __________ __________ class.

M No problem.

12

W Luke, can you tell me __________ __________

__________ kimchi fried rice?

M Okay. Prepare a __________ __________, kimchi, cooked rice, oil, and __________.

W What should I do then?

M __________, __________ the kimchi and cube the ham. __________, heat the pan and add some oil.

W Okay, that's easy.

M Now put all the __________ __________ in the pan, __________ __________ the rice. Mix them. Then __________ __________ __________ in the pan, and mix them __________.

W It doesn't sound hard. I will try to make it. Thanks.

13

W Hi, Gabriel. __________ __________ __________ __________. I'm glad to see you.

M I'm glad to see you, too. How have you been?

W __________ __________. And you?

M I'm fine. __________ __________ __________, do you still practice the oboe every Sunday?

W Yes, but not this Sunday. I have a __________ __________ in math and English. The __________ __________ are starting next week.

M I see. __________ __________ on __________ __________.

14

① W Victoria reads the most __________ __________ __________.

② W Olivia reads __________ __________ Natalie.

③ W Andrew reads more than Joshua.

④ W Natalie reads __________ __________ Olivia.

⑤ W Joshua reads five books __________ __________.

15

M Please tell me my __________ __________.

W You __________ __________ __________ with Dr. Costner at 3 o'clock.

M What about my meeting with Professor Herrington?

W He's scheduled for 5:40 this __________. I sent you the __________ of the __________ you will need to sign via email.

M Thank you. Can you __________ some drinks and snacks for my guests, please?

W Sure. I'll do that now.

M Okay. I'll __________ __________ my email, then.

16

① W __________ __________ __________?

M Yes. I'm going to get married next month.

② W Where are you from?

M __________ __________ Chicago.

③ W How do you __________ __________ __________?

M My dad takes me to school.

④ W __________ __________ to the movies.

M Sounds great!

⑤ W How much is that __________?

M It is 3 dollars.

17

M Did you sign up for a __________?

W No. I don't even know __________ __________ and __________ __________ __________ clubs there are in this school.

M There are __________ __________. Since it is __________, you should __________ at least one.

W I know. Which one do you __________

__________?

M I belong to the __________ __________.

W That __________ like fun. I think I'll join up, too.

18

M Carol is a __________ __________. She is __________ that passengers must turn off __________ __________ like mp3 players, __________, and cell phones. It is because their __________ may __________ with the plane's __________ __________. At that time, she sees a man take his mp3 player out and try to __________ it __________. In this situation, what would Carol most likely say to the man?

19

W Do you want to go to the __________ __________ this weekend?

M __________ __________ __________ go but my mom has to say 'Yes' first.

W __________ __________ __________ __________ her now and ask her about it?

M Okay, __________ __________. [pause]

W __________ did she say?

M She said it will be a good experience for me.

20

M Can I __________ my book __________? I need it for the test.

W I'm sorry. I __________ it at __________ this morning. If you need it, I will go home and get it.

M Well, you don't have to.

W Are you sure?

M I will just __________ the __________ __________ from the library.

W Thank you. It's a __________ __________ __________.

M No problem. I often forget things, too.

Vocabulary Review

Vocabulary Review

	ride	타다
01	beautiful	아름다운
	for a while	잠시
	be out of	~이 떨어지다
02	convenience store	편의점
	quite	꽤
	hundreds of	수백의
03	neither	~도 아니다
	section	구역
	have a reservation	예약되어 있다
04	dine	식사하다
	party	일행
05	deal	거래
	additional	추가의
	pose for	~을 위해 자세를 취하다
06	magnificent	웅장한
	have lunch	점심 식사를 하다
	these days	요즈음
07	since	~이므로
	at the moment	지금은
08	Go ahead.	그렇게 하세요.
	be from	~ 출신이다
	sleeping bag	침낭
09	though	(문장 끝에서) 그러나
	equipment	장비
	get married	결혼하다
10	keep ~ secret	~을 비밀로 하다
	look good together	잘 어울리다
	principal	교장선생님
11	school newsletter	가정통신문

	submit	제출하다
	permission slip	허가서
	stay healthy	건강을 유지하다
12	nutritional supplement	영양제
	keep in shape	건강을 유지하다
	decide on	~을 결심하다
13	gather	모으다
	look forward to -ing	~하기를 고대하다
14	take a nap	낮잠을 자다
	go out	외출하다
15	catch a cold	감기에 걸리다
	mention	언급하다
16	comic book	만화책
	stranger	낯선 사람
	festival	축제
	various	다양한
17	entertain	즐겁게 하다
	participant	참가자
	be limited to	~로 제한되다
18	wait for	~을 기다리다
	situation	상황
	check out	확인하다
19	try to-V	~하려고 노력하다
	envy	부러워하다
	on one's way home	집에 가는 길에
20	grab	움켜쥐다
	set the table	상을 차리다

Vocabulary Review

01	between A and B	A와 B 사이에
	laptop	노트북 컴퓨터
02	popular	인기 있는
	friendly	친근한
	bald	대머리의
03	stomach	배
	bother	힘들게 하다
	under the weather	몸이 좋지 않은
	food poisoning	식중독
04	How's it going?	어떻게 지내세요?
	deposit	입금하다
	check	수표
	open an account	계좌를 개설하다
05	parcel	소포
	by regular mail	일반 우편으로
	weigh	(무게가) ~ 나가다
	cost	(돈이) 들다
06	excitement	즐거움
	culture	문화
	climate	기후
07	because of	~ 때문에
	sweet	다정한
08	participation	참여
	attendance	출석
	assignment	과제
	total	합계하다
09	refrigerator	냉장고
	run out of	~이 다 떨어지다
10	spare	여분의
	every other day	이틀에 한 번씩
11	move over	자리를 좁히다
12	tip	비결
13	wear odd shoes	신발을 짝짝이로 신다
	laugh at	~을 보고 웃다
	embarrassed	당황스러운
	in a hurry	서두른
14	not only A but also B	A뿐만 아니라 B 또한
	healthy	건강한
	slim	날씬한
15	final paper	기말 (논문)과제
	survey	설문
	take	(시간이) 걸리다
16	grow up	자라다
17	How have you been?	어떻게 지냈니?
	used to-V	~하곤 했다
	amusement park	놀이공원
18	have no idea	전혀 모르다
	be interested in	~에 흥미가 있다
	probably	아마도
19	attend	참석하다
	leave a message	메시지를 남기다
	call back	회답 전화를 하다
20	free	한가한
	plan to-V	~할 계획이다
	nursing home	양로원

Vocabulary Review

01	chubby	통통한
	active	활동적인
02	go straight	직진하다
	across from	~의 건너편에
03	rip	찢다
	as soon as	~하자 마자
	make a copy of	~을 복사하다
04	have a runny nose	콧물이 흐르다
	cough	기침하다
	flu	독감
	prescribe	처방하다
05	absent	결석한
	including	~을 포함하여
	except for	~을 제외하고
06	laundry	세탁
	fold	(옷 등을) 개다
	rate	가격
	delivery	배달
07	whether ~ or not	~인지 아닌지
	ingredient	재료
	first of all	우선
08	feel airsick	비행기 멀미하다
	remain	~인 채로 있다
09	structure	구조
	stem	줄기
	function	기능
10	memorize	암기하다
	had better+동사원형	~하는 것이 낫다
11	destroy	파괴하다
	either A or B	A 또는 B
	injure	다치게 하다
	donate	기부하다
12	suitable	적당한
	detergent	세제
	after a while	잠시 후에
13	work out	운동하다
	regularly	규칙적으로
	be good for	~에 좋다
	gain weight	살이 찌다
14	Speaking.	(전화) 전데요.
	invite	초대하다
15	apology	사과
	have a hard time -ing	~하는 데 애를 먹다
16	How far ~?	얼마나 멀리 ~?
	How long ~?	얼마나 오랫동안 ~?
	How often ~?	얼마나 자주 ~?
17	take off	벗다
	inside	내부에서
	Westerner	서양인
18	overseas	해외에
	arrange	계획을 짜다
	urgent	급한
19	fortunately	다행스럽게도
	explain	설명하다
	Don't mention it.	천만에.
20	science fiction	공상과학
	at least	최소한

04 Vocabulary Review

01	whole	전체의
	curly hair	곱슬머리
02	dessert	후식
	peach	복숭아
03	worry	걱정시키다, 걱정하다
	prepare	준비하다
	enough	충분한
04	fill a prescription	약을 조제하다
	pill	알약
	~ times a day	하루에 ~ 번
	skip	거르다
05	be made of	~로 만들어지다
	pretty	꽤
	possible	가능한
	discount	할인
06	care about	~에 관심을 가지다
	fit	건강한
	for oneself	혼자 힘으로
07	wake up	깨다
	get up	일어나다
	record	녹음하다, 녹화하다
08	take a break	휴식을 취하다
	by the way	그런데
	be good at	~를 잘하다
09	available	이용 가능한
	monthly rent	월세
10	heavy traffic	교통 혼잡
11	pick up	고르다
	suit	~에게 어울리다
	fitting room	탈의실

12	Congratulations!	축하해!
	preview	예습하다
	review	복습하다
13	mad	화난
	on time	제시간에
	patience	인내심
14	thriller	스릴러
	have ~ in common	~을 공통으로 가지다
	run	상영되다
15	have a headache	두통이 있다
	stand	참다
	go around	(병 등이) 퍼지다
	take medicine	약을 먹다
16	What do you think of ~?	~에 대해 어떻게 생각해?
	look around	둘러보다
17	vacation	방학
	Europe	유럽
	fantastic	환상적인
18	homeroom teacher	담임선생님
	honestly	솔직하게
	strict	엄격한
19	on the way to	~로 가는 길에
	sick	아픈
	slip	미끄러져 넘어지다
20	breathe	숨을 쉬다
	out of order	고장 난
	Pardon?	뭐라고요?

Vocabulary Review

01	take care of	~를 돌보다
	exhausted	녹초가 된
	yawn	하품하다
02	nephew	조카
	stuffed	봉제한
03	terrific	아주 멋진
	souvenir	기념품
04	catch a flight	비행기를 타다
	as+부사+as possible	가능한 한 ~하게
	traffic jam	교통 체증
05	break	(돈을 작은 단위로) 바꾸다
	rest	나머지
	Here you go.	여기 있습니다.
06	introduce	소개하다
	impression	인상
	advice	충고
	entire	전체의
07	shaggy	털투성이의
	look great on	~에게 잘 어울리다
	come along	동행하다
08	receive	받다
	vase	꽃병
	on purpose	고의로
	fall down	쓰러지다
09	grapefruit	자몽
	seedless	씨 없는
	be fond of	~를 좋아하다
10	lazy	여유로운, 느긋한
	wet	젖은
	raindrop	빗방울
11	take a picture	사진을 찍다
	go on a picnic	소풍을 가다
	access	접속하다
	Why don't you ~?	~하는 게 어때?
12	wrong	잘못된
	back	되돌려
	exchange	교환하다
	refund	환불
	inconvenience	불편함
13	lie	눕다
	How about -ing?	~하는 건 어때?
	several	몇몇의
14	restaurant	식당, 레스토랑
	buffet	뷔페
15	environment	환경
	save	절약하다
	recycle	재활용하다
16	try on	입어[신어]보다
	police officer	경찰관
17	choose	선택하다
	expensive	비싼
	be in one's mind	염두에 두다
18	tourist spot	관광명소
	fancy	화려한
	leave a tip	팁을 남기다
19	excited	신이 난
	competition	시합
	for free	공짜로
20	It's time to-V	~할 시간이다
	go to bed	잠자리에 들다

Vocabulary Review

01	either	(부정문에서) 또한
	What if ~?	만약 ~라면 어쩌지?
02	turn right	오른쪽으로 돌다
	Not at all.	천만에요.
03	eat out	외식하다
	borrow	빌리다
	purse	(여성용) 지갑, 핸드백
	treat	대접하다
04	shelf	선반
	reserve	따로 남겨 두다
05	August	8월
	May	5월
06	limited	제한된
	resources	자원
	material	자재
	pollute	오염시키다
07	go to the movies	영화 보러 가다
	sometimes	때때로
08	make an appointment	약속을 정하다
	see a doctor	진료를 받다
09	make a call	전화 걸다
	text message	문자
10	be late for	~에 지각하다
	miss	놓치다
	lend	빌려주다
	share	공유하다
11	checkout	체크아웃, 퇴실
	extend	연장하다
12	home appliance	가전제품
	metal	금속
13	cause	야기시키다
	start a fire	화재를 일으키다
	spill	엎지르다
	repairman	수리공
	recover	복구하다
14	business hours	영업 시간
	membership fee	회원가
	per	~마다
15	costume	복장
	remind	상기시키다
	stop by	~에 들르다
16	February	2월
17	brochure	소책자
	special price	특별가
	early bird	일찍 오는 사람
18	ignore	무시하다
	noise	소음
	fall asleep	잠이 들다
	neighbor	이웃
19	release stress	스트레스를 해소하다
	process	과정
	one day	언젠가는
20	regret	후회하다
	be supposed to-V	~하기로 되어 있다

07 Vocabulary Review

01	weather report	일기예보
	degree	도(℃)
	stay tuned	계속 시청하다
02	job interview	취업 면접
	prefer A to B	B보다 A를 더 좋아하다
	go with	~와 잘 어울리다
03	be opposite to	~와 정반대이다
	celebrate	기념하다
	amazing	놀라운
04	passport	여권
	immigration	입국
	purpose	목적
	on business	사업차
05	close	친한
	dozen	열두 개
	wrap	포장하다
06	raise	기르다
	feed	먹이를 주다
07	textbook	교과서
	extra	여분의
	backpack	배낭
08	Who's calling?	(전화상에서) 누구세요?
	package	소포, 꾸러미
	security office	경비실
	appreciate	감사하다
	consideration	배려
09	order	주문
10	have a great time	즐거운 시간을 보내다
	fall	폭포
	scenery	경치

11	look for	~을 찾다
	especially	특히
	taste	취향
	recommend	추천하다
12	cancel	취소하다
	confirm	확인하다
	representative	상담원; 대표자
	repeat	반복하다
13	already	이미
14	clearance sale	재고 정리 세일
	from A to B	A부터 B까지
	on sale	세일 중인
15	remember	기억하다
	move	이사하다
16	pay in cash	현금으로 지불하다
	nervous	불안한
17	mean	의미하다
18	give an excuse	변명을 하다
	lecture	훈계하다
	behavior	행동
19	have a seat	자리에 앉다
	in a minute	곧
20	due to	~ 때문에
	typhoon	태풍
	heavy rain	폭우
	thunderstorm	심한 뇌우

08 Vocabulary Review

01	be ready to-V	~할 준비가 되다
	back to back	등을 맞대고
	polka-dot	물방울 무늬의
02	lettuce	양상추
	a head of	한 포기의
03	accept	받아들이다
	come true	실현되다
04	terrible	심한
	cold medicine	감기약
	work well	(약이) 잘 듣다
05	else	그 밖의
	change	잔돈, 거스름돈
06	shop online	인터넷 쇼핑하다
	personal data	개인정보
	expose	노출하다
07	toilet	변기
	overflow	넘쳐 흐르다
	food waste	음식물 쓰레기
	amount	양
	What a day!	정말 힘든 하루다!
08	major in	~을 전공하다
	history	역사
09	water	물을 주다
	plant	식물
10	housework	집안일
	wash the dishes	설거지하다
	do the laundry	빨래하다
	do the vacuuming	진공청소기로 청소하다
11	Long time no see.	오랜만이야.
	give birth	출산하다

12	newborn baby	신생아
	in front of	~ 앞에서
	while	~하는 동안
	neat	깔끔한
13	concentrate on	~에 집중하다
	addict	중독되게 하다
	serious	진지한
	ruin	망치다
15	dish	음식; 접시
	housewarming party	집들이
16	on foot	걸어서
	due date	마감 기한
	lose	잃어버리다
17	Cheer up!	힘내!
	afraid	두려워하는
	report card	성적표
	do one's best	최선을 다하다
18	drop	떨어뜨리다
	wallet	지갑
	ground	땅
19	bridge	다리
	of course	물론
	believe	믿다
20	search	검색하다
	a pair of	~ 한 켤레
	I'm broke.	난 빈털터리야.

Vocabulary Review

01	row	줄
02	travel	여행하다
	hike	도보여행을 하다
	hot spring	온천
	plum	자두
03	be sick of	~에 진절머리가 나다
04	stain	얼룩
	sleeve	소매
	remove	제거하다
	by tomorrow	내일까지
05	book	예약하다
	tax	세금
06	device	장치
	transfer	옮기다
	be able to-V	~할 수 있다
	keep track of	~을 추적하다
07	awful	끔찍한
	boring	따분한
	bore	따분한 사람
08	side dish	반찬
	have a bite to eat	(가벼운) 식사를 하다
09	press	누르다
	bill	계산서
	stairs	계단
10	salesclerk	판매원
	counter	계산대
	wrapping paper	포장지
11	match	경기
	wish	소망하다
	obviously	확실히
12	turn on	켜다
	warm up	예열하다
	surface	표면
	lastly	마지막으로
13	Welcome to ~.	~에 온 것을 환영합니다.
	check in	체크인하다, 투숙하다
	spell	철자를 말하다
	last name	성
14	December	12월
	contact	연락, 접촉
16	sick in bed	몸져누운
	starve	굶주리다
17	actually	실제로
	in stock	재고가 있는
18	receptionist	접수 담당자
	dental clinic	치과
	directly	곧바로
	walk-in	불쑥 찾아온 방문자
19	have no plan	계획이 없다
	take a rest	휴식을 취하다
	perfect	완벽한
20	arrive	도착하다
	airport	공항
	welcome party	환영 파티

10 Vocabulary Review

01	cucumber	오이
	You bet.	물론이지.
02	elder sister	언니, 누나
	two-story	이층의
03	secretary	비서
	single	1인용의
	floor	층
	behind	~ 뒤에
04	play baseball	야구 하다
	sweat	땀 흘리다
05	forget	잊다
	leave	두고 오다
06	beat	이기다
	as long as	~하는 한
	safeguard	안전요원
	drown	익사하다
07	abroad	해외로, 해외에서
	Thailand	태국
	wonder	경이로움
08	movie theater	극장
09	full	배가 부른
	I beg your pardon?	뭐라고요?
10	turn down	줄이다
	still	여전히
	waste	낭비하다
11	My goodness!	맙소사!
	autograph	사인, 서명
	brave	용감한
	kindness	친절
	public restroom	공중 화장실
12	install	설치하다
	washstand	세면대
	rub	비비다
13	wall paper	벽지
	calm	차분한
	relax	편하게 하다
14	Language Arts	(과목) 언어, 국어
	least	가장 적게
15	conference	회의
	public transportation	대중교통
16	holiday	휴가
	get	가져다 주다
17	car accident	차 사고
	bad	심하게
	unfortunately	불행하게도
18	be absent from	~에 결석하다
	bad cold	독감
	Social Studies	(과목) 사회
19	enroll in	~에 등록하다
	timetable	시간표
20	have no choice	선택의 여지가 없다
	suppose	생각하다
	adult	성인

11 Vocabulary Review

01	bottom	바닥
	kite	연
	Good job!	잘했어!
02	road sign	도로표지판
	keys of a piano	피아노 건반
	crosswalk	횡단보도
03	blood	피
	dead	죽은
	make-up artist	분장사
04	French	프랑스의
05	exhibition	전시회
	convenient	편리한
	receipt	영수증
06	invention	발명품
	in person	직접
	play a major role in	~에 중요한 역할을 하다
	global	지구의
07	lake	호수
	flat	공기가 빠진
	That's nice of you.	너 참 착하구나.
08	be out	외출 중이다
09	bring	가지고 오다
10	neighborhood	사는 지역
	quiet	조용한
	area	지역
	apartment	아파트
11	declaration	신고
	help out	도와주다
	fill out	작성하다
	die from	~로 사망하다
12	death	사망
	prevent	예방하다
	brush one's teeth	양치하다
13	escalator	에스컬레이터
	be full of	~로 가득 차다
	trouble	고통
14	all year round	일년 내내
	entrance fee	입장료
	elderly	노인의
15	be sold out	매진되다
	within	~ 안에
16	get angry	화가 나다
	hallway	복도
	meat	육류
17	fall off	~에서 떨어지다
	elbow	팔꿈치
	knee	무릎
18	decide to-V	~할 것을 결심하다
	unnecessary	불필요한
	proverb	속담
19	clear	(날씨가) 맑은
20	dress up	옷을 차려 입다
	I'm afraid that	유감스럽지만 ~이다
	illness	질병

12 Vocabulary Review

01	yard sale	야드 세일
	stuff	물건
02	dresser	화장대
	drawers	서랍장
	closet	옷장
03	statement	진술
	leather	가죽
	registration	등록
04	have a stomachache	배가 아프다
	excuse	변명
05	national museum	국립 박물관
06	musical instrument	악기
	turn A into B	A를 B로 바꾸다
	comb	빗
	xylophone	실로폰
07	feel sick	아프다
	shot	주사
	cure	치료하다
	No way!	절대 안돼!
08	be mean to	~에게 못되게 굴다
	not ~ anymore	더 이상 ~할 수 없는
	awkward	어색한
09	upside-down	거꾸로 된
	triangle	삼각형
	trunk	(코끼리의) 코
10	slender	날씬한
	jog	천천히 달리다, 조깅하다
	companion	동행(인)
11	night market	야시장
	moreover	게다가
12	elementary school	초등학교
	depend on	~에 달려있다
	traffic	교통(량)
13	make it to	~ 시간에 대다
	appointment	약속
	high fever	고열
14	P. E.	체육
15	in a way	한편으로는
	penalty	벌
	fee	요금
	cut off	중단하다
	account transfer	계좌 이체
16	how to-V	~하는 방법
17	scary	무서운
	smooth	부드러운
	bite	물다
18	average	평균
	be disappointed	실망하다
19	tasty	맛있는
	awesome	끝내주는
20	floral	꽃의
	pattern	무늬
	striped	줄무늬의

13 Vocabulary Review

01	next to	~의 옆에
	beard	턱수염
	shave	면도하다
02	finish -ing	~하는 것을 끝내다
	milk a cow	우유를 짜다
	a piece of cake	아주 쉬운 일
03	go wrong	잘못되다
	be nice to	~에게 친절하게 대하다
	trip on	~에 걸려 넘어지다
04	take a look	훑어보다
	infect	감염시키다
05	term paper	학기말 리포트[보고서]
	due	마감이 ~까지인
	remaining	남아 있는
06	shoot out	쏘다
	according to	~에 따라서
	surroundings	주위 환경
07	volunteer	자원봉사자
	apply for	~에 지원하다
	film director	영화감독
08	organize	정리하다
	file documents	서류를 철하다
	mind -ing	~하는 것을 꺼리다
09	take a test	시험을 보다
	eraser	지우개
	comfortable	편안한
10	take an order	주문을 받다
	serve	(음식을) 차려내다
11	up to	최대 ~까지
	present	선물
12	chore	허드렛일
	separate	분리하다
	recyclable	재활용품
13	hum	(노래를) 흥얼거리다
	actor	배우
	shake one's hand	~와 악수하다
14	working hours	근무 시간
	flexible	융통성 있는
	applicant	지원자
15	apologize	사과하다
	cafeteria	구내식당
	a while ago	조금 전에
16	Watch your step.	발 조심해.
	subject	과목
17	chance	가능성
	take an umbrella	우산을 가져가다
	weatherman	일기예보자
	outdoor activity	야외 활동
18	have a dead battery	배터리가 나가다
	get nervous	불안해하다
19	meal	식사
	smell	~한 냄새가 나다
20	be done with	~을 끝내다
	solve	풀다
	talent	재능

14 Vocabulary Review

01	rental car	렌터카
	search for	~을 찾다
	pack	짐을 싸다
	as well	역시
02	flat	납작한
	sneakers	운동화
	cool	멋진
03	delete	지우다
	restore	복구하다
	That's it.	그게 다야.
04	dye	염색하다
	natural	타고난, 자연스러운
05	both	둘 다
	pay by credit card	신용카드로 지불하다
06	tone	분위기
	mood	기분
	poem	시
07	be lost	길을 잃다
	chest	흉부
	eye clinic	안과
08	agree	동의하다
	make a fire	불을 피우다
	alone	혼자
	instant noodle	즉석 면, 라면
09	Do you have the time?	몇 시예요?
	have the wrong number	전화 잘못 걸다
10	out of shape	몸 상태가 나쁜
	in shape	몸 상태가 좋은
11	return	반납하다
	check out	(절차를 밟고) 빌리다
	do ~ a favor	~의 부탁을 들어주다
12	chop	다지다
	cube	네모로 자르다
	heat	가열하다
	mix	섞다
13	be glad to-V	~하게 되어 기쁘다
	practice	연습하다
	makeup class	보충 수업
15	be scheduled for	~로 일정이 잡히다
	contract	계약서
	via	~을 거쳐
	guest	손님
16	take A to B	A를 B로 데려가다
17	sign up for	~에 가입하다
	mandatory	의무적인
	belong to	~에 속해 있다
18	flight attendant	비행기 승무원
	electric device	전자 기기
	interfere with	~을 방해하다
	navigation	운항
19	senior's center	양로원
	experience	경험
20	get back	돌려 받다
	need	필요로 하다
	Are you sure?	정말?

MEMO

MEMO

MEMO

MEMO

내신 및 시 · 도 교육청 영어듣기평가 완벽 대비

Listening 올리고

Level 2

중학영어 듣기 모의고사

정답 및 해석

DARAKWON

Listening 올리고 2

Level 2

중학영어듣기 모의고사

정답 및 해석

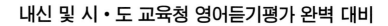

01 Listening Test 정답

p. 10

01 ①	02 ⑤	03 ③	04 ⑤	05 ②
06 ④	07 ④	08 ①	09 ③	10 ②
11 ③	12 ⑤	13 ①	14 ③	15 ⑤
16 ③	17 ②	18 ④	19 ①	20 ②

01

W Let's go to the Han River after school.
M Why do you want to go there?
W I want to ride a bike or in-line skate.
M Wow! That sounds great. We will have fun there, it's a beautiful day.
W That's the point. Let's forget about our tests and homework for a while.
M You're right. Today is a perfect day to get some fresh air.
W I couldn't agree with you more.

여 방과 후에 한강에 가자.
남 너는 왜 그곳에 가고 싶니?
여 자전거나 인라인 스케이트를 타고 싶어.
남 우와! 괜찮은데. 우리는 거기서 즐겁게 시간 보낼 거야. 멋진 날이니까.
여 내 말이. 시험이나 숙제는 잠시 잊어버리자.
남 네 말이 맞아. 오늘이 신선한 공기를 쐬기엔 최적의 날이다.
여 네 말에 전적으로 동의해.

ride 타다 **beautiful** 아름다운 **That's the point.** 그게 핵심이야. **for a while** 잠시 **I couldn't agree with you more.** 네 말에 전적으로 동의해.

02

W Sam, we're out of milk. Could you go to the convenience store and get some, please?
M Now? I have to go out to meet Tom.
W What time will you be back then?
M I'll be back around 9 p.m.
W That's quite late. I would be glad if you could buy some for me now.
M Okay. What kind of milk do you want? Plain, low-fat, or fat-free?
W A carton of low fat milk would be great. If another kind is on sale, you could get that.

여 Sam, 우유가 다 떨어졌네. 편의점에 가서 좀 사오겠니?
남 지금요? 하지만 저는 Tom을 만나러 나가야 해요.
여 그러면 언제 돌아오는데?
남 밤 9시쯤요.
여 꽤 늦네. 네가 지금 사다줄 수 있으면 참 좋겠어.
남 알겠어요. 어떤 종류의 우유를 사올까요? 일반 흰 우유, 저지방 우유, 아니면 무지방 우유요?
여 저지방 우유 한 팩이면 좋겠구나. 만일 다른 종류의 우유가 세일 중이라면 그것으로 사와도 돼.

be out of ~이 떨어지다 **convenience store** 편의점 **quite** 꽤 **glad** 기쁜 **low-fat** 저지방의 **fat-free** 무지방의 **a carton of** ~ 한 팩

03

M Look! There are hundreds of types of food.
W I don't know what to eat first.
M Me neither. I think I will try the Italian section first. What about you?
W I will have a salad first as usual. Then I think I will try some sushi.
M What should I eat next? Should I have a salad or try some steak?
W Oh, no. I wonder how I can taste all of these different foods.
M Let's start. I am starving to death.

남 봐! 수백 가지의 음식들이 있어.
여 무엇을 먼저 먹어야 할지 모르겠네.
남 나도 그래. 나는 제일 먼저 이탈리아 음식을 먹어볼 거야. 너는?
여 나는 항상 그렇듯 샐러드를 먼저 먹을 거야. 그리고선 초밥을 먹을 생각이야.
남 난 그 다음엔 무엇을 먹지? 샐러드를 먹어야 하나, 아니면 스테이크를 먹어야 하나?
여 오, 이런. 이 모든 종류의 음식들을 어떻게 다 맛볼 수 있을지 고민된다.
남 일단 먹자. 배고파 죽겠어.

① 실망한 ② 무서워하는 ③ 신이 난
④ 화난 ⑤ 짜증난

●●
hundreds of 수백의 **neither** ~도 아니다 **section** 구역 **as usual** 평소처럼 **sushi** 초밥 **starve to death** 굶어 죽다

04

W Welcome to Pho Pho. Do you have a reservation, sir?

M No, I don't.

W Will you be dining alone?

M No. There are five people in my party including me.

W I see. Please take this number and wait to be seated. I'll call your number when it's your turn.

M Okay.

W Here is the menu. You can take a look at this while you wait.

M That's very kind of you. Thank you very much.

여 포포식당에 오신 걸 환영합니다. 예약하셨습니까?
남 아니오.
여 혼자서 드시는 것인가요?
남 아니오. 저를 포함해서 5명입니다.
여 알겠습니다. 이 번호를 받고 자리가 날 때까지 기다려주세요. 차례가 되면 번호를 불러 드리겠습니다.
남 알겠습니다.
여 여기 메뉴 판이 있어요. 기다리시는 동안 보세요.
남 참 친절하시네요. 정말 감사합니다.

① 쇼핑몰 ② 부엌 ③ 파티장
④ 약국 ⑤ 식당

●●
welcome to ~에 온 것을 환영하다 **have a reservation** 예약되어 있다 **dine** 식사하다 **party** 일행 **including** ~을 포함하여 **turn** 순서 **take a look at** ~을 훑어보다

05

W Did you check the social commerce website, Pang Pang?

M Yes. I saw a special discount on tickets for our trip.

W Sounds good. How much is it?

M It's 5,000 won for adults, 1,700 won for kids, and free for children under the age of 4.

W That means 10,000 won for two of us? That's a good deal.

M What's more, if I pay by visa card, they give additional 5% discount. Fortunately, I have one.

여 소셜커머스 웹사이트 Pang Pang을 확인해 봤니?
남 응. 우리 여행에 대한 특별 할인 티켓을 봤어.
여 잘됐네. 얼마야?
남 성인은 5천원, 어린이는 1,700원, 그리고 4세 이하는 무료야.
여 그럼 우리 둘이 10,000원이라고? 괜찮은 가격이네.
남 더구나 비자카드로 결제하면 추가 5% 할인이 돼. 운 좋게도 난 그 카드를 가지고 있어.

●●
social commerce 소셜 커머스 **discount** 할인 **adult** 성인 **free** 무료의 **deal** 거래 **pay by** ~로 지불하다 **additional** 추가의 **fortunately** 운 좋게도

06

W Good morning. Before starting our day, I'd like to let you know today's schedule. First, we're going to visit the Statue of Liberty. You can see one of the tallest statues ever made. If you pose for the photograph next to it, I will take pictures for you. After that, we will visit the Empire State Building. It is one of the world's tallest buildings. You will be surprised by how magnificent it is. Then we will have lunch at a Chinese restaurant. I hope you enjoy today's tour.

여 좋은 아침입니다. 하루를 시작하기 전에, 오늘의 일정에 대해서 알려드리겠습니다. 먼저, 자유의 여신상을 방문할 것입니다. 지금까지 만들어진 것 중 가장 높은 동상 중의 하나이지요. 동상 옆에서 자세를 취하시면 제가 사진을 찍어 드리겠습니다. 그런 후, Empire State Building을 방문할 것입니다. 세계에서 가장 높은 빌딩들 중의 하나입니다. 얼마나 웅장한지 놀라실 것입니다. 그런 다음 우리는 중국 식당에서 점심을 먹을 것입니다. 즐거운 여행 되시길 바랍니다.

●●
let + 목적어 + 동사원형 ~가 …하게 놔두다 **pose for** ~을 위해 자세를 취하다 **one of the + 복수명사** ~들 중 하나 **magnificent** 웅장한 **have lunch** 점심 식사를 하다

07

W Did you make a reservation for the musical this weekend?

M Not yet. I am very busy with work these days.

W Have you decided which musical we are going to see then?

M Yes. I searched the Internet and chose one. The title is *Those Days*.

W That sounds good. I'll go home and make a reservation.

M Thank you very much. I have to finish writing this report since it is due tomorrow.

W It's no problem. I have nothing to do at the moment.

여 이번 주말 뮤지컬 예약했니?

남 아직. 나 요즘 일하느라 무척 바빠.

여 그러면 어떤 뮤지컬을 볼지는 결정했니?

남 응. 인터넷에서 찾아서 하나 골랐어. 제목이 〈그날들〉이야.

여 재미있겠다. 내가 집에 가서 예매할게.

남 정말 고마워. 이 보고서가 내일까지라 작성을 끝내야 해서.

여 괜찮아. 난 지금 할 일도 없는 걸.

make a reservation 예약을 하다 **these days** 요즈음 **since** ~이므로 **due** 기한이 된 **at the moment** 지금은

08

M Excuse me. Can I ask you something?

W Why not? Go ahead.

M Do you know where the nearest bookstore is? I believe that it is somewhere near ABC bank.

W I'm sorry, I don't know where that is. I am not from around here. Why don't you ask someone else?

M Okay. I think I will have to. Thank you, anyway.

W No problem. I hope you can find it.

남· 실례합니다. 뭐 좀 여쭤봐도 될까요?

여 네. 말씀하세요.

남 가장 가까운 서점이 어디에 있는지 아세요? ABC은행 근처에 있는 것 같은데요.

여 죄송해요. 어디에 있는지 모르겠습니다. 제가 이곳 출신이 아니라서요. 다른 사람들에게 물어보는 것이 어떠세요?

남 네. 그렇게 해야겠네요. 어쨌든, 감사합니다.

여 별말씀을요. 찾으시길 바랄게요.

Go ahead. 그렇게 하세요. **be from** ~ 출신이다 **Why don't you ~?** ~하는 게 어때?

09

W John, did you make a shopping list for our camping trip?

M Of course, I did. We'll need a tent, a chair, a sleeping bag, a lantern, and some portable pots and pans.

W That's quite a lot. By the way, we have a lantern, don't we?

M We used to have one, but not now. I can borrow a tent from Jason, though.

W That's good. A tent is the most expensive piece of equipment.

M You're right. We can save a lot by borrowing one.

여 John, 캠핑 여행에 필요한 쇼핑 리스트를 만들었니?

남 물론이지. 텐트, 의자, 침낭, 손전등, 코펠이 필요할 거야.

여 꽤 많네. 그런데, 우리 손전등 있잖아, 그렇지?

남 옛날엔 있었지만 지금은 없어. 하지만 내가 Jason에게 텐트를 빌릴 순 있겠어.

여 잘됐네. 텐트가 가장 비싼 장비잖아.

남 네 말이 맞아. 그거 빌림으로써 절약이 많이 되겠는 걸.

sleeping bag 침낭 **lantern** 손전등 **portable** 휴대용의 **borrow A from B** B에게서 A를 빌리다 **though** (문장 끝에서) 그러나 **expensive** 비싼 **equipment** 장비

10

M Did you hear the news about Jessie and Thomas?

W No. What happened to them?

M They are going to get married next month. They have been dating for three years.

W For three years? Wow! How could they keep it secret such a long time?

M I know! Anyway, they look good together.

W You're right.

남 Jessie와 Thomas에 관한 소식 들었니?

여 아니, 무슨 일인데?

남 그들은 다음 달에 결혼한대. 3년 동안 연애했다는데.

여 3년 동안? 우와! 어떻게 그렇게 오랫동안 비밀로 할 수가 있지?

남 그러게 말이야. 어쨌든, 둘이 잘 어울려.
여 네 말이 맞아.

••
What happened to ~? ~에게 무슨 일이 일어났니? **get married** 결혼하다 **keep ~ secret** ~을 비밀로 하다 **such** 그렇게나 **look good together** 잘 어울리다

11

M Dear students. This is Michael Hanks, your principal. We are going to go on a field trip to Gyeongbokgung in October. We have already sent a school newsletter to your parents about the trip. Please get your parent's signature by Friday and submit your permission slip to your homeroom teacher. Without your parent's signature, you won't be able to go on the trip. If you'd like to join, please talk to your parents and turn the slip in to your teacher on time. Thank you.

남 학생 여러분. 저는 Michael Hanks 교장입니다. 우리는 10월에 경복궁으로 견학을 갑니다. 견학에 대해 이미 부모님들께 가정통신문을 보냈습니다. 금요일까지 부모님의 사인을 받아 담임선생님께 허가서를 제출하세요. 부모님의 사인이 없으면, 견학을 갈 수가 없을 것입니다. 가고 싶다면, 부모님과 상의하여 제 시간에 허가서를 선생님께 제출하세요. 감사합니다.

••
principal 교장선생님 **field trip** 견학 **October** 10월 **school newsletter** 가정통신문 **submit** 제출하다 **permission slip** 허가서 **homeroom teacher** 담임선생님 **turn in** ~을 제출하다 **on time** 제 시간에

12

W Hey, Steve. I heard that you were in the hospital. Are you okay now?
M Yes. I feel much better than before.
W It's good to hear that. Are there any special things that you do to stay healthy?
M Well, I jog every morning. I eat less meat and also lots of vegetables. I also have regular checkups.
W I see. Do you take vitamins and other nutritional supplements?
M Of course I do. They're one of the basic steps to keeping in shape.

여 이봐, Steve. 너 병원에 입원했었다고 들었어. 지금은 괜찮니?
남 응. 이전보다 훨씬 나아졌어.
여 다행이다. 건강 유지를 위해 특별히 하는 것들이 있니?
남 음, 매일 아침 조깅을 해. 육류를 적게 먹을 뿐 아니라 채소를 많이 먹어. 정기 건강검진도 받고.
여 그렇구나. 비타민이나 다른 영양제도 섭취하니?
남 물론이지. 건강을 유지하기 위한 기본적인 방법들 중의 하나잖아.

••
feel better 낫다 **stay healthy** 건강을 유지하다 **regular checkup** 정기 건강검진 **nutritional supplement** 영양제 **keep in shape** 건강을 유지하다

13

[Beep]
W Hello, Peter. I'm leaving this message because you're not answering your phone. We have to decide on a topic and start gathering information for the final report. Since we have to work as a pair, I'd like to share some ideas with you. As soon as you get this message, please call me on my cell phone. My number is 010-0000-7979. I'm looking forward to hearing from you soon. Bye.

여 안녕, Peter. 전화를 받지 않아서 메시지를 남겨. 우리 기말 보고서 주제도 정하고 정보 수집도 시작해야 해. 우리 둘이 짝으로 해야 해서 너와 의견을 나누고 싶어. 이 메시지를 받는 즉시 내 휴대전화로 전화해 줘. 내 번호는 010-0000-7979야. 네가 곧 전화 주기를 기다릴게. 안녕.

••
leave a message 메시지를 남기다 **decide on** ~을 결심하다 **gather** 모으다 **pair** 짝, 한 쌍 **would like to-V** ~하고 싶다 **as soon as** ~하자마자 **look forward to -ing** ~하기를 고대하다

14

① W I'm going to clean my room on Saturday morning.
② W I'm going to go to church on Sunday morning.
③ W I'm going to see a movie on Saturday evening.
④ W I'm going to take a nap on Sunday afternoon.
⑤ W I'm going to go out to eat on Sunday evening.

Sue의 주말 일과			
	오전	오후	저녁
토요일	방 청소하기	영화 보기	숙제 하기
일요일	교회 가기	낮잠 자기	외식 하기

① 여 나는 토요일 아침에 내 방 청소를 할 것이다.
② 여 나는 일요일 아침에 교회에 갈 것이다.
③ 여 나는 토요일 저녁에 영화를 보러 갈 것이다.
④ 여 나는 일요일 오후에 낮잠을 잘 것이다.
⑤ 여 나는 일요일 저녁에 외식을 할 것이다.

●●
go to church 교회에 가다 **take a nap** 낮잠을 자다 **go out** 외출하다

15

W What do you want to do, Sean?
M Let's go swimming, mom.
W Sweetie, I'm sorry, but we can't. It's too cold to swim in the sea. You might catch a cold.
M I see. Maybe we can go to an indoor swimming pool sometime. Shall we try to catch some little crabs this time then?
W That sounds good. But how about making a sand castle?
M I already made one yesterday with dad.
W Okay. Let's do what you mentioned a while ago.

여 Sean, 무엇을 하기를 원하니?
남 수영하러 가요, 엄마.
여 얘야, 미안하지만 안되겠구나. 바다에서 수영을 하기에는 너무 추워. 너 감기에 걸릴지도 몰라.
남 알겠어요. 언젠가 다음에 실내 수영장에 가죠 뭐. 그러면 이번에는 작은 게를 한번 잡아볼까요?
여 재미있겠구나. 하지만 모래성을 만드는 것은 어떠니?
남 어제 이미 아빠와 만들었는 걸요.
여 알겠다. 조금 전에 네가 말했던 것으로 하자.

●●
too ~ to-V 너무 ~해서 …할 수 없다 **catch a cold** 감기에 걸리다 **indoor** 실내의 **crab** 게 **sand castle** 모래성 **mention** 언급하다

16

① M Do you know where I can find some comic books?
W Yes. I will show you where they are.
② M I like this mobile phone case a lot.
W Are you sure you want to buy it?
③ M Do you need any help finding a book?
W No, I like this book very much.
④ M Where is the nearest bus stop?
W I am sorry. I'm a stranger here, too.
⑤ M Let's meet at ten o'clock.
W Sure, why not?

① 남 만화책을 어디서 찾을 수 있는지 아세요?
여 네. 제가 어디에 있는지 보여드릴게요.
② 남 나는 이 휴대전화 케이스가 정말 마음에 들어.
여 너 정말 그것을 사고 싶니?
③ 남 책을 찾는 데 도움이 필요하세요?
여 아니요, 저는 이 책을 정말 좋아해요.
④ 남 가장 가까운 버스 정류장이 어디인가요?
여 죄송해요. 저도 초행길이라서요.
⑤ 남 10시에 만나자.
여 좋아.

●●
comic book 만화책 **mobile phone** 휴대전화 **stranger** 낯선 사람

17

W Welcome to the Tomato Festival. This is a wonderful event for tomato lovers. We have various activities ready to entertain you. For children between 7 and 10, there will be a tomato-picking contest. After that, children can bake a pizza and eat it with their parents. We are also having a pizza-eating contest after that. The participants in the contest are limited to adults, though. The person who eats the most pizza will win some prize money.

여 토마토 축제에 오신 것을 환영합니다. 이 축제는 토마토를 사랑하시는 분들께 멋진 행사입니다. 저희는 여러분들을 즐겁게 할 다양한 활동들을 준비했습니다. 7살에서 10살 사이의 어린이들은 토마토 따기 대회를 할 것입니다. 그런 후 어린이들은 피자를 구워서 부모님들과 함께 먹을 수 있습니다. 그 다음엔 피자 먹기 대회도 있습니다. 하지만 이 대회는 성인들만 참가할 수 있습니다. 가장 많은 피자를 먹는 사람에게 약간의 상금이 주어집니다.

●●
festival 축제 **various** 다양한 **entertain** 즐겁게 하다 **between A and B** A와 B 사이에 **participant** 참가자 **be limited to** ~로 제한되다 **prize** 상

18

M Subin and Taeho like playing tennis. Every Saturday morning, they play tennis in the park together. Today, Taeho got up late and came to the park late. Subin was waiting for him for 30 minutes. In this situation, what would Taeho say to Subin?

남 수빈이와 태호는 테니스 치는 것을 좋아합니다. 매주 토요일 아침, 그들은 함께 공원에서 테니스를 칩니다. 오늘, 태호는 늦잠을 잤고 공원에 늦게 나갔습니다. 수빈이는 30분 동안 태호를 기다렸습니다. 이 상황에서 태호는 수빈이에게 무엇이라고 말할까요?

① 제 시간에 오렴.
② 나는 테니스 치는 것을 무척 좋아해.
③ 너는 몇 시에 잠자리에 들었니?
④ 늦어서 정말 미안해.
⑤ 지금 우리 테니스 치자.

wait for ~을 기다리다 **situation** 상황

19

M Hey, check this out. I got a new cell phone.
W How nice! Did your parents get it for you?
M Yeah. You know it was my birthday yesterday.
W Do they always buy you the things you want?
M Yes. They try to get them for me.
W Wow, I envy you.

남 이것 좀 봐. 나 새 휴대전화가 생겼어.
여 정말 좋네! 부모님께서 사주셨니?
남 응. 어제가 내 생일이었잖아.
여 네 부모님께서는 네가 원하는 것들을 항상 사주시니?
남 응. 그분들은 내게 사주시려고 노력하셔.
여 야, 네가 부럽다.

① 야, 네가 부럽다.
② 나는 네게 휴대전화를 사주고 싶어.
③ 나는 새 휴대전화를 갖고 싶어.
④ 네 생일 파티는 정말 재미있었어.
⑤ 우리 부모님은 내게 모든 것을 사줄 형편이 안되셔.

check out 확인하다 **cell phone** 휴대전화 **birthday** 생일 **try to-V** ~하려고 노력하다 **envy** 부러워하다

20

[Telephone rings.]
W Hello. It's me, honey. Where are you now?
M I am on my way home. Do you want me to grab anything?
W No. I finished doing all of the grocery shopping this afternoon.
M Then what's up?
W I just want to know when you'll be here so that I can set the table.
M I think I'll be there within 20 minutes.
W Okay. See you then.

[전화벨이 울린다.]
여 여보세요. 여보, 저예요. 지금 어디세요?
남 집에 가고 있는 길인데. 내가 뭐 사다 줄 게 있어요?
여 아니에요. 오늘 오후에 장은 다 보았어요.
남 그러면 무슨 일이에요?
여 그냥 당신이 언제 여기 오는지 알고 싶어서요. 그래야 상을 차릴 수 있어서요.
남 내 생각에는 20분 정도 걸릴 것 같은데.
여 알겠어요. 그럼 그때 봐요.

① 맘껏 드세요.
② 알겠어요. 그럼 그때 봐요.
③ 상을 차리는 것은 쉽지 않아요.
④ 나는 식료품점에 가고 있어요.
⑤ 장보기는 매우 재미있어요.

on one's way home 집에 가는 길에 **grab** 움켜쥐다 **grocery shopping** 장보기 **What's up?** 무슨 일이야? **set the table** 상을 차리다 **within** ~ 안에

Further Study 정답

p. 14

1 She wants to ride a bike or in-line skate.
2 He will come home around 9 p.m.
3 They will get them from a social commerce site.
4 They are a chair, a sleeping bag, a lantern, and some portable pots and pans.
5 The students have to submit the permission slip by Friday.

6 The reason is that Peter is not answering his phone.
7 He made a sand castle with his dad.
8 The winner will be the person who eats the most pizza. The winner will get some prize money.

On Your Own 모범답안

p. 15

A

Yes, I have. I learned how to ride a bike (1)when I was 10. (3)My dad taught me how to ride. Now, I usually ride my bike (2)in the school yard with (3)my classmates. At first, I was (4)scared. However, after a while, I was (4)excited and was able to ride my bike very well. I think riding a bike is one of the most exciting outdoor activities you can do.

자전거 타기			
(1) 언제	(2) 어디서	(3) 누가	(4) 느낌
10살 때 지난 주 지난 달 2년 전 방과 후	학교 운동장에서 놀이터에서 공원에서 길거리에서	친구 급우 엄마 / 아빠 언니 (누나, 여동생) / 오빠 (형, 남동생) 선생님	행복한 신나는 자신감 있는 무서운 걱정되는

네, (자전거를 타본 적이) 있습니다. 저는 10살 때 자전거 타는 법을 배웠습니다. 아빠가 어떻게 타는지 가르쳐 주셨습니다. 이제는 대개 급우들과 학교 운동장에서 자전거를 탑니다. 처음에는 무서웠습니다. 그러나 좀 지나선 재미있어졌고 잘 탈 수 있었습니다. 저는 자전거를 타는 것은 여러분들이 할 수 있는 가장 재미있는 야외 활동들 중의 하나라고 생각합니다.

B

My Weekend Schedule			
	In the morning	In the afternoon	In the evening
Saturday	go jogging	clean my room	do my homework
Sunday	go to church	take a nap	watch TV

I'm going to talk about what I usually do on the weekend. I go jogging on Saturday morning. On Saturday afternoon, I clean my room, and I do my homework in the evening. Every Sunday morning, I go to church with my family. I usually take a nap in the afternoon. On Sunday evening, I mostly watch TV. My weekends are quite busy.

나의 주말 일과			
	오전	오후	저녁
토요일	조깅 하기	방 청소하기	숙제 하기
일요일	교회 가기	낮잠 자기	TV 보기

나는 내가 일반적으로 주말에 무엇을 하는지에 대해 이야기할 것입니다. 나는 토요일 아침에 조깅을 하러 갑니다. 토요일 오후에는 방 청소를 하고, 저녁에는 숙제를 합니다. 일요일 아침마다 나는 가족과 함께 교회에 갑니다. 나는 오후에는 대체로 낮잠을 잡니다. 일요일 저녁에는 대부분 TV를 봅니다. 나의 주말은 꽤 바쁩니다.

02 Listening Test 정답

중학영어듣기 모의고사 02회

p. 20

01 ③	02 ④	03 ①	04 ⑤	05 ③
06 ④	07 ②	08 ⑤	09 ②	10 ②
11 ②	12 ①	13 ⑤	14 ①	15 ③
16 ③	17 ①	18 ③	19 ⑤	20 ④

01

M Mom, have you seen my watch?
W No. Why do you ask?
M Because I can't see it anywhere.
W Did you look on your desk?
M Yes, but it wasn't there.
W Did you look in your coat pocket? It seems that you sometimes leave it there.

M No, not yet. It isn't here, either. Oh, mom I found it. It's between the laptop and the speakers on the desk.

남 엄마, 내 시계 보셨어요?
여 아니. 왜 물어보는 거니?
남 시계가 아무 데도 없어요.
여 책상 위에 봤니?
남 네, 하지만 거기에 없었어요.
여 외투 주머니 안을 확인해 봤니? 너는 가끔 거기에 시계를 넣어 두는 것 같더라.
남 아뇨. 아직 확인 안 했어요. 여기에도 없네요. 오! 엄마, 찾았어요. 책상 위에 있는 노트북 컴퓨터와 스피커 사이에 있어요.

coat pocket 외투 주머니 **either** (부정문에서) 또한 **between A and B** A와 B 사이에 **laptop** 노트북 컴퓨터

02

W Have you met the new science teacher?
M No, not yet. But I heard he is really popular with the students.
W I've already met him and he was very funny and friendly.
M Is he handsome?
W Hmm. He's very short and fat with a shiny bald head.
M Oh, that's surprising. He must have a good sense of humor.

여 새로 오신 과학선생님 만나봤어?
남 아니, 아직. 근데 그 분이 학생들에게 아주 인기 있다는 말은 들었어.
여 난 만나봤는데 그 선생님은 아주 재미있고 다정하셔.
남 잘생기셨어?
여 음, 작고 뚱뚱하고 반짝이는 대머리셔.
남 오, 의외인데. 그럼 분명 유머 감각이 좋으신가봐.

popular 인기 있는 **friendly** 친근한 **shiny** 반짝이는 **bald** 대머리의 **sense of humor** 유머 감각

03

M Why didn't you come to school yesterday?
W My stomach was bothering me a lot.
M Did it get any better?
W Well, I'm still feeling a bit under the weather.
M Did you take some medicine?
W Yes, I did. I went to see a doctor and he told me that I had mild food poisoning.
M I hope you feel better soon.

남 어제 왜 학교에 안 왔어?
여 배가 너무 아팠어.
남 좀 나아졌니?
여 음, 아직도 조금 안 좋아.
남 약은 먹었니?
여 응. 진찰 받으러 갔었는데 의사선생님이 가벼운 식중독이라고 하셨어.
남 곧 나아지길 바래.

① 걱정하는 ② 마음 상한 ③ 답답한
④ 즐거운 ⑤ 신이 난

stomach 배 **bother** 힘들게 하다 **a bit** 약간, 조금 **under the weather** 몸이 좋지 않은 **mild** 가벼운 **food poisoning** 식중독

04

W How's it going?
M I'm good.
W How can I help you?
M I'd like to deposit this check for 230 dollars, please.
W Do you have an account with us?
M No, I don't.
W Then you should open an account first. What sort of account would you like to open?

여 어떻게 지내세요?
남 좋습니다.
여 무엇을 도와드릴까요?
남 이 230달러 수표를 입금하고 싶습니다.
여 우리 은행에 계좌가 있으세요?
남 없습니다.
여 그러면 먼저 계좌를 개설하셔야 돼요. 어떤 종류의 계좌를 개설하고 싶으세요?

① 우체국 ② 상점 ③ 헬스클럽
④ 음식점 ⑤ 은행

How's it going? (안부를 물을 때) 어떻게 지내세요? **deposit** 입금하다 **check** 수표 **account** 계좌 **open an account** 계좌를 개설하다

05

W Next! What can I do for you?

M I'd like to mail this parcel to the United States by regular mail.

W What is in the parcel?

M Only some clothes.

W Okay, let me see how much it weighs. It's about 2.5kgs. That will be 15 dollars and 25 cents.

M I'd like to insure my parcel.

W Then it will cost an additional 2 dollars and 15 cents.

여 다음 분 오세요. 무엇을 도와드릴까요?

남 이 소포를 일반 우편으로 미국에 보내고 싶어요.

여 소포 안에는 무엇이 있나요?

남 옷만 조금 있어요.

여 네, 무게를 한 번 재볼게요. 약 2.5킬로네요. 그럼 15.25달러입니다.

남 소포에 보험을 들겠습니다.

여 그러면 추가로 2.15달러를 더 내셔야 합니다.

●●

mail (우편물을) 보내다 **parcel** 소포 **by regular mail** 일반 우편으로 **weigh** (무게가) ~ 나가다 **insure** 보험에 들다 **cost** (돈이) 들다 **additional** 추가의

06

M There is a special excitement in writing to a pen pal who lives far away. The culture, holidays and even the climate may be different from your own. It is interesting to learn about another country from someone your own age. Also, you will be making a new friend at the same time. How can you find a pen pal? Follow these directions carefully.

남 멀리 떨어져 사는 펜팔에게 편지를 쓰는 것에는 특별한 재미가 있습니다. 문화, 휴일 그리고 기후조차 여러분이 사는 곳과는 다를지 모릅니다. 여러분들 또래의 누군가로부터 다른 나라에 대해 배우는 것은 재미있습니다. 또한, 여러분들은 새로운 친구도 동시에 사귈 것입니다. 어떻게 펜팔을 찾을 수 있냐구요? 이 지침들을 신중하게 따르세요.

●●

excitement 즐거움 **far away** 멀리 떨어져 **culture** 문화 **climate** 기후 **interesting** 재미있는 **at the same time** 동시에 **direction** 지침

07

M You look a little different today.

W Oh, that's because of my new glasses. Do you think they look good on me?

M Absolutely yes. You look even younger in them.

W That's very sweet of you. By the way, would you do me a favor?

M Of course. What is it?

W Can you help me carry these books to the library?

M No problem.

남 너 오늘 조금 달라 보인다.

여 오, 내 새 안경 때문이야. 나한테 어울리는 것 같니?

남 응 정말 잘 어울려. 훨씬 더 어려 보여.

여 넌 정말 다정해. 그런데, 부탁 하나 들어줄래?

남 물론이지. 그게 뭔데?

여 내가 이 책들을 도서관까지 옮기는 걸 도와줄래?

남 그래.

●●

because of ~ 때문에 **look good on** ~에게 잘 어울리다 **even** (비교급 앞에서) 훨씬 **sweet** 다정한 **do ~ a favor** ~의 부탁을 들어주다 **No problem.** (부탁을 들어줄 때) 그래.

08

W I was wondering how you decide on our grades.

M I consider many things: class participation, attendance, assignments, and tests.

W How do you total our scores?

M The mid-term test and the final-term test are fifty percent of your grade; assignments, attendance, and class participation total the remaining fifty percent.

W Will you let us know if we have a serious problem?

M Of course, I will be letting you know what you need to work on.

여 선생님이 우리 점수를 어떻게 결정하시는지 궁금해요.

남 나는 수업 참여, 출석, 과제, 시험 등 많은 요소들을 고려해.

여 점수는 어떻게 합산되나요?

남 중간고사, 기말고사는 50퍼센트 반영되고, 과제, 출석, 그리고 수업 참여는 나머지 50퍼센트에 반영된다.

여 우리가 심각한 문제가 있으면 말씀해주시나요?

남 물론이지. 너희들이 무엇을 더 신경 써야 하는지 알려줄게.

●●
grade 점수 **participation** 참여 **attendance** 출석 **assignment** 과제 **total** 합계하다 **let + 목적어 + 동사원형** ~가 …하게 해주다

09

M Good morning, Mom. That smells really good. It's making me hungry.

W Breakfast is ready. Can you take the milk out of the refrigerator and put it on the table?

M Sure, I can. May I pour some milk into my glass?

W Yes. Here are some eggs and toast. Do you need some sausages?

M That sounds good. And I need the butter and strawberry jam.

W I'm sorry but we've run out of strawberry jam.

남 안녕히 주무셨어요, 엄마. 냄새가 정말 좋아요. 맛있는 냄새가 배고프게 만드네요.

여 아침식사 준비 다 됐다. 냉장고에서 우유 꺼내서 테이블 위에 올려줄래?

남 물론이죠. 컵에 우유 따를까요?

여 그래. 달걀과 토스트 여기 있다. 소시지 먹을래?

남 좋아요. 그리고 버터와 딸기잼도 주세요.

여 미안하지만, 딸기잼은 다 먹고 없단다.

●●
take A out of B A를 B에서 꺼내다 **refrigerator** 냉장고 **pour A into B** A를 B에 붓다 **run out of** ~이 다 떨어지다

10

W Luke, what kind of sports do you do in your spare time?

M I go hiking with my family on Saturdays when the weather is good. And I jog every other day.

W Good. I like table tennis. Do you play table tennis?

M Yes. I'm really good at playing it. I have a strong serve.

W Really? Me, too!

M Why don't we play it tomorrow then?

여 Luke, 넌 여가 시간에 어떤 종류의 스포츠를 하니?

남 나는 날씨가 좋으면 토요일마다 가족들과 하이킹을 가. 그리고 이틀에 한 번씩 조깅해.

여 좋은데. 나는 탁구 치는 걸 좋아해. 너 탁구 치니?

남 응. 나 탁구 진짜 잘 쳐. 난 서브를 강하게 해.

여 정말? 나도 그래.

남 그럼 우리 내일 탁구 치는 거 어때?

●●
spare 여분의 **go hiking** 하이킹 가다 **jog** 조깅하다 **every other day** 이틀에 한 번씩 **be good at** ~을 잘하다 **serve** 서브

11

W Excuse me. Is this seat taken?

M Sorry. What did you say?

W Oh. Is anyone going to sit in this seat?

M I don't think so. I think you can take it if you want.

W Could you move over one seat, so my boyfriend and I can sit together?

M No problem.

여 실례합니다. 여기 자리 있나요?

남 죄송합니다. 뭐라고 하셨죠?

여 오. 이 자리에 누가 앉을 건가요?

남 그런 것 같지 않은데요. 제 생각에는 원하시면 앉으셔도 될 것 같아요.

여 제 남자친구와 제가 같이 앉을 수 있게 옆으로 한 좌석 좁혀 앉아 주실래요?

남 그럼요.

●●
Is this seat taken? 자리 임자 있나요? **sit in** ~에 앉다 **move over** 자리를 좁히다

12

M Helen, do you sleep well?

W Yes. Why?

M I can't sleep very well these days. Can you give me some tips on how to sleep better at night?

W Why don't you try not drinking coffee or tea in the evening? Also, don't take a nap during the day.

M Sounds helpful. Anything else?

W I think watching TV late at night is not very good, either. I heard that drinking warm milk before going to bed, or doing some exercises is also helpful.

M Thank you very much.

남 Helen, 너는 잠을 잘 자니?
여 응, 왜?
남 나는 요즘 잠을 잘 못 자겠어. 밤에 잠을 잘 자는 법 좀 알려줄래?
여 저녁에는 커피나 차를 마시지 마. 또한 낮 동안에 잠을 자지 마.
남 도움이 되겠네. 다른 것은?
여 밤 늦게 TV를 보는 것도 좋지 않은 것 같아. 잠 자기 전에 따뜻한 우유를 마시거나, 운동을 조금 하는 것도 도움이 된다고 들었어.
남 정말 고마워.

sleep well 잠을 잘 자다 **these days** 요즈음 **tip** 비결 **at night** 밤에 **in the evening** 저녁에 **take a nap** 낮잠을 자다

13

W Oh, Tony. Look! You are wearing odd shoes.
M Oh, no! People were laughing at me on the way to school, but I didn't know why.
W Didn't anyone tell you?
M No. I was very embarrassed. Now I know why they were laughing.
W Were you in a hurry?
M Yes. I woke up late. So...
W I see. You should be more careful next time.

여 오, Tony. 봐봐! 너 신발을 짝짝이로 신었어.
남 오, 이런! 학교에 오는 길에 사람들이 나를 보며 웃었지만 왜 그러는지 몰랐었어.
여 아무도 네게 이야기해 주지 않았니?
남 아니. 나는 무척 민망했어. 이제야 그 사람들이 왜 웃었는지 알겠네.
여 서둘렀니?
남 응. 늦잠을 잤어. 그래서...
여 그렇구나. 다음 번에는 조금 더 조심해.

wear odd shoes 신발을 짝짝이로 신다 **laugh at** ~을 보고 웃다 **embarrassed** 당황스러운 **in a hurry** 서두른

14

W Do you like dancing? Do you want to learn how to dance? Why don't you visit our club and join us? Dancing not only makes you happy but also healthy and slim. You can make new friends, too. We meet at 10 o'clock in the morning at the ABC Center on Saturdays. Anyone who is interested in dancing is welcome to come along. Please come and join us.

댄스클럽에 가입하세요

- 만나는 시간
  ① 매주 토요일 오후 ABC 센터에서
- 이점들
  ② 춤추는 법을 배움
  ③ 건강하고 날씬해짐
  ④ 새 친구를 사귐
- 가입 자격
  ⑤ 춤에 관심 있는 누구나

여 춤추는 것을 좋아하세요? 춤추는 법을 배우고 싶으세요? 저희 클럽을 방문하시고 참여하시는 것은 어때요? 춤추는 것은 당신을 행복하게 해줄 뿐만 아니라 건강하고 날씬하게도 해줍니다. 새 친구도 사귈 수 있습니다. 우리는 매주 토요일 ABC센터에서 오전 10시에 만납니다. 춤에 관심이 있으신 분은 누구든지 오시는 것을 환영합니다. 오셔서 참여하세요.

like -ing ~하는 것을 좋아하다 **not only A but also B** A뿐만 아니라 B 또한 **healthy** 건강한 **slim** 날씬한 **be interested in** ~에 흥미가 있다

15

W Jaeil, do you have time?
M Yes. What's up?
W Can you help me with my final paper?
M Sure. What can I do for you?
W Please answer these survey questions. It will take about 15 minutes.
M Okay. Give me the survey.
W Thank you very much. I will get you something to drink to thank you.

여 재일아, 너 시간 있니?
남 응. 무슨 일이야?
여 내 기말 보고서 좀 도와줄래?
남 물론이지. 무엇을 하면 되는데?
여 여기 설문에 응답해줘. 15분 정도 걸릴 거야.
남 그래. 설문지 이리 줘.
여 정말 고마워. 고마움의 표시로 내가 음료수 살게.

have time 시간이 있다 **final paper** 기말 (논문)과제 **survey** 설문 **take** (시간이) 걸리다

16

① M What are you going to do this weekend?
W I am going to see a movie with my friend.
② M I don't think I did very well on my English test.
W Don't worry. You can do better next time.
③ M What do you want to be when you grow up?
W I want to swim in the sea.
④ M Did you finish your science homework?
W Not yet.
⑤ M What's your favorite season?
W I like summer best.

① 남 너 이번 주말에 무엇을 할 거니?
여 나는 친구와 영화를 보러 갈 거야.
② 남 나는 영어시험을 망친 것 같아.
여 걱정 마. 다음에 더 잘할 수 있어.
③ 남 너는 커서 무엇이 되고 싶니?
여 나는 바다에서 수영하고 싶어.
④ 남 너 과학 숙제 끝냈니?
여 아직.
⑤ 남 네가 좋아하는 계절은 무엇이니?
여 나는 여름을 가장 좋아해.

••
do well 잘하다 **grow up** 자라다

17

M Hey, Lisa. How have you been?
W I'm doing great. What about you, David?
M I'm good, too. Where are you living now?
W I'm living in Los Angeles. I used to live in New York.
M I see. Are you married?
W Yes. I have one daughter and one son.
M It's good to see you here in this amusement park after so long.

남 Lisa, 어떻게 지냈니?
여 잘 지내고 있어. David 너는?
남 나도 잘 지내지. 지금은 어디서 살고 있니?
여 나는 로스앤젤레스에서 살고 있어. 이전에는 뉴욕에서 살았었어.
남 그렇구나. 결혼은 했니?
여 응. 딸 하나 아들 하나 있어.
남 이곳 놀이공원에서 이렇게 오랜 후에 널 보다니 참 반갑다.

••
How have you been? 어떻게 지냈니? **live in** ~에서 살다 **used to-V** (과거에) ~하곤 했다 **amusement park** 놀이공원

18

M Peter is talking to his daughter, Jessica. He asks her what she wants to be when she grows up. She says she has no idea. She is not interested in anything. In this situation, what will Peter most probably say to his daughter?

남 Peter는 그의 딸 Jessica에게 이야기하고 있다. 그는 그녀가 커서 무엇이 되고 싶은지 묻는다. 그녀는 전혀 모르겠다고 말한다. 그녀는 그 어떤 것에도 흥미가 없다. 이 상황에서 Peter는 그의 딸에게 무어라 하겠는가?

① 너의 노력이 참 기특하구나.
② 나는 네가 직업을 갖는 것을 원하지 않아.
③ 목표를 정하는 것은 매우 중요하단다.
④ 나는 네가 음악에 관심이 있는 줄 몰랐구나.
⑤ 나는 네가 이렇게 컸다는 게 믿어지지 않는구나.

••
have no idea 전혀 모르다 **be interested in** ~에 흥미가 있다 **probably** 아마도

19

[Telephone rings.]
W Hello, may I talk to Dr. Han, please?
M Sorry, but he is not here. He is attending a meeting now.
W Do you know when he is coming back?
M Probably around 4 o'clock this afternoon. Who's calling please?
W This is Hanna from Seoul. May I leave a message?
M Sure. Go ahead.
W Please tell him to call me back.

[전화벨이 울린다.]
여 여보세요. 한선생님과 통화할 수 있을까요?
남 죄송하지만 여기에 안 계십니다. 그는 지금 회의에 참석하고 있어요.
여 언제쯤 돌아오실 것 같은가요?
남 아마도 오늘 오후 4시쯤요. 누구시죠?

여 서울에 사는 한나라고 해요. 메시지를 남겨도 될까요?
남 물론이죠. 말씀하세요.
여 제게 전화 좀 해달라고 전해주세요.

① 즐거운 하루 보내세요.
② 메시지를 남겨주세요.
③ 전화 주셔서 감사합니다.
④ 전화 잘못 거셨습니다.
⑤ 제게 전화 좀 해달라고 전해주세요.

attend 참석하다 **come back** 돌아오다 **leave a message** 메시지를 남기다 **call back** 회답 전화를 하다

20

M Do you have any plans for this Sunday?
W No. I'm free. Why?
M I'm planning to visit a nursing home. Would you like to join me?
W A nursing home? What would I have to do there?
M You could chat with the elderly. They will be very happy to talk to you.
W Sounds interesting. I'll join you.

남 너 이번 일요일에 일 있니?
여 아니, 한가해. 왜?
남 난 양로원을 방문할까 계획 중이야. 나랑 같이 갈래?
여 양로원? 거기에서 무얼 해야 해?
남 할머니, 할아버지들과 얘기 나눌 수도 있지. 너랑 얘기하면 무척 즐거워하실 거야.
여 재미있겠네. 너랑 같이 갈게.

① 나랑 같이 가자.
② 우리 얘기 좀 해.
③ 너랑 같이 가게 돼서 기뻐.
④ 재미있겠네. 너랑 같이 갈게.
⑤ 이번 주말에 뭐 할 거야?

free 한가한 **plan to-V** ~할 계획이다 **nursing home** 양로원 **the elderly** 어르신들

Further Study 정답

p. 24

1 The reason was that she had mild food poisoning so her stomach was bothering her a lot.
2 He wants to deposit $230.
3 He wants to send it to the United States.
4 He considers class participation, attendance, assignments, and tests.
5 The reason was that she wants to sit with her boyfriend.
6 ① Do not drink coffee or tea in the evening.
② Do not take a nap during the day.
③ Drink warm milk before going to bed.
④ Do some exercises.
7 She asked him to help her with her final paper.
8 He is planning to visit a nursing home.

On Your Own 모범답안

p. 25

A

About My Classmate	
(1) What is your name?	Luke
(2) What do you like to do?	watch TV
(3) Where do you like to spend time?	at home
(4) What sports do you like to play?	soccer
(5) How often do you play it?	once a week
(6) What would you like to be?	a doctor
(7) Why do you want that job?	wants to take care of sick people

My classmate's name is (1)Luke. When he has spare time, he likes to (2)watch TV. He likes to spend time (3)at home. His favorite sport is (4)soccer. He plays it with his friends (5)once a week. He would like to be (6)a doctor because (7)he wants to take care of sick people.

나의 학급 친구에 관하여	
(1) 이름이 뭐니?	Luke
(2) 무엇을 하는 것을 좋아하니?	TV 보기
(3) 어디서 시간 보내길 좋아하니?	집에서
(4) 어떤 스포츠를 좋아하니?	축구
(5) 얼마나 자주 그 운동을 하니?	일주일에 한 번
(6) 무엇이 되고 싶니?	의사
(7) 왜 그 일을 하고 싶니?	아픈 사람들을 보살피고 싶어서

나의 학급 친구 이름은 Luke입니다. 그는 여가 시간에 TV 보는 것을 좋아합니다. 그는 집에서 시간을 보내는 것을 좋아합니다. 그가 가장 좋아하는 스포츠는 축구입니다. 그는 친구들과 함께 일주일에 한 번 축구를 합니다. 그는 아픈 사람들을 돌봐주기를 원해서 의사가 되고 싶어 합니다.

B

I Want to Be a(n)...	
(1) What do you want to be?	a doctor
(2) What does he/she usually do?	cures sick people
(3) Where does he/she work?	in a hospital or a clinic
(4) Why do you want to be a(n) ...?	could help sick people, cure their diseases
(5) Do you know anyone who is a(n) ...?	my father

I want to be a (1)doctor. A (1)doctor (2)cures sick people. A (1)doctor usually works (3)in a hospital or a clinic. The reasons why I want to be a (1)doctor are that (4)I could help sick people and cure their diseases. (5)My father is my role model. I think his passion for his work is very impressive.

나는 …가 되고 싶습니다	
(1) 무엇이 되고 싶나요?	의사
(2) 그/그녀는 일반적으로 무엇을 하나요?	아픈 사람을 치료함
(3) 그/그녀는 어디에서 일을 하나요?	병원이나 진료소에서
(4) 왜 …가 되고 싶나요?	아픈 사람들을 도와서 그들의 병을 치료해줄 수 있으므로
(5) …인 사람을 알고 있나요?	우리 아버지

저는 의사가 되고 싶습니다. 의사는 아픈 사람들을 치료해줍니다. 의사는 대개 병원이나 진료소에서 일을 합니다. 제가 의사가 되고 싶은 이유는 아픈 사람들을 도와서 그들의 병을 치료해줄 수 있기 때문입니다. 저의 아버지가 제 롤모델이십니다. 저는 아버지의 일에 대한 열정이 매우 감명적이라고 생각합니다.

03 Listening Test 정답

p. 30

01 ⑤	02 ③	03 ⑤	04 ③	05 ①
06 ④	07 ①	08 ②	09 ②	10 ②
11 ⑤	12 ②	13 ④	14 ④	15 ①
16 ③	17 ③	18 ④	19 ⑤	20 ①

01

M Do you have a pet?

W Yes, I have a cat. Her name is Mittens.

M What does she look like?

W She's black and white. She has a long tail and her hair is short. How about you? Do you have a pet?

M Yes. I have a dog whose name is Rover.

W What does Rover look like?

M He has long black hair and a short tail. He's a little bit chubby but he's very active.

남 너 애완동물 있니?

여 응, 고양이 한 마리 키워. 이름이 Mittens야.

남 어떻게 생겼니?

여 희고 검어. 꼬리가 길고 털이 짧아. 너는 어때? 애완동물 있니?

남 응, 나는 개를 기르는데 이름이 Rover야.

여 Rover는 어떻게 생겼어?

남 털이 길고 검고, 꼬리가 짧아. 조금 통통하긴 하지만 아주 활동적이야.

pet 애완동물 **What do(es) + 주어 + look like?** ~가 어떻게 생겼니?
chubby 통통한 **active** 활동적인

02

W Excuse me. Could you tell me how to get to Mega Box?

M Of course. Go straight for two blocks. You'll see AK Plaza on the left. At that corner, turn left.

W Oh, wait. I walk two blocks and turn left at AK Plaza?

M Yes. Then go one block and the theater is just on the corner. It's across from a bank.

W Okay, I go one block and the theater is just on the corner, right?

M That's right. Enjoy the movie!

W Thanks a lot.

여 실례합니다. Mega Box에 가는 방법을 말씀해주실 수 있으세요?

남 물론이죠. 두 블록 직진하세요. 왼편에 AK Plaza가 보이실 거예요. 그 모퉁이에서 왼쪽으로 도세요.

여 아, 잠깐만요. 두 블록 직진하고 AK Plaza에서 왼쪽으로 돌라고요?

남 네. 그러고 나서 한 블록 더 가시면 그 블록 모퉁이에 극장이 있습니다. 극장 건너편에는 은행이 있습니다.

여 그러니까, 한 블록 더 가면 모퉁이에 극장이 있어요. 맞나요?

남 맞습니다. 영화 재미있게 보세요.

여 정말 감사합니다.

how to-V ~하는 방법 **go straight** 직진하다 **on the left** 왼편에 **across from** ~의 건너편에 **That's right.** 맞아.

03

M I have to say I'm sorry.

W Why? What's wrong?

M My little sister ripped several pages out of the notebook which you lent me yesterday.

W Oh my God! What should I do? I can't study without that notebook.

M I can't tell you how sorry I am. However, as soon as I borrowed your notes, I made copies of them.

남 너에게 미안하다고 말을 해야겠어.

여 왜? 무슨 일이야?

남 내 여동생이 네가 어제 나에게 빌려준 공책에서 몇 쪽을 찢어버렸어.

여 오! 맙소사. 어떻게 하지? 나는 그 공책 없이는 공부를 못해.

남 얼마나 미안한지 말로 할 수 없을 정도야. 하지만, 너의 공책을 빌리자마자 복사를 해두었어.

① 미안한 → 걱정하는 ② 행복한 → 화난
③ 두려워하는 → 분노한 ④ 미안한 → 즐거운
⑤ 속상한 → 안도하는

What's wrong? 무슨 일이야? **rip** 찢다 **out of** ~에서 **several** 몇 개의 **lend** 빌려주다 **as soon as** ~하자 마자 **make a copy of** ~을 복사하다

04

W How can I help you?

M I think I have a bad cold. I took some medicine but it didn't work at all.

W What seems to be the problem?

M I have a sore throat, and a runny nose. Also, I can't stop coughing.

W Let me see your throat.

M How does it look?

W You have the flu but it is not very serious. I'll prescribe you some medicine.

여 무엇을 도와드릴까요?

남 심한 감기에 걸린 것 같아요. 약을 먹었지만 전혀 효과가 없네요.

여 어디가 아픈 것 같아요?

남 목이 아프고 콧물이 나요. 기침도 계속 나요.

여 목 좀 볼게요.

남 어때요?

여 독감이지만 별로 심각하지는 않아요. 약을 좀 처방해 드릴게요.

① 식당 ② 약국 ③ 병원
④ 백화점 ⑤ 극장

bad cold 심한 감기 **work** 효과가 있다 **sore** 아픈 **have a runny nose** 콧물이 흐르다 **cough** 기침하다 **flu** 독감 **prescribe** 처방하다

05

M Let's do a class survey!

W That sounds good. Then, we have to count the number of the students first. Is there anyone absent?

M No one. We are all here so there are twenty students.

W There are eight girls and twelve boys, including us.

M How many students wear glasses?

W Three girls and four boys.

M How many students have a cell phone?

W Everyone except for me.

남 학급 설문조사 하자.

여 좋아. 그러면, 먼저 학생 수부터 세야 해. 결석한 학생 있어?

남 없어. 모두 출석해서 20명이야.
여 우리를 포함해서, 여학생 8명이고 남학생 12명이야.
남 안경을 쓴 학생은 몇 명이야?
여 여학생 3명과 남학생 4명이야.
남 휴대전화가 있는 학생은 몇 명이야?
여 나를 제외하고 모두 다.

do a survey 설문 조사하다 **absent** 결석한 **There be** ~가 있다 **including** ~을 포함하여 **except for** ~을 제외하고

06

W Laundry can often make you tired and take up a lot of your valuable time. Are you a person who hates doing laundry? Here is good news for you. We offer home or office pick-up services for your laundry. As we wash, dry and fold it separately, your laundry is not mixed with anyone else's. Also, you can get it back the very next day! Please visit our website www. laundryking.co.kr. Cheap rates! Next day delivery!

여 세탁은 종종 당신을 피곤하게 만들고 당신의 많은 귀중한 시간을 빼앗아 갑니다. 당신은 세탁하는 것을 싫어하는 사람인가요? 여기 좋은 소식이 있습니다. 저희는 가정이나 회사로 세탁물을 수거하는 서비스를 제공합니다. 우리는 당신의 세탁물을 분리해서 빨고 말리고 개기 때문에 당신의 세탁물은 다른 어떤 사람의 세탁물과도 섞이지 않습니다. 또한, 세탁물을 맡긴 바로 다음날 받으실 수 있습니다. 저희 웹사이트 www.laundryking.co.kr을 방문해주세요. 싼 가격! 바로 다음날 배달!

laundry 세탁 **valuable** 귀중한 **offer** 제공하다 **fold** (옷 등을) 개다 **the very next day** 바로 다음날 **rate** 가격 **delivery** 배달

07

M I want to make mom happy. Do you have any good ideas?
W Why don't we make some chocolate muffins for her? She likes sweet things.
M Oh, that's a good idea. But I don't know how to make them. Can you help me?
W Sure. Let me check whether we have all the ingredients we need or not. [pause] Perfect. We have everything.
M Then, what should I do first?
W First of all, we should wash our hands.

남 엄마를 기쁘게 해드리고 싶어. 좋은 생각 있니?
여 엄마를 위해서 초콜릿 머핀을 만드는 게 어때? 엄마는 달콤한 것을 좋아하시잖아.
남 오, 좋은 생각이야. 하지만, 난 머핀을 만드는 방법을 몰라. 나를 도와줄래?
여 물론이지. 필요한 재료가 다 있는지 없는지 확인해볼게. 완벽해. 재료가 다 있어.
남 그럼, 나는 뭐부터 할까?
여 우선, 우리는 손부터 씻어야 해.

make + 목적어 + 형용사 ~를 …하게 만들다 **Why don't we ~?** ~하는 게 어때? **whether ~ or not** ~인지 아닌지 **ingredient** 재료 **first of all** 우선

08

M Excuse me. I am feeling a little airsick.
W Oh, I see. Why don't you put your seat back a little? Any better?
M I feel a bit better. Thanks.
W My pleasure. Do you need anything to drink?
M Do you have any orange juice?
W Yes, I'll be right back. Please remain seated and take some rest.
M Thank you so much.

남 실례합니다. 저 비행기 멀미 하는 것 같아요.
여 오, 알겠습니다. 좌석을 조금 뒤로 젖혀 보시겠어요? 조금 나아요?
남 조금 낫네요. 감사합니다.
여 천만에요. 마실 것 좀 드릴까요?
남 오렌지 주스 있나요?
여 네, 곧 가져다 드릴게요. 좌석에 앉아서 쉬고 계세요.
남 감사합니다.

feel airsick 비행기 멀미하다 **back** 뒤로 **a little** 조금 **feel better** 기분이 나아지다 **right** 바로 **remain** ~인 채로 있다 **take some rest** 휴식을 취하다

09

W Hi, Mike. Is it all right if I sit next to you?

M Sure, Jennifer. I'm reviewing today's lesson from science class.

W That's why you always get the best score. Can I join you?

M Why not? We learned about the structure of plants; the roots, stem and the leaves.

W The function of flowers was mentioned, too.

M That's right. Also, vegetables like carrots and radishes are actually roots.

여 안녕, Mike. 네 옆에 앉아도 되니?

남 물론이지, Jennifer. 나는 오늘 과학 시간에 배운 내용을 복습하고 있는 중이야.

여 그것이 네가 항상 최고 점수를 받는 이유이구나. 나도 함께 해도 돼?

남 물론이지. 우리는 식물의 구조가 뿌리, 줄기, 잎으로 구성되어 있다고 배웠어.

여 꽃의 역할도 언급되었어.

남 맞아. 또한, 당근과 무와 같은 채소는 실제로는 뿌리야.

next to ~의 옆에 **review** 복습하다 **always** 항상 **structure** 구조 **root** 뿌리 **stem** 줄기 **leaf** 잎 **function** 기능 **vegetable** 채소 **radish** 무

10

W What time do you go to bed?

M I go to bed around 9. I like to wake up early and memorize English words.

W What time do you get up then?

M I usually get up at 6.

W That's too early. I like studying late at night and sleeping late.

M That's why you're always late to class. You'd better go to bed earlier so you're not late again.

여 넌 몇 시에 자니?

남 나는 대략 9시 정도에 자. 나는 일찍 일어나서 영어 단어 암기하는 것을 좋아해.

여 그럼 몇 시에 일어나니?

남 나는 대개 6시에 일어나.

여 너무 이르다. 나는 밤 늦게까지 공부하고 늦게 자는 것을 좋아해.

남 그래서 네가 항상 수업에 지각하는 거야. 다시 지각하지 않기 위해서 너는 좀더 빨리 자는 게 좋겠어.

go to bed 잠자리에 들다 **around** 대략 **memorize** 암기하다 **get up** 일어나다 **usually** 대개 **late** 늦게 **always** 항상 **had better + 동사원형** ~하는 것이 낫다

11

M Did you hear the news? A tsunami hit several cities in Japan last night.

W My goodness. Really?

M Some buildings were destroyed and many people are either injured or dead.

W That's terrible. Is there anything we can do to help out the people there?

M I heard that we can donate money over the phone.

W Do you have the number?

M Yes. I will text it to you.

남 너 뉴스 들었어? 지난 밤에 쓰나미가 일본 몇몇 도시를 강타했대.

여 오 이런. 정말?

남 일부 건물들은 파괴됐고, 많은 사람들이 다치거나 죽었어.

여 끔찍하네. 그 곳 사람들을 위해 우리가 도울 것이 있니?

남 전화로 돈을 기부할 수 있다고 들었어.

여 전화번호 가지고 있니?

남 응. 문자 보내줄게.

tsunami 쓰나미 **destroy** 파괴하다 **either A or B** A 또는 B **injure** 다치게 하다 **help out** 도와주다 **donate** 기부하다 **text** 문자를 보내다

12

M First, put the dirty dishes, pans, and glasses inside the machine. Second, put a suitable amount of detergent into the machine. Third, turn the machine on. After a while, you will hear a sound that lets you know the washing has finished. Then, take the clean dishes, pans, and glasses out of the machine.

남 첫 번째로, 더러운 접시들과 냄비들, 그리고 유리컵들을 기계 안에 넣으세요. 두 번째로, 적당량의 세제를 기계 안에 넣으세요. 세 번째로, 기계를 켜세요. 잠시 후에 세척이 끝났음을 알리는 소리가 들릴 것입니다. 그러면 깨끗한 접시들과 냄비들, 그리고 유리컵들을 꺼내세요.

●●
dish 접시 **pan** (손잡이가 달린) 냄비 **suitable** 적당한 **detergent** 세제 **turn on** ~을 켜다 **after a while** 잠시 후에 **out of** ~에서

13

W Sam, do you think I should start working out?

M Exercising regularly will be good for your health. Why do you ask?

W Well… I am gaining weight little by little. And all of my friends are slim. I think I'm the only one who is fat.

M Don't think like that. You look good as you are.

W Really? Thank you, Sam.

여 Sam, 너는 내가 운동을 시작해야 한다고 생각하니?

남 규칙적인 운동을 하는 것은 네 건강에 좋지. 왜 물어보는 건데?

여 음… 나는 조금씩 살이 찌고 있어. 그리고 내 친구들은 모두 말랐어. 나 혼자만 뚱뚱한 것 같아.

남 그렇게 생각하지 마. 너는 지금 그대로 좋아 보여.

여 정말? 고마워, Sam.

●●
work out 운동하다 **exercise** 운동하다 **regularly** 규칙적으로 **be good for** ~에 좋다 **gain weight** 살이 찌다 **little by little** 조금씩 **slim** 날씬한 **fat** 뚱뚱한

14

[Telephone rings.]

W Hello. May I speak to George?

M Speaking. Who's calling?

W Hi, George. This is Terra. I'd like to invite you to my birthday party. Can you come?

M When is it?

W It's the last Saturday of this month.

M Oh, it's this Saturday! I can come. Please tell me the place and the time.

W Thank you. It will be in my house at 2.

[전화벨이 울린다.]

여 여보세요? George와 통화할 수 있을까요?

남 전데요. 누구시죠?

여 안녕, George. 나 Terra야. 나는 너를 내 생일파티에 초대하고 싶어. 올 수 있니?

남 언젠데?

여 이번 달 마지막 토요일이야.

남 오, 이번 주 토요일이네! 갈 수 있어. 장소와 시간을 말해줘.

여 고마워. 2시에 우리 집이야.

●●
Speaking. (전화) 전데요. **invite** 초대하다 **month** 월 **October** 10월

15

W What are you doing here alone?

M I'm writing a letter of apology.

W A letter of apology?

M Yes. My teacher told me to do it because I didn't do my homework. I had a hard time finding the right book to use.

W Oh, no. Let's go to the library together after this. I'll help you finish your homework.

M Really? Thank you.

W No problem. I'll wait for you.

여 너 혼자 여기에서 뭐 하니?

남 나는 반성문을 쓰고 있어.

여 반성문?

남 응. 내가 숙제를 해오지 않아서 선생님께서 쓰라고 하셨어. 나는 사용할 마땅한 책을 찾는 게 힘들었거든.

여 오, 이런. 이거 다 쓰고 같이 도서관에 가자. 내가 너 숙제 끝내는 것을 도와줄게.

남 정말? 고마워.

여 문제 없어. 기다릴게.

●●
alone 혼자 **apology** 사과 **do one's homework** 숙제를 하다 **have a hard time -ing** ~하는 데 애를 먹다 **wait for** ~을 기다리다

16

① M When did you move to Atlanta?
W Last month.

② M How far is the TBC Bank from here?
W It's about 5 minutes walk from here.

③ M How long have you been in Chicago?
W It's not long.

④ M Do you have any pets?
W Yes. I have a pet dog.

⑤ M How often do you ride your bike?

W Every day.

① 남 너는 언제 Atlanta로 이사했니?
여 지난 달에.
② 남 여기에서 TBC 은행까지 얼마나 머니?
여 대략 걸어서 5분 정도 걸려.
③ 남 너는 얼마 동안 Chicago에 있었니?
여 그것은 길지 않아.
④ 남 너 애완 동물 있니?
여 응. 나는 애완견이 있어.
⑤ 남 너는 얼마나 자주 자전거를 타니?
여 매일.

move to ~로 이사하다 **How far ~?** 얼마나 멀리 ~? **How long ~?** 얼마나 오랫동안 ~? **pet** 애완동물 **How often ~?** 얼마나 자주 ~?

17

W Brian, can you take your shoes off before coming into my house, please?

M Sure, it's no problem.

W Koreans do not wear their shoes inside. We always take off.

M Yeah, some Westerners do as well, but some don't.

W How about you? Do you take off your shoes inside?

M I usually do not, but this time I will. Haha.

여 Brian, 우리 집에 들어오기 전에 신발을 벗어줄래?
남 알았어, 얼마든지.
여 한국 사람들은 집에서 신발을 신지 않아. 우리는 항상 신발을 벗어.
남 응, 일부 서양인들도 그렇게 해. 하지만 일부는 그렇게 하지 않지.
여 넌 어때? 넌 실내에서 신발을 벗니?
남 보통은 안 벗지. 하지만 지금은 벗을 거야. 하하.

take off 벗다 **come into** ~에 들어가다 **inside** 내부에서 **Westerner** 서양인

18

W Becky and Steve have been friends since they were 7. Steve was overseas studying and came back last week for a vacation. Becky has arranged to have dinner with Steve this evening at an Italian restaurant to greet him. However, something urgent has come up at Becky's home, so she won't be able to have dinner with him. In this situation, what would Becky say to Steve?

여 Becky와 Steve는 7살 때부터 친구이다. Steve는 해외에서 공부하고 있었고 방학을 보내기 위해 지난 주에 왔다. Becky는 그를 맞이하기 위해 이탈리아음식점에 오늘 저녁 식사 자리를 마련했다. 그런데, Becky의 집에 급한 일이 생겨 그와의 저녁 식사를 할 수 없게 되었다. 이 상황에서 Becky는 Steve에게 무엇이라 말하겠는가?

① 큰 도움이 될 거야.
② 나는 이탈리아 음식을 좋아해.
③ 예약을 하는 게 어때?
④ 정말 미안해. 오늘 만나지 못할 것 같아.
⑤ 방학 동안 무엇을 할 거니?

since ~ 이후로 **overseas** 해외에 **arrange** 계획을 짜다 **greet** 반갑게 맞이하다 **urgent** 급한 **come up** 생기다 **be able to-V** ~할 수 있다

19

M You look so sad. What's wrong with you?

W I have to solve these math problems by tomorrow but I can't. Can you help me?

M Sure. Let me see.

W Do you think you can solve them?

M Fortunately, I can. Do you want me to explain now?

W Yes, please. I don't know how to thank you.

M Don't mention it. What are friends for?

남 너 무척 슬퍼 보여. 무슨 일이니?
여 이 수학 문제들을 내일까지 풀어야 하는데 못 풀겠어. 나 좀 도와줄래?
남 물론이지. 보자.
여 너는 그것들을 풀 수 있을 것 같니?
남 다행스럽게도 할 수 있어. 지금 설명해 줄까?
여 응, 부탁해. 네게 어떻게 고마움을 표해야 할지 모르겠네.
남 천만에. 친구 좋다는 게 뭐니?

① 내가 설명할게.
② 걱정하지 마. 행복하렴!
③ 미안하지만 안되겠어.
④ 내가 가장 좋아하는 과목은 수학이야.
⑤ 천만에. 친구 좋다는 게 뭐니?

solve a problem 문제를 풀다 **fortunately** 다행스럽게도 **explain** 설명하다 **Don't mention it.** 천만에.

20

M Jessica, what do you usually do in your free time?
W I usually read books.
M What kinds of books do you like best?
W Well, I like all kinds of books, but science fiction is my favorite.
M I enjoy reading science fiction, too. I usually read science fiction at least once a month.
W It's nice to hear that. Why don't we go to the bookstore and get some science fiction books together?
M I'd love to. Let's go now.

남 Jessica, 너는 여가 시간에 주로 무엇을 하니?
여 나는 대체로 책을 읽어.
남 너는 어떤 종류의 책을 가장 좋아하니?
여 글쎄, 나는 모든 종류의 책을 다 좋아하지만 공상과학을 가장 좋아해.
남 나도 공상과학 읽는 것을 좋아하는데. 나는 보통 최소한 한 달에 한 권을 읽어.
여 반가운 소리네. 서점에 같이 가서 공상과학 책을 좀 살까?
남 좋아. 지금 가자.

① 좋아. 지금 가자.
② 너는 얼마나 자주 책을 읽니?
③ 공상과학 구역이 어디죠?
④ 나는 여가 시간을 책을 읽으며 보내.
⑤ 미안. 난 이 지역이 익숙하지 않아.

free time 여가 시간 **science fiction** 공상과학 **enjoy -ing** ~하는 것을 즐기다 **at least** 최소한 **once a month** 한 달에 한 번

Further Study 정답

p. 34

1 She has a cat. Its color is black and white. It has short hair and a long tail.
2 The reason was that his little sister ripped several pages out of the woman's notebook.
3 Nineteen students have cell phones.
4 A plant consists of roots, a stem and leaves.
5 Put the dirty dishes, pans, and glasses inside the machine.
6 The reason was that she wants to invite him to her birthday party.
7 She has to solve some math problems by tomorrow, but she can't.
8 She usually reads books in her free time.

On Your Own 모범답안

p. 35

A

About My Class		
Questions	Boys	Girls
How many students are there?	10	10
How many students wear glasses?	8	2
How many students have cell phones?	8	8
How many students are wearing caps?	2	1
How many students have curly hair?	2	3

There are twenty students in my class: ten boys and ten girls. Eight boys and two girls wear glasses. On the other hand, there are ten students without glasses. Sixteen students have cell phones but two boys and two girls don't have one. Today, three students are wearing caps and there are five students who have curly hair: two boys and three girls.

우리 반에 대해		
질문	남	여
학생들은 몇 명입니까?	10	10
안경 쓴 학생은 몇 명입니까?	8	2
휴대전화가 있는 학생은 몇 명입니까?	8	8
모자를 쓴 학생은 몇 명입니까?	2	1
곱슬머리인 학생은 몇 명입니까?	2	3

우리 반에는 남자 10명과 여자 10명, 총 20명의 학생이 있습니다. 8명의 남학생과 2명의 여학생이 안경을 씁니다. 반면에 10명의 학생은 안경을 쓰지 않습니다. 16명의 학생은 휴대전화를 가지고 있지만 2명의 남학생과 2명의 여학생은 휴대전화가 없습니다. 오늘 3명의 학생이 모자를 쓰고

있고 남학생 2명, 여학생 3명, 총 5명의 학생이 곱슬머리입니다.

B

My Free Time	
(1) What do you do?	listen to music
(2) When did you start to do it?	7 years old
(3) Why do you like to do it?	makes me calm, peaceful
(4) How do you like it?	one of the greatest ways to spend my free time

I'm going to talk about what I usually do in my free time. I usually (1)listen to music in my free time. I first started to do it when (2)I was seven. I like to do it because (3)it makes me calm and peaceful. I think (1)listening to music is (4)one of the greatest ways to spend my free time.

나의 여가 시간	
(1) 무엇을 합니까?	음악 듣기
(2) 언제 처음 시작했나요?	7살 때
(3) 그것을 좋아하는 이유는 무엇인가요?	차분하고 평화롭게 만들어 줘서
(4) 그것은 어떤가요?	나의 여가 시간을 보내는 최고의 방법들 중 하나

저는 제가 여가 시간에 대개 무엇을 하는지에 대해 이야기하겠습니다. 저는 여가 시간에 대체로 음악을 듣습니다. 저는 7살 때 처음으로 시작했습니다. 저는 그것이 저를 차분하고 평화롭게 만들어줘서 좋아합니다. 저는 음악을 듣는 것이 나의 여가 시간을 보내는 가장 좋은 방법들 중의 하나라고 생각합니다.

04 Listening Test 정답

중학영어듣기 모의고사 04회

p. 40

01 ⑤	02 ②	03 ①	04 ④	05 ③
06 ③	07 ①	08 ⑤	09 ④	10 ②
11 ②	12 ⑤	13 ①	14 ②	15 ④
16 ④	17 ⑤	18 ④	19 ③	20 ③

01

W Here is my old family photo.
M Oh, I like it. Tell me about it.
W This is my whole family: my parents, my older sister, my younger sister and me.
M Which one are you?
W I am the one who has long, straight hair and glasses.
M Then, who is this person that is slim and has short and curly hair?
W That's my older sister.

여 여기 우리 집 옛날 가족 사진이야.
남 오, 사진 좋은데. 사진에 대해서 말해줘.
여 나의 부모님, 언니, 여동생, 그리고 나, 이렇게 우리 전체 가족이야.
남 어떤 사람이 너니?
여 긴 생머리에 안경을 쓰고 있는 사람이 나야.
남 그러면, 날씬하고 짧은 곱슬머리인 이 사람은 누구니?
여 그 사람은 나의 언니야.

family photo 가족 사진 **whole** 전체의 **slim** 날씬한 **curly hair** 곱슬머리

02

M May I take your order?
W I'd like to have a chicken salad, a cheese burger, and French fries.
M Would you like anything to drink?
W I'll have an ice tea, please.
M What would you like for dessert?
W What do you have?

M We have apple pie, chocolate cake, and peach and vanilla ice cream.

W I'll have peach ice cream, please.

남 주문하시겠습니까?

여 치킨 샐러드, 치즈 버거, 그리고 프렌치 프라이 주세요.

남 음료는 어떻게 하시겠습니까?

여 아이스 티 주세요.

남 후식은 무엇으로 하시겠습니까?

여 뭐가 있나요?

남 사과 파이, 초콜릿 케이크 그리고 복숭아와 바닐라 아이스크림이 있습니다.

여 복숭아 아이스크림으로 주세요.

take one's order 주문을 받다 **dessert** 후식 **peach** 복숭아

03

W You look worried. Are you all right?

M I didn't prepare for the mid-term exams yet.

W Don't worry too much about it. You still have a week before the exams.

M But a week is not enough to cover every subject. I don't understand math at all.

W I am almost ready for the math test. Do you need some help?

M Really? Thank you very much.

여 걱정스러워 보여. 너 괜찮아?

남 나 중간고사 준비를 아직 못했어.

여 너무 걱정하지 마. 아직 중간고사까지 일주일이나 남아 있어.

남 하지만 일주일은 모든 과목을 다 공부하기에는 충분하지 않아. 나는 수학은 전혀 이해가 안돼.

여 나는 수학 시험은 거의 준비가 다 됐어. 도움이 좀 필요하니?

남 정말? 진짜 고마워.

① 도움을 주는 ② 활기 넘치는 ③ 부정적인
④ 수줍어하는 ⑤ 이기적인

worry 걱정시키다, 걱정하다 **prepare** 준비하다 **mid-term exam** 중간고사 **yet** (부정문에서) 아직 **still** 여전히, 아직도 **be ready for** ~에 준비가 되다 **enough** 충분한

04

M How may I help you?

W Can you fill this prescription?

M Yes, one moment, please.

W Okay. [pause]

M Your prescription's ready. You should take one of these pills after each meal.

W Then, do I have to take them three times a day?

M Exactly. Don't skip a meal!

W Okay, I won't. How much is it?

남 어떻게 도와드릴까요?

여 이 처방전대로 약을 조제해주시겠어요?

남 네. 잠시만 기다려 주세요.

여 네.

남 다 준비되었습니다. 이 알약들을 매 식사 후에 한 알씩 드셔야 합니다.

여 그럼, 하루에 세 번 먹어야 하나요?

남 맞습니다. 식사 거르지 마세요.

여 네. 안 그럴게요. 얼마예요?

① 호텔 ② 병원 ③ 기차 역
④ 약국 ⑤ 식료품점

fill a prescription 약을 조제하다 **pill** 알약 **~ times a day** 하루에 ~번 **after meal** 식사 후에 **skip** 거르다

05

W Hello, sir. May I help you?

M I'm looking for a scarf for my mother.

W What do you think of this? It is made of silk.

M That looks pretty good. How much is it?

W It costs only fifty dollars.

M It's a little expensive. Is it possible to get a discount?

W How about a ten percent discount? That's the best that I can do.

M That's okay. I'll take it.

여 안녕하세요. 무엇을 도와드릴까요?

남 어머니에게 드릴 스카프를 찾고 있어요.

여 이건 어떠세요? 실크로 만들어진 거예요.

남 상당히 좋아 보이네요. 얼마입니까?

여 50달러밖에 하지 않아요
남 조금 비싸네요. 할인 가능한가요?
여 10% 할인 어떠세요? 제가 할 수 있는 최대입니다.
남 좋아요. 살게요.

●●
be made of ~로 만들어지다 **pretty** 꽤 **possible** 가능한 **discount** 할인

06

M Do you care about having good health? You know that eating the right foods will help you stay strong and fit. Since most of you live alone, you need to prepare your own meals for yourself. Therefore, you should know the best way to prepare healthy meals. Today, I am going to show you how to plan healthy meals and safe ways to prepare food.

남 당신은 건강을 유지하는 데 관심이 있습니까? 알다시피 바른 음식을 먹는 것은 당신이 강인하고 건강하게 되는 데 도움이 될 것입니다. 여러분들 대부분은 혼자 살기 때문에, 스스로 식사를 준비해야 합니다. 따라서, 여러분들은 건강한 식단을 준비하는 최상의 방법을 알아야 합니다. 오늘 저는 여러분에게 건강한 식단을 짜는 방법과 안전하게 음식을 준비하는 방법에 대해서 보여드릴 것입니다.

●●
care about ~에 관심을 가지다 **right** 올바른 **fit** 건강한 **since** ~ 때문에 **alone** 혼자 **for oneself** 혼자 힘으로 **healthy** 건강한

07

W Hi, Andrew. Did you have a good night's sleep?
M No, I didn't. I really feel sleepy as I woke up very early this morning.
W Why did you get up early?
M I watched the soccer game.
W You mean the game with Iraq? How was it?
M It was so exciting. Do you want to see it? I recorded it.
W Really? I'd love to see it. Thank you.

여 안녕, Andrew. 간밤에 잘 잤니?
남 아니. 오늘 아침에 아주 일찍 깨서 너무 잠 와.
여 왜 일찍 일어났어?
남 축구 경기를 봤거든.
여 이라크와의 경기 말하는 거야? 어땠어?
남 정말 재미있었어. 너 그 경기 보고 싶니? 나 녹화했거든.
여 정말? 보고 싶어. 고마워

●●
have a good sleep 잘 자다 **wake up** 깨다 **get up** 일어나다 **record** 녹음하다, 녹화하다

08

M I'm happy that we're finally taking a break.
W It's too hot here. I need something cold to drink.
M Me, too. By the way, how was the class?
W The English infinitive form is difficult to understand. I can't do the homework about it.
M I think I'm pretty good at it. Can I help you with our homework?
W That would be great. Why don't we do our homework together today?
M Okay. Let's study together after school.

남 드디어 쉬는 시간이어서 좋아.
여 여기 너무 더워. 뭔가 차가운 마실 것이 필요해.
남 나도. 그런데 수업 어땠어?
여 영어 부정사는 이해하기가 어려워. 그것에 대한 숙제는 못할 것 같아.
남 난 부정사는 꽤 잘 이해하는 것 같아. 내가 너 숙제 하는 것 도와줄까?
여 아주 좋아. 오늘 우리 숙제 같이 하는 것 어때?
남 그래. 방과 후에 같이 공부하자.

●●
take a break 휴식을 취하다 **by the way** 그런데 **infinitive** (문법) 부정사 **be good at** ~을 잘하다 **after school** 방과 후에

09

W Hello, what can I do for you?
M I'm looking for a one-bedroom apartment to rent.
W I have one. It is located right across the street. When do you need it?
M As soon as possible. Can you tell me more about the apartment you have available?
W The monthly rent is $400. There are enough parking spaces for every resident without extra charge.
M Sounds good. Can I take a look at it now?

여 안녕하세요. 무엇을 도와드릴까요?
남 저는 침실 한 개짜리 임대 아파트를 찾고 있습니다.
여 하나 있어요. 바로 길 건너편에 있지요. 언제 필요하세요?
남 가능한 한 빨리요. 갖고 계신 아파트에 대해서 좀 더 말씀해주시겠어요?
여 월세는 400달러입니다. 주차 공간은 모든 거주자에게 충분하고 추가 비용은 없습니다.
남 좋네요. 지금 볼 수 있을까요?

available 이용 가능한 **monthly rent** 월세 **parking space** 주차 공간 **resident** 거주민 **extra charge** 추가 비용

10

M What time does your train leave?
W It leaves at eleven in the morning.
M When do you have to be at the station?
W Just fifteen minutes early. I already bought my ticket.
M Without heavy traffic, it takes about thirty minutes to get to the station.
W Hmm, thirty minutes…
M But it is better to be early than to be late. So, why don't we leave the house at nine fifty?
W Yes, Dad.

남 네가 탈 기차는 몇 시에 출발하니?
여 오전 11시에 출발해요.
남 언제까지 역에 도착해야 하니?
여 15분만 일찍 도착하면 돼요. 이미 표를 샀거든요.
남 교통이 혼잡하지 않다면, 역까지 가는 데 30분 정도 걸리지.
여 음, 30분이면…
남 하지만 일찍 도착하는 게 늦는 것보다 더 나아. 9시 50분에 집에서 나가는 것 어떠니?
여 좋아요, 아빠.

leave 떠나다 **heavy traffic** 교통 혼잡 **It takes + 시간 + to-V** ~하는 데 …의 시간이 걸리다

11

M Melanie, why are you taking so long?
W Steve, I can't decide which one looks better.
M Why don't you just pick the one up that you like more?
W I like this red dress and that white skirt.
M Hmm... How about trying them both on?
W Okay. Please tell me which one suits me better.
M All right. Go to the fitting room and try them.

남 Melanie, 왜 그렇게 오래 걸리니?
여 Steve, 어떤 것이 더 좋아보이는지 모르겠어.
남 네가 더 좋아하는 것을 고르면 되잖아.
여 나는 이 빨간 드레스와 흰색 치마가 좋아.
남 음… 두 개 다 입어보는 것이 어때?
여 좋아. 어떤 것이 나에게 더 잘 어울리는지 이야기해줘.
남 알았어. 탈의실에 가서 입어봐.

decide 결심하다 **pick up** 고르다 **try on** ~을 입어보다 **suit** ~에게 어울리다 **fitting room** 탈의실

12

M Congratulations! You are the top student in school again.
W Thanks.
M Do you have any special tips for studying?
W Well, I always preview and review. I also write down each day's study plan in my diary.
M Anything else?
W I make a note of the answers I get wrong in tests.
M Wow. I will try to follow your method.

남 축하해! 너 학교에서 이번에도 전교 1등이네.
여 고마워.
남 공부하는 데 대한 특별한 비법이라도 있니?
여 음. 나는 항상 예습과 복습을 해. 나는 또한 수첩에 매일의 공부 계획을 적어 둬.
남 다른 것은?
여 시험에서 내가 틀리는 답들은 적어두지.
남 우와. 네 방법들을 따라 해 봐야겠다.

Congratulations! 축하해! **preview** 예습하다 **review** 복습하다 **study plan** 공부 계획 **make a note of** ~을 적어두다 **method** 방법

13

W Aren't you going to say a single word?
M There's nothing to say.

W Are you mad?

M I can't say no but I'll be okay soon. Just leave me alone for a while.

W Come on. Please...

M Listen. You are never on time. You always make me wait for you. I'm running out of patience.

W I'm very sorry. I won't be late again.

여 너 한마디도 안 할 거니?

남 할 말 없는데.

여 화났어?

남 아니라고는 말할 수 없지만 곧 괜찮아질 거야. 그냥 잠시 혼자 놔둬 줘.

여 왜 그래. 제발…

남 들어봐. 너는 절대 제시간에 오지 않아. 너는 항상 내가 너를 기다리게 해. 나는 인내심이 바닥났어.

여 정말 미안해. 다시는 늦지 않을게.

mad 화난 **for a while** 잠시 동안 **on time** 제시간에 **run out of** ~을 다 써버리다 **patience** 인내심

14

M Shall we choose a movie to watch together tonight?

W Sure. What kinds of movies do you like? I like action, comedy and romance movies.

M I like action movies, too. I also like both thriller and horror movies.

W Good. We have one in common. Let me check if there are any action movies running now.

M If possible I'd like to see after 6 p.m.

W Okay.

	여자	남자
① 로맨스	♥	
② 스릴러	♥	♥
③ 호러		♥
④ 코미디	♥	
⑤ 액션	♥	♥

남 오늘 밤에 같이 볼 영화 고를까?

여 그래. 너는 어떤 종류의 영화를 좋아하니? 나는 액션, 코미디, 그리고 로맨스 영화를 좋아해.

남 나도 액션 영화 좋아하는데. 나는 스릴러와 공포영화도 좋아해.

여 잘됐다. 공통 부분이 하나 있네. 지금 상영되는 액션 영화가 있는지 확인해 볼게.

남 가능하다면 오후 6시 이후로 해줘.

여 알겠어.

choose 선택하다 **thriller** 스릴러 **horror** 공포 **have ~ in common** ~을 공통으로 가지다 **run** 상영되다

15

M What's the matter?

W I have a terrible headache. I can't stand it.

M Do you also have a fever?

W Yes, but it is very slight.

M Well, I think you have a bad cold. It is going around.

W What should I do, then?

M Take this medicine, drink a lot of water and get lots of rest. Drinking warm lemon tea would be helpful, too.

W OK. Thank you.

남 무슨 문제세요?

여 두통이 너무 심해서요. 참을 수가 없네요.

남 열도 있습니까?

여 네, 그렇지만 미열이에요.

남 음. 제 생각에는 독감에 걸리신 것 같아요. 감기가 유행이거든요.

여 그러면 제가 어떻게 해야 하죠?

남 이 약 드시고, 물을 많이 마시고, 충분한 휴식을 취하세요. 따뜻한 레몬차를 마시는 것도 도움이 될 겁니다.

여 네. 감사합니다.

have a headache 두통이 있다 **stand** 참다 **fever** 열 **have a cold** 감기에 걸리다 **go around** (병 등이) 퍼지다 **take medicine** 약을 먹다

16

① W What do you think of this sweater?

M It looks warm and fashionable.

② W How often do you play the piano?

M Every day.

③ W How many pages do you have to write down?

M About 7 pages.

④ W How was your weekend?

M I'm going to see a concert on the weekend.

⑤ W How may I help you?
M No. I'm just looking around.

① 여 이 스웨터 어때?
남 따뜻하고 예뻐 보여.
② 여 너는 얼마나 자주 피아노를 치니?
남 매일.
③ 여 몇 페이지나 써야 해?
남 대략 7 페이지.
④ 여 주말 어떻게 보냈니?
남 나는 주말에 콘서트 보러 갈 거야.
⑤ 여 무엇을 도와드릴까요?
남 아니요. 그냥 둘러보는 겁니다.

What do you think of ~? ~에 대해 어떻게 생각하니? **look around** 둘러보다

17

W Are you going somewhere this vacation?
M I'm planning to go to Europe with my family.
W Really? Fantastic! What countries are you going to?
M We are thinking about visiting France, Switzerland, and Italy.
W Wow. How long are you going to be away?
M For about two weeks.
W Sounds wonderful! I wish I could go with you.

여 너 이번 방학에 어디 가니?
남 가족과 함께 유럽에 갈 계획이야.
여 정말? 환상적이네! 어느 나라에 갈 거니?
남 프랑스, 스위스, 그리고 이탈리아를 방문할까 생각하고 있어.
여 우와. 얼마 동안 가 있을 거니?
남 대략 2주 정도.
여 멋지다! 나도 너랑 같이 가면 좋겠다.

vacation 방학 **plan to-V** ~할 계획이다 **Europe** 유럽 **fantastic** 환상적인

18

W I want to talk about my homeroom teacher. Honestly, my first impression of him was quite scary. He looked really strict and cold. My classmates and I were frightened. However, as time passed, we found out that he has a warm heart and is kind to everyone. All of the students in my class like him very much. So do I.

여 저는 저의 담임선생님에 대하여 이야기하고자 합니다. 솔직하게, 제게 선생님의 첫인상은 꽤 무서웠습니다. 그는 매우 엄격하고 차갑게 보였습니다. 학급친구들도 나도 두려웠습니다. 그러나, 시간이 가면서 우리는 그가 매우 따뜻하고 모든 사람들에게 친절하다는 것을 알게 됐습니다. 우리 반에 있는 모든 학생들은 그를 좋아합니다. 저도 그렇습니다.

① 고통 없이는 얻는 것도 없다.
② 엎질러진 물은 다시 담을 수 없다.
③ 백지장도 맞들면 낫다.
④ 겉모습만 보고 판단하지 마라.
⑤ 한 가지 일에 전부를 걸지 마라.

homeroom teacher 담임선생님 **honestly** 솔직하게 **quite** 꽤 **strict** 엄격한 **cold** 차가운 **frightened** 무서워 하는

19

M Hi, Amy. Where are you going?
W I'm on the way to the hospital.
M Why? Are you sick?
W No, not me. My grandmother is in the hospital.
M Oh, no. What happened to her?
W She slipped on the tiles in the bathroom this morning and she broke her right leg.
M I'm sorry to hear that.

남 안녕, Amy. 너 어디 가니?
여 나는 병원에 가는 길이야.
남 왜? 아프니?
여 아니, 내가 아니야. 할머니가 병원에 계셔.
남 오, 이런. 무슨 일이니?
여 오늘 아침에 화장실 타일에서 미끄러지셨는데 오른 쪽 다리가 부러졌어.
남 안됐구나.

① 고마워. 그녀에게 말할게.
② 행운을 빌어.
③ 안됐구나.
④ 농담이지? 어디 보자.
⑤ 병원이 어디에 있는지 아니?

on the way to ~로 가는 길에 **sick** 아픈 **slip** 미끄러져 넘어지다
break one's leg 다리가 부러지다

20

M Oh, no! I can't breathe. It's so hot in here.
W Why don't you turn on the air conditioner? Here is the remote control.
M Unfortunately, it's out of order. I have been meaning to fix it but I have been too busy lately.
W What should we do?
M Would you mind if I opened the window?
W Pardon?
M Can I open the window?

남 오, 이런! 숨을 못 쉬겠어. 여기 정말 덥다.
여 에어컨을 켜지 그래? 여기 리모컨이 있어.
남 불행하게도, 고장 났어. 계속 고치려곤 했는데 내가 최근에 너무 바빴어.
여 어떻게 해야 하지?
남 창문을 열어도 될까?
여 뭐라고?
남 창문을 열어도 돼?

① 천만에.
② 다신 그렇게 말하지 마.
③ 창문을 열어도 돼?
④ 나는 네가 더운 날씨를 좋아하는 줄 몰랐어.
⑤ 고객센터가 어디야?

breathe 숨을 쉬다 **remote control** 리모컨 **unfortunately** 불행하게도 **out of order** 고장 난 **mean to-V** ~할 작정이다 **lately** 최근에
Would you mind ~? ~해도 괜찮겠습니까? **Pardon?** 뭐라고요?

Further Study 정답

p. 44

1 She has long, straight hair and wears glasses.
2 They have seven days before the exams.
3 He is going to help her with her homework about the English infinitive form which is too difficult for her to understand.
4 She is expected to arrive there at 10:20.
5 The reason was that she is the top student in school again.
6 The woman likes action, comedy, and romance movies. The man likes action, thriller, and horror movies.
7 He is going to go to Europe with his family.
8 The reason was that he looked really strict and cold.

On Your Own 모범답안

p. 45

A

My Vacation	
Where you are	Hawaii
Describe the weather	terrific; warm, sunny
Describe the food	really tasty
What you did today	visited the Big Island; saw volcanoes and visited a black sand beach
What you are going to do	spend my entire time swimming, snorkeling, and relaxing on the beach

Hi, there!
I'm having a wonderful time in Hawaii. The weather is terrific. It is warm and sunny. Also, the food is really tasty. Today I visited the Big Island. It was great to see volcanoes and visit a black sand beach. Tomorrow I'm going to spend my entire time swimming, snorkeling and relaxing on the beach. See you soon!

나의 휴가	
있는 곳	하와이
날씨 묘사	너무 좋음; 따뜻하고 화창함
음식 묘사	진짜 맛있음
오늘 한 일	빅아일랜드를 감; 화산을 보고, 검은 모래 해변도 감
앞으로 할 일	하루 종일 수영하고, 스노클링도 하고, 해변에서 휴식을 취하면서 보낼 것임

안녕!
나는 하와이에서 환상적인 시간을 보내고 있어. 날씨는 너무 좋아. 따뜻하고 화창해. 또 음식도 진짜 맛있어. 오늘은 빅아일랜드를 갔어.

화산도 보고, 검은 모래 해변도 갔는데 아주 좋았어. 내일은 하루 종일 수영도 하고, 스노클링도 하고, 해변에서 휴식을 취하면서 보낼 거야. 곧 만나자!

B

My Favorite Teacher	
(1) His/Her name	Raymond Lee
(2) What he/she looks like	tall, slim, handsome
(3) The subject he/she teaches	English
(4) Your first impressions of him/her	kind, sweet
(5) Why you like him/her	teaches English very well

I'm going to talk about my favorite teacher. The name of my favorite teacher is (1)Raymond Lee. He is (2)tall and slim. He is (2)handsome, too. He teaches (3) English. His first impressions were (4)kind and sweet. I like him very much because he (5)teaches English very well.

내가 가장 좋아하는 선생님	
(1) 선생님 이름	Raymond Lee
(2) 선생님의 생김새	키가 크고 날씬하고 잘생김
(3) 가르치시는 과목	영어
(4) 첫인상	친절하고 다정함
(5) 좋아하는 이유	영어를 잘 가르치심

나는 내가 가장 좋아하는 선생님에 대해서 이야기할 것입니다. 내가 가장 좋아하는 선생님의 이름은 Raymond Lee입니다. 그는 키가 크고 말랐습니다. 그는 또한 잘 생기셨습니다. 그는 영어선생님입니다. 그의 첫 인상은 친절하고 다정했습니다. 나는 그 선생님이 영어를 아주 잘 가르쳐 주셔서 무척 좋아합니다.

p. 50

01 ④	02 ⑤	03 ⑤	04 ③	05 ③
06 ①	07 ③	08 ①	09 ②	10 ②
11 ④	12 ④	13 ①	14 ①	15 ②
16 ⑤	17 ③	18 ②	19 ④	20 ④

01

W Hey, look at Joe! He's sleeping again.

M Well, as his mom is sick at the moment, he has to take care of his little brothers. He must be really exhausted.

W Sam is tired, too. He is yawning.

M Look at Mike. He's laughing about the picture on the board.

W Yeah, because Jessica is drawing a funny character who looks like Jimmy.

M It sure looks like Jimmy.

여 이봐, Joe 좀 봐! 또 자고 있네.

남 음, 엄마가 지금 편찮으셔서 그는 어린 남동생들을 돌봐야 해. 정말 피곤함에 틀림없어.

여 Sam도 피곤한가 봐. 하품하고 있어.

남 Mike 좀 봐. 칠판에 그려진 그림을 보고 웃고 있어.

여 맞아. Jessica가 Jimmy를 닮은 웃긴 인물을 그리고 있기 때문이야.

남 진짜 Jimmy처럼 보여.

take care of ~를 돌보다 **exhausted** 녹초가 된 **yawn** 하품하다 **character** 인물 **look like + 명사** ~처럼 보이다

02

M Excuse me, can you help me? I want to buy a toy for my two-year old nephew.

W How about this stuffed teddy bear? It is really popular with kids.

M Hmm. What about this tricycle?

W It's nice but he might be too young for it.

M Oh, I see.

W Then, how about that red truck that the little boy over there is playing with?

M That would be great. My nephew will love it. I'll take that one.

남 실례지만 좀 도와주시겠어요? 두 살 된 조카에게 장난감을 사주려고 해요.

여 이 봉제 곰 인형은 어때요? 아이들에게 진짜 인기가 많아요.

남 흠. 이 세발자전거는 어떤가요?

여 좋긴 하지만, 그 자전거를 타기에는 조카가 너무 어릴지도 모르겠네요.

남 네, 그렇군요.

여 그럼, 저기 어린 소년이 가지고 놀고 있는 빨간 트럭은 어때요?

남 그거 좋겠네요. 제 조카가 좋아할 거예요. 저것으로 사겠습니다.

nephew 조카 **stuffed** 봉제한 **teddy bear** 곰 인형 **be popular with** ~에게 인기가 있다

03

W Our family is planning to go to Canada during the summer vacation.

M That sounds terrific. How long are you going for?

W My parents want to go for ten days and nine nights.

M I wish I was going on a trip like you.

W I hope you do something fun, too.

M Will you bring me back a souvenir?

W Of course I will.

여 우리 가족은 여름방학 동안 캐나다로 갈 계획이야.

남 아주 멋지다. 얼마나 머물 예정이야?

여 부모님은 9박 10일 머물기를 원하셔.

남 나도 너처럼 여행을 가면 좋을 텐데.

여 너도 뭔가 재미난 일을 하길 바랄게.

남 기념품 사다 줄 거지?

여 물론 그럴 거야.

① 희망에 찬 ② 신이 난 ③ 당황한
④ 외로운 ⑤ 부러워하는

plan to-V ~할 계획이다 **during + 기간** ~동안 **terrific** 아주 멋진 **go on a trip** 여행을 가다 **souvenir** 기념품

04

M Good evening. Where would you like to go?

W Can you take me to Kimpo Airport?

M Sure. Are you going to catch a flight?

W Yes. It's a nine o'clock flight. I have to be there by seven o'clock. So can you drive as fast as possible?

M Oh, we are in a traffic jam now, but I will try my best.

W Thank you.

남 안녕하세요. 어디로 모실까요?

여 김포 공항으로 가주시겠어요?

남 물론이죠. 비행기를 타실 건가요?

여 네. 9시 비행기를 탈 거예요. 7시까지는 도착해야 하고요. 그러니까 가능한 한 빨리 가주시겠어요?

남 오, 지금 교통 체증이 있긴 하지만 최선을 다해 보겠습니다.

여 감사합니다.

① 비행기 ② 공항 ③ 택시
④ 버스 ⑤ 지하철

take A to B A를 B로 데려가다 **catch a flight** 비행기를 타다 **as + 부사 + as possible** 가능한 한 ~하게 **traffic jam** 교통 체증

05

W How can I help you?

M Can you break a hundred-dollar bill for me?

W Of course. How do you want it?

M Can I get three twenties, two tens, and the rest in ones?

W I am afraid that I don't have enough one-dollar bills. Are two fives fine with you?

M That's all right.

W Here you go.

여 어떻게 도와드릴까요?

남 100달러짜리 지폐를 잔돈으로 좀 바꿔주시겠어요?

여 물론이죠. 어떻게 바꿔드릴까요?

남 20달러 3장, 10달러 2장, 그리고 나머지는 1달러 지폐로 받을 수 있을까요?

여 죄송하지만, 1달러 지폐가 충분하지 않네요. 5달러짜리 2장도 괜찮으세요?

남 괜찮아요.
여 여기 있습니다!

●●
break (돈을 작은 단위로) 바꾸다 **rest** 나머지 **enough** 충분한 **Here you go.** 여기 있습니다.

06

M How you introduce yourself to others is important. First impressions can leave either a good or bad impression of you. Here are two pieces of advice for making a great first impression. First, always begin with a smile. Second, try to speak an equal amount in the conversation. No one likes a person who talks by himself or herself the entire time.

남 당신 자신을 다른 사람들에게 어떻게 소개하는지는 중요합니다. 첫인상은 당신에 대한 좋은 인상을 남길 수도, 나쁜 인상을 남길 수도 있습니다. 좋은 첫인상을 만드는 두 가지 조언이 여기 있습니다. 첫 번째, 항상 미소로 시작하세요. 두 번째, 대화에서 상대방과 동등한 양의 말을 하려고 노력하세요. 어떤 사람도 대화 내내 혼자서만 이야기하는 사람을 좋아하지 않습니다.

●●
introduce 소개하다 **others** 다른 사람들 **impression** 인상 **advice** 충고 **equal** 동등한 **entire** 전체의

07

W Your hair is getting really long.
M I know. My little sister says I look like a bear with shaggy hair.
W I agree with her. Why don't you get it cut?
M Okay, then how about I get it cut like Won Bin's in the movie *The Man from Nowhere*?
W Wow! I think that hairstyle would look great on you.
M Do you want to come along with me?
W Sure. Let's go right now!

여 너 머리가 너무 길어지고 있네.
남 나도 알아. 내 여동생은 내가 털투성이 곰 같아 보인다고 말을 해.
여 나도 네 여동생과 동감이야. 머리 좀 자르는 게 어때?
남 좋아. 그러면 영화 〈아저씨〉에 나오는 원빈 머리처럼 자르는 건 어떨까?
여 와우! 내 생각에 그 헤어스타일은 너에게 아주 잘 어울릴 것 같아.
남 나랑 같이 갈래?
여 물론이야. 지금 당장 가자!

●●
shaggy 털투성이의 **How about ~?** ~는 어때? **look great on** ~에게 잘 어울리다 **come along** 동행하다

08

W I received a phone call from your teacher today.
M Oh, no. What did she say?
W She said you broke a vase on her desk. Is it true?
M Yes, but I didn't do it on purpose.
W What happened then?
M When I passed by Dave's desk, I tripped on one of its legs and fell down, breaking the vase.
W Weren't you hurt? You need to be more careful.

여 오늘 너의 선생님으로부터 전화가 왔었어.
남 오, 안되는데. 선생님께서 뭐라고 하셨어요?
여 네가 선생님 책상에 있는 꽃병을 깼다고 하셨어. 정말이니?
남 네, 하지만 일부러 그런 것이 아니에요.
여 그럼, 어떻게 된 일이니?
남 Dave의 책상을 지나갈 때, 걔 책상 다리 한 짝에 걸려서 넘어지면서 그 꽃병을 깼어요.
여 다치진 않았니? 더 조심해.

●●
receive 받다 **vase** 꽃병 **on purpose** 고의로 **trip on** ~에 발이 걸려 넘어지다 **fall down** 쓰러지다

09

M What is your favorite fruit, Kelly?
W I love all kinds of fruit.
M So do I. But which fruit do you like the best?
W Well, I like grapefruits very much.
M What other types of fruit do you like?
W I love oranges, cherries, and seedless grapes. What about you?
M I am fond of apples and watermelons.

남 네가 가장 좋아하는 과일은 뭐야, Kelly?
여 나는 모든 종류의 과일을 좋아해.
남 나도 그래. 하지만 어떤 과일을 가장 좋아하니?

여 글쎄, 자몽을 무척 좋아해.
남 네가 좋아하는 다른 종류의 과일은 뭐가 있어?
여 나는 오렌지, 체리 그리고 씨 없는 포도를 좋아해. 너는 어때?
남 나는 사과와 수박을 좋아해.

●●
favorite 가장 좋아하는 **grapefruit** 자몽 **seedless** 씨 없는 **be fond of** ~를 좋아하다

10

M What do you like to do on rainy days?
W I like to stay in bed and watch TV all day. I feel lazy on rainy days. How about you?
M I like to take a walk in the rain. It makes me feel refreshed.
W Don't you get wet?
M A little. However, it is really interesting to listen to the sound of raindrops outside. Why don't you join me sometime?
W No thanks!

남 너는 비 오는 날에 무엇을 하는 것을 좋아하니?
여 나는 침대에 누워서 종일 TV 보는 것을 좋아해. 비 오는 날은 여유로운 느낌이야. 너는 어때?
남 나는 빗속에서 산책하는 것을 좋아해. 그러면 난 상쾌한 느낌이 들어.
여 비에 젖지 않니?
남 조금. 하지만 밖에서 빗방울 소리를 듣는 것은 정말 재미있어. 언제 같이 해볼래?
여 고맙지만, 사양할게.

●●
rainy day 비 오는 날 **lazy** 여유로운, 느긋한 **take a walk** 산책하다 **refreshed** 상쾌한 **wet** 젖은 **raindrop** 빗방울

11

W I heard that you took some pictures when we went on the picnic.
M Yes. I uploaded most of them to my blog.
W My laptop was broken last week, so it's hard for me to access the Internet.
M I see. Why don't you get it fixed then?
W I will, but could you send some of the photos to my cell phone, please?
M Sure.
W Thank you. I can't wait to see them.

여 우리 소풍 갔을 때 네가 사진을 좀 찍었다고 들었어.
남 응. 내 블로그에 그것들 대부분을 올렸는데.
여 지난 주에 내 노트북 컴퓨터가 고장 나서 내가 인터넷에 접속하기가 어려워.
남 알았어. 그러면 왜 고치지 않는 거야?
여 그럴 거야. 그런데 내 휴대전화로 그 사진들 중 몇 장을 좀 보내줄래?
남 그래.
여 고마워. 사진 빨리 보고 싶어.

●●
take a picture 사진을 찍다 **go on a picnic** 소풍을 가다 **access** 접속하다 **fix** 수리하다 **Why don't you ~?** ~하는 게 어때?

12

[Telephone rings.]
W Hello, Bonnie Books. How may I help you?
M Hello. I ordered a book from your homepage, and I received it today.
W Uh-huh.
M However, you sent me the wrong one.
W Oh, I'm sorry. Do you want your money back or would you like to exchange it?
M I'd like to get a refund.
W Okay. Send us the book and we will give you your money back. Sorry for the inconvenience.

[전화벨이 울린다.]
여 여보세요. Bonnie Books입니다. 무엇을 도와 드릴까요?
남 여보세요. 제가 그쪽 홈페이지에서 책을 주문하고 오늘 받았습니다.
여 그런데요?
남 그런데 책을 잘못 보내셨어요.
여 오, 죄송합니다. 환불해 드릴까요, 아니면 교환해 드릴까요?
남 환불해 주세요.
여 알겠습니다. 저희 쪽으로 책을 보내주시면, 환불해 드리겠습니다. 불편을 드려 죄송합니다.

●●
order 주문하다 **receive** 받다 **wrong** 잘못된 **back** 되돌려 **exchange** 교환하다 **refund** 환불 **inconvenience** 불편함

13

M What a beautiful day!
W I wish that I were at the beach.

M Lying on the beach and drinking a cup of iced coffee would be perfect.

W How about going to the beach this weekend? Are you busy?

M I have no plans yet. Are you serious?

W Yes. We haven't gone on a trip for several months.

M Yeah, you're right. Let's go.

W I am so happy.

남 정말 아름다운 날이다!
여 해변에 있으면 좋을 텐데.
남 해변에 누워 냉커피 한 잔을 마신다면 완벽할 텐데.
여 이번 주말에 해변에 가는 것 어때? 너 바빠?
남 아직 계획 없어. 정말이야?
여 응. 몇 달 동안 여행 못 갔잖아.
남 그래, 네 말이 맞아. 가자.
여 정말 좋아.

lie 눕다 **a cup of** 한 잔의 ~ **perfect** 완벽한 **How about -ing?** ~하는 건 어때? **several** 몇몇의

14

① W The restaurant closes at 11 in the evening.
② W The restaurant opens at 11 in the morning.
③ W The restaurant is a buffet restaurant.
④ W The restaurant is at 23 Main Street, Los Angeles.
⑤ W People can call the restaurant at 310-231-3456.

델리 하우스 레스토랑
매일 오전 11시부터 밤 10시까지 영업합니다.
신선한 해산물 뷔페를 즐기세요.
로스앤젤레스시, Main가 23번지
☎ 310-231-3456

① 여 레스토랑은 밤 11시에 문을 닫는다.
② 여 레스토랑은 오전 11시에 문을 연다.
③ 여 레스토랑은 뷔페 레스토랑이다.
④ 여 레스토랑은 로스앤젤레스시의 Main가 23번지에 있다.
⑤ 여 레스토랑 전화번호는 310-231-3456번이다.

restaurant 식당, 레스토랑 **buffet** 뷔페

15

W What do you think we can do to keep our environment clean?

M Well. There are many things we can do.

W Like what? Save energy?

M That would be one thing. We should turn off lights when we leave rooms. We should also recycle paper, cans and bottles.

W Anything else?

M We can take the subway or buses instead of cars.

W Oh, we can do the first before we leave.

여 환경을 깨끗하게 하기 위해 우리가 무엇을 할 수 있다고 생각하니?
남 글쎄. 우리가 할 수 있는 일들이 많이 있어.
여 어떤 거? 에너지 절약하는 거?
남 그것도 한 방법이지. 방에서 나갈 때 불을 꺼야 해. 또 종이, 캔, 그리고 병을 재활용해야 해.
여 다른 건 없니?
남 자동차 대신 지하철이나 버스를 타면 돼.
여 아, 우리가 방에서 나가기 전에 제일 처음 것을 할 수 있겠다.

environment 환경 **clean** 깨끗한 **save** 절약하다 **turn off** ~을 끄다 **recycle** 재활용하다 **instead of** ~ 대신에

16

① M When's your birthday?
W It's on June 8th.
② M Where are you from?
W I'm from Jeju Island.
③ M Can I try this on?
W Sure, go ahead.
④ M What do you want to be when you grow up?
W I want to be a police officer.
⑤ M What's your favorite subject?
W I hate math.

① 남 너 생일이 언제니?
여 6월 8일이야.
② 남 어디 출신이니?
여 제주도에서 왔어.
③ 남 이거 입어봐도 되나요?
여 물론이죠. 그렇게 하세요.

④ 남 너는 커서 무엇이 되고 싶니?
  여 나는 경찰관이 되고 싶어.
⑤ 남 가장 좋아하는 과목이 무엇이니?
  여 나는 수학을 싫어해.

●●
be from ~ 출신이다 **try on** (옷, 신발 등을) 입어[신어] 보다 **grow up** 자라다 **police officer** 경찰관 **favorite** 가장 좋아하는 **hate** 싫어하다

17

M Are you looking at the student exchange program?
W Yeah. It's hard to choose where to go.
M Weren't you interested in Britain?
W I was. But it's too expensive there, so I have given up on going there.
M Which countries are in your mind then?
W I might go to New Zealand, because my uncle lives there.
M That's good.
W Yeah, I think I can get some help from him if I go there.

남 교환학생 프로그램을 보고 있는 거니?
여 응. 어디로 갈지 선택하는 게 어렵네.
남 영국에 관심 있었던 것 아니니?
여 그랬어. 하지만 그곳은 너무 비싸. 그래서 거기 가는 것은 포기했어.
남 그러면 어느 나라들을 염두에 두고 있니?
여 뉴질랜드로 갈 수도 있어. 왜냐하면 삼촌이 그곳에 사시거든.
남 그거 괜찮네.
여 응, 내가 거기 가면 삼촌 도움을 좀 받을 수 있을 거라 생각해.

●●
exchange program 교환 프로그램 **choose** 선택하다 **be interested in** ~에 흥미가 있다 **expensive** 비싼 **be in one's mind** 염두에 두다

18

M Nikko is visiting Jihyun, one of her Korean friends, in Seoul. Jihyun has taken her to several tourist spots. They've visited places like the Han River, N Seoul Tower, 63 Building, and Yeouido Park. Now they are at a fancy restaurant located in Gwanghwamun. They've finished eating a nice dinner, and they are about to leave. Nikko is wondering whether she has to leave a tip for the waiter on the table or not. In this situation, what would she say to Jihyun?

남 Nikko는 서울에 살고 있는 그녀의 한국 친구들 중 한 명인 지현이를 방문 중이다. 지현이는 그녀를 여러 관광 명소로 데려가 주었다. 그들은 한강, N 서울 타워, 63빌딩, 여의도공원과 같은 곳들을 방문했다. 이제 그들은 광화문에 위치해 있는 화려한 식당에 있다. 그들은 맛있는 저녁 식사를 끝냈고, 이제 막 떠날 참이다. Nikko는 테이블에 웨이터를 위한 팁을 남겨 놓아야 하는지 아닌지 고민하고 있다. 이 상황에서 그녀는 지현이에게 무어라 말하겠는가?

① 비용은 각자 내자.
② 한국에서는 팁을 주니?
③ 음식이 얼마니?
④ 고맙다는 말 외엔 다른 무슨 말을 해야 할지 모르겠다.
⑤ 오늘 정말로 관광과 음식이 좋았어.

●●
tourist spot 관광 명소 **fancy** 화려한 **whether ~ or not** ~인지 아닌지 **leave a tip** 팁을 남기다

19

M Hooray! I can't believe this.
W What is it? Why are you so excited?
M I entered a competition on a radio program last month. Fortunately, they chose me as the winner.
W Really?
M YES! And I won two tickets to Europe. That means we can go to Europe for free.
W Let's check our schedule to see when we can go.

남 야호! 믿을 수가 없어.
여 뭔데? 왜 그렇게 신이 나 있어?
남 지난 달에 라디오 프로그램 경연에 참여했어. 운이 좋게도 프로그램 담당자들이 나를 승자로 뽑아줬어.
여 정말?
남 그래! 그리고 유럽 가는 표 두 장을 받았어. 우리가 공짜로 유럽을 갈 수 있다는 얘기지.
여 우리 언제 갈 수 있는지 일정을 확인해 보자.

① 나는 중국에 가고 싶어.
② 유럽 여행 어땠니?
③ 나는 네가 왜 그렇게 신이 났는지 모르겠어.
④ 우리 언제 갈 수 있는지 일정을 확인해 보자.
⑤ 나는 라디오 프로그램에 보낼 편지를 쓰고 있어.

●●
Hooray! 야호! **excited** 신이 난 **enter** 참여하다 **competition** 시합 **fortunately** 운이 좋게도 **choose** 선택하다 **Europe** 유럽 **for free** 공짜로

20

M Honey, the sun is already high in the sky. It's time to wake up.

W I am so sleepy. Can I stay in bed for 20 more minutes?

M Didn't you say that you will start jogging in the park this week?

W No, not today. I will start next week.

M What time did you go to bed last night?

W I stayed up until 1 o'clock in the morning.

남 얘야, 해가 이미 중천에 떴어. 일어날 시간이야.
여 너무 졸려요. 20분만 더 누워있으면 안돼요?
남 너 이번 주에 공원에서 조깅 시작할 거라고 말하지 않았니?
여 아뇨, 오늘 말고요. 다음 주부터 할래요.
남 어젯밤에 몇 시에 잠자리에 들었니?
여 새벽 1시까지 깨어 있었어요.

① 지금 현재 2시 15분이에요.
② 나는 공원에서 조깅하는 것을 좋아해요.
③ 나는 대체로 10시경에 잠자리에 들어요.
④ 새벽 1시까지 깨어 있었어요.
⑤ 나는 새 침대를 샀는데 매우 편안해요.

●●
It's time to-V ~할 시간이다 **stay in bed** 침대에 누워있다 **go to bed** 잠자리에 들다 **until** ~ 때까지

Further Study 정답 p. 54

1 She is planning to go to Canada for ten days and nine nights.
2 She breaks it into 3 twenties, 2 tens, 2 fives and 10 ones.
3 He did it by mistake because he tripped on a desk leg and fell down.
4 He likes to take a walk in the rain.
5 He uploaded them to his blog.
6 He wants to lie on the beach and drink a cup of iced coffee.
7 She is looking at a student exchange program.
8 He entered a competition on a radio program and he was chosen as the winner.

On Your Own 모범답안 p. 55

A

My Favorite Song	
(1) The title of the song	You Can Get Through It
(2) The singer of the song	Kang Saneh
(3) The theme of the song	You should not regret what you have done and you can do whatever you want with a strong heart.
(4) Reasons you like the song	helps me have respect for and trust myself

The song I like most is (1) *You Can Get Through It*. It is sung by (2) Kang Saneh. The song is about the fact that (3) you should not regret what you have done and that you can do whatever you want with a strong heart. I like this song because (4) it helps me have respect for and trust myself.

내가 가장 좋아하는 노래	
(1) 제목	넌 할 수 있어
(2) 가수	강산에
(3) 주제	당신이 이미 한 일을 후회하면 안되고 당신은 강한 마음으로 원하는 뭐든지 할 수 있다.
(4) 좋아하는 이유	나 자신을 존중하고 믿을 수 있게 도와줌

내가 가장 좋아하는 노래는 〈넌 할 수 있어〉입니다. 그것은 강산에가 부릅니다. 그 노래는 당신이 이미 한 일을 후회하지 말아야 한다는 것과 강한 마음만 있으면 원하는 뭐든지 할 수 있다는 사실에 대한 것입니다. 나는 이 노래가 나 자신을 존중하고 믿을 수 있게 도와줘서 좋아합니다.

B

If I Had a Chance to Study Abroad...	
(1) Which country would you like to go?	the U.S.
(2) Why do you want to go there?	learn English, visit Ivy League universities, see the Statue of Liberty
(3) What language do they speak?	English
(4) Can you speak the language?	a little
(5) Does anyone you know live there?	my cousin

If I had a chance to study abroad, I would like to go to (1)the U.S. The reasons why I would like to study there are that I could (2)learn English, visit Ivy League universities, and see the Statue of Liberty. People in the country speak (3)English. I can speak (4)English a little. Actually, (5)my cousin lives and studies there. I wish I could go to (1)the U.S. and study there one day.

내게 만약 유학을 할 기회가 온다면...	
(1) 어느 나라를 가고 싶습니까?	미국
(2) 왜 그곳에 가고 싶습니까?	영어를 배우고, 아이비리그 대학들을 방문하고, 자유의 여신상을 볼 수 있어서
(3) 그 나라에서는 어떤 말을 합니까?	영어
(4) 그 나라 말을 할 수 있습니까?	조금
(5) 그곳에서 사는 사람을 알고 있습니까?	사촌

제게 만일 유학을 할 수 있는 기회가 온다면, 저는 미국에 가고 싶습니다. 그곳에서 공부하고 싶은 이유는 영어를 배울 수 있고, 아이비리그 대학들을 방문할 수 있고, 또 자유의 여신상을 볼 수 있기 때문입니다. 그 나라 사람들은 영어를 사용합니다. 저는 영어로 조금 말할 줄 압니다. 사실 제 사촌이 그곳에서 살면서 공부합니다. 저는 언젠가 미국에 가서 공부할 수 있기를 소망합니다.

06 Listening Test 정답

p. 60

01 ④	02 ②	03 ①	04 ③	05 ②
06 ⑤	07 ④	08 ②	09 ④	10 ①
11 ③	12 ②	13 ②	14 ①	15 ①
16 ⑤	17 ⑤	18 ③	19 ②	20 ⑤

01

M Mom! I can't find Minnie anywhere. She isn't in the living room, and in the kitchen.

W What about the laundry room? You know she likes to hide there.

M No, she's not there, either.

W Don't worry too much. I'm sure she's somewhere.

M What if she's lost? What should I do?

W Oh, look! There she is. She's under your bed!

남 엄마! 어디에서도 Minnie를 찾을 수가 없어요. 거실에도 없고, 부엌에도 없어요.

여 세탁실은 어때? Minnie는 거기에 숨는 것을 좋아하잖아.

남 아뇨. 거기에도 없어요.

여 너무 걱정하지 마. 어딘가 주변에 있을 거야.

남 만약에 길을 잃어버린 거라면 어떻게 하죠? 어떻게 해야 해요?

여 오, 봐! 저기에 있어. 네 방 침대 밑에 있어.

anywhere 어디에도 **either** (부정문에서) 또한 **living room** 거실 **laundry** 세탁 **what if ~?** 만약 ~라면 어쩌지?

02

W Excuse me, sir. Can you tell me where the nearest post office is?

M Sure. Go down one block and turn right.

W One block down and turn right?

M Yes, you will find it on your left. It's the second building from the corner. You can't miss it.

W Thank you for helping me.

M Not at all.

여 실례합니다. 가장 가까운 우체국이 어디에 있는지 말씀해주시겠어요?
남 물론이죠. 한 블록 간 후 오른쪽으로 도세요.
여 한 블록 내려간 후 오른쪽으로 돈다고요?
남 네, 왼편에서 우체국을 발견할 수 있을 거예요. 모퉁이에서 두 번째 건물입니다. 찾기 쉬워요.
여 정말 감사합니다.
남 천만에요.

●●
post office 우체국 **turn right** 오른쪽으로 돌다 **You can't miss it.** 찾기 쉬워요. **Not at all.** 천만에요.

03

M It's already 1 o'clock. Let's eat out for lunch.
W Can I borrow some money from you? I didn't bring my purse to work today.
M You don't need to. I'll treat you today.
W Are you sure? You are so nice.
M And I look handsome, too?
W Of course, you do. So, where are you taking me?
M What about Sue's Kitchen?

남 벌써 1시야. 점심 나가서 먹자.
여 돈 좀 빌려줄래? 오늘 회사 오면서 지갑을 안 가지고 왔어.
남 그럴 필요 없어. 오늘 내가 사줄게.
여 정말? 너 진짜 마음씨 좋다.
남 그리고 또한 잘 생겼지?
여 물론이지. 그럼 어디로 나를 데리고 갈 거야?
남 Sue's Kitchen 어때?

① 후한 ② 무례한 ③ 이기적인
④ 엄격한 ⑤ 주의 깊은

●●
already 벌써 **eat out** 외식하다 **borrow** 빌리다 **purse** (여성용) 지갑, 핸드백 **work** 직장 **treat** 대접하다

04

W May I help you?
M I couldn't find the book that I want to read.
W Did you check the database?
M Yes, it said the book was on the shelf but it was not there.
W Maybe we have lost it. We'll get a new copy of it soon. Do you want me to reserve it for you?
M Yes, please. Thanks a lot.

여 도와드릴까요?
남 제가 읽고 싶은 책을 찾을 수가 없어요.
여 데이터베이스 확인하셨어요?
남 네, 그 책이 선반에 있다고 했는데, 거기에 없어요.
여 아마도 저희가 잃어버린 것 같네요. 새 것으로 한 권을 곧 구입해놓을 거예요. 새 책이 오면 당신을 위해 따로 놔둘까요?
남 네, 그렇게 해주세요. 감사합니다.

① 장난감 가게 ② 편의점 ③ 도서관
④ 주민 센터 ⑤ 박물관

●●
want to-V ~하기를 원하다 **database** 데이터베이스 **shelf** 선반 **copy** (같은 책의) 권 **soon** 곧 **reserve** 따로 남겨 두다

05

W When is your birthday?
M Mine is on August the 14th. How about yours?
W My birthday is on May the 13th.
M Oh, there are 10 days left until your birthday. Are you planning to have a party?
W Yes, I am. Would you like to come to my birthday party?
M That would be great. Thank you for inviting me.

여 네 생일이 언제니?
남 8월 14일이야. 네 생일은 언제야?
여 내 생일은 5월 13일이야.
남 오, 네 생일까지 10일 남았네. 파티를 열 계획이야?
여 응. 내 생일 파티에 올래?
남 좋아. 초대해 줘서 고마워.

●●
August 8월 **May** 5월 **plan to-V** ~할 계획이다 **invite** 초대하다

06

W Our earth has a limited amount of resources. If we don't save but just waste our resources, there will be no materials that our grandchildren can use. Also, wasting resources can pollute the environment, so we have to recycle the materials we have used. When we recycle cans, bottles, and paper, we are saving resources for future use.

여 우리 지구에는 제한된 양의 자원이 있습니다. 만약 우리가 자원을 절약하지 않고 단지 낭비한다면, 우리의 손자, 손녀들이 사용할 수 있는 물자는 없을 것입니다. 또한 자원을 낭비하는 것은 환경을 오염시킬 수 있습니다. 그래서 우리는 우리가 사용한 물자들을 재활용해야 합니다. 우리가 캔, 병, 종이를 재활용한다면, 우리는 미래의 사용을 위해서 자원을 절약하는 중인 것입니다.

earth 지구 **limited** 제한된 **amount** 양 **resources** 자원 **material** 자재 **pollute** 오염시키다 **grandchildren** 손주 **recycle** 재활용하다 **bottle** 병

07

M Do you like to go out?

W Yes. I like to go out with my friends. What about you?

M I love to stay home, reading books or watching movies. Where do you usually go out?

W We usually go to the movies. Sometimes we go to the library to read books.

M Would you like to come to my house this Saturday, then? I have lots of interesting movies and books.

W That would be great.

남 너는 외출하는 것을 좋아하니?

여 응. 나는 친구들과 외출하는 것을 좋아해. 너는 어떠니?

남 나는 책을 읽거나, 영화를 보면서 집에 있는 것을 좋아해. 너는 외출하면 보통 어디를 가니?

여 우리는 대개 영화 보러 가. 가끔 책 읽으러 도서관에 가기도 해.

남 그럼, 이번 주 토요일에 우리집에 올래? 나한테 재미있는 영화랑 책이 많이 있어.

여 좋아.

go to the movies 영화 보러 가다 **sometimes** 때때로 **lots of** 많은 **interesting** 재미있는

08

[Telephone rings.]

W Hello. Dr. Kim's office.

M I'd like to make an appointment for an eye exam, please.

W Have you seen the doctor before?

M No, I haven't.

W Can I have your name please, sir?

M This is Mike Park.

W All right. How about this Thursday afternoon at 2?

[전화벨이 울린다.]

여 여보세요. Dr. Kim's 진료소입니다.

남 눈 검사를 위한 예약을 좀 하고 싶습니다.

여 전에 저희 진료소에서 진료를 받으신 적이 있으세요?

남 아니요. 없습니다.

여 이름을 좀 말씀해 주시겠어요?

남 저는 Mike Park입니다.

여 네. 이번 주 목요일 오후 두 시 어떠세요?

make an appointment 약속을 정하다 **see a doctor** 진료를 받다

09

M I need a new cell phone, mom.

W Why? Is yours broken? I just bought it for you a few months ago.

M A few months? No. It has been almost a year. I can't take photos with it very well.

W I bought you a cell phone, not a camera. There is no problem with making calls, and sending text messages, right?

M But mom, please.

W My answer is no.

남 새 휴대전화가 필요해요, 엄마.

여 왜? 네 휴대폰이 고장 났니? 몇 달 전에 사줬잖아.

남 몇 달 전이라고요? 아니에요. 거의 1년이 다 되었어요. 이 휴대전화로는 사진이 잘 안 찍혀요.

여 나는 너에게 카메라가 아니라 휴대전화를 사준 거야. 전화 걸고, 문자 보내는 데 아무런 문제가 없지, 그렇지?

남 하지만 엄마, 제발요.

여 내 대답은 안돼야.

make a call 전화 걸다 **text message** 문자 **a few months ago** 몇 달 전에

10

W Why were you late for class?

M I missed the bus. Oh, I forgot to bring my pencil case. Can you lend me a pencil?

W Of course. Here you are.

M I didn't bring my textbook, either. Can you share yours with me?

W Sure. Then what did you bring in your bag today?

M Nothing. Something is wrong with me today.

여 너 왜 수업시간에 지각했어?

남 버스를 놓쳤어. 오, 필통 가지고 오는 것을 잊어버렸어. 연필 좀 빌려줄래?

여 물론이지. 여기 있어.

남 교과서도 안 가지고 왔네. 네 책 좀 같이 볼 수 있을까?

여 물론이야. 그럼 너 오늘 가방에 뭘 가지고 온 거야?

남 아무것도 없어. 오늘 내가 제정신이 아닌 거 같아.

●●

be late for ~에 지각하다 **miss** 놓치다 **forget to-V** ~할 것을 잊어버리다 **pencil case** 필통 **lend** 빌려주다 **textbook** 교과서 **share** 공유하다

11

W Good morning. May I help you?

M What is the checkout time here?

W It's twelve o'clock. I mean noon.

M I see. Is it possible to extend the checkout time? My flight is at 7 p.m.

W Sure. When do you want to check out then?

M If possible, at 3 o'clock, please.

여 안녕하세요. 무엇을 도와드릴까요?

남 여기 퇴실 시간이 어떻게 됩니까?

여 12시입니다. 그러니까 정오입니다.

남 알겠습니다. 퇴실 시간을 연장할 수 있을까요? 제 비행기가 오후 7시라서요.

여 물론이죠. 그럼 언제 퇴실하시기를 원하십니까?

남 만일 가능하다면, 3시로 해주세요.

●●

checkout 체크아웃, 퇴실 **noon** 정오 **extend** 연장하다

12

M This is a very useful home appliance that almost every household has. This will warm up food not only easily but also quickly. What you have to do is open the door, place some food on the tray, close the door, press the timing button, and press the start button. You should use a special bowl and should not put metal inside this appliance. Metal will cause sparks and might start a fire.

남 이것은 매우 유용한 가전제품이기에 거의 모든 가정에서 가지고 있습니다. 이것은 음식을 쉽고도 빠르게 데워 줍니다. 당신은 문을 열어 접시에 음식을 올려 놓고, 문을 닫은 후 시간 조절 버튼을 누르고, 시작 버튼을 누르면 됩니다. 당신은 특별한 그릇을 사용해야 하며, 금속은 이 전기 제품 안에 넣으면 안됩니다. 금속은 불꽃을 야기시켜 화재를 일으킬 수도 있습니다.

●●

home appliance 가전제품 **household** 가구 **warm up** 데우다 **not only A but also B** A뿐만 아니라 B까지도 **tray** 접시 **metal** 금속 **cause** 야기시키다 **spark** 불꽃 **start a fire** 화재를 일으키다

13

W Are you okay? You look angry.

M My friend spilled coffee on my laptop computer.

W My goodness. Did you take it to the repair shop?

M Yes. But the repairman said that he can't recover my data. Even worse, I didn't back my data up.

W I'm so sorry to hear that.

M Now I have to start rewriting my final report.

여 너 괜찮니? 화가 나 보여.

남 내 친구가 내 노트북 컴퓨터에 커피를 엎질렀어.

여 이런. 수리점에 가져갔었니?

남 응. 그런데 수리공이 내 데이터는 복구할 수 없대. 더 심각한 것은, 내가 데이터를 백업하지 않았다는 거야.

여 안됐구나.

남 이제 나는 기말 리포트를 다시 쓰기 시작해야 해.

●●

spill 엎지르다 **repair shop** 수리점 **repairman** 수리공 **recover** 복구하다

14

W Waves Fitness Center opening on August 28th. We are located on the second floor of Guro station. Our business hours are from 6 in the morning till

11 at night. We offer you a free locker, workout clothes and towels. Our membership fee is 35,000 won per month. Please come and join us. We will be looking forward to seeing you!

대 개장!
웨이브즈 휘트니스 센터

① 개장일 : 8월 20일
② 위치 : 구로역 2층
③ 영업 시간 : 오전 6시에서 오후 11시까지
④ 특별 제공 : 무료 락커
: 무료 운동복과 수건
⑤ 회원가 : 한 달 35,000원

여 웨이브즈 휘트니스 센터가 8월 28일에 개장할 예정입니다. 저희 센터는 구로역 2층에 위치해 있습니다. 영업 시간은 새벽 6시부터 밤 11시까지입니다. 저희는 락커, 운동복, 그리고 수건을 무료로 제공합니다. 회원가는 매달 35,000원입니다. 오셔서 가입하세요. 당신을 만날 것을 고대하겠습니다.

••
business hours 영업 시간 **offer** 제공하다; 제공 **membership fee** 회원가 **per** ~마다 **look forward to -ing** ~하기를 고대하다

15

W Would you like to go shopping with me after school?
M Sure. What do you want to buy?
W I want to buy a costume for the Halloween party.
M Oh, I have to buy one, too. I totally forgot about that. Thanks for reminding me.
W You're welcome. I'm so excited about the party.
M Me too. Let's meet at the school gate in 10 minutes. I have to stop by the library quickly.
W Okay.

여 방과 후에 같이 쇼핑 갈래?
남 물론이야. 무엇을 사고 싶은데?
여 핼러윈 파티 복장을 사고 싶어.
남 오, 나도 하나 사야 하는데. 나 그거 완전히 잊고 있었어. 생각나게 해줘서 고마워.
여 천만에. 파티를 생각하면 정말 신나.
남 나도 그래. 10분 후에 학교 정문에서 만나자. 나 얼른 도서관에 들러야 해.
여 알았어.

••
costume 복장 **totally** 완전히 **remind** 상기시키다 **gate** 정문 **stop by** ~에 들르다

16

① W How do you like this scarf?
M It's so pretty.
② W Where are you going?
M I'm on my way to a meeting.
③ W Would you like to go hiking on the weekend?
M Of course I would.
④ W When's your birthday?
M It's on February 28th.
⑤ W Are you sick?
M No, I have a headache.

① 여 이 스카프 어때?
남 정말 예뻐.
② 여 너 어디 가니?
남 회의에 가는 중이야.
③ 여 주말에 하이킹 갈래?
남 물론 가지.
④ 여 너 생일이 언제니?
남 2월 28일이야.
⑤ 여 너 아프니?
남 아니, 머리가 아파.

••
scarf 스카프 **on one's way to** ~로 가는 길에 **February** 2월 **have a headache** 두통이 있다

17

W Have you ever been to Las Vegas?
M No, I haven't. Why?
W I'm looking at a travel brochure and the city looks fantastic.
M Yeah, I saw it on TV. If I have a chance, I really want to go.
W Why don't we make a reservation to go there during this vacation? They offer a special price for the early bird reservations.
M Sounds great. Let's do that.

여 라스베이거스에 가본 적 있니?
남 아니, 없어. 왜?
여 여행 책자를 보고 있는데 도시가 정말 환상적으로 보여.
남 응, 나도 TV에서 봤어. 기회가 있다면 나도 정말 가고 싶어.
여 이번 휴가 동안에 거기에 가게 예약하는 것 어때? 조기 예약자들에게 특별가를 제공한대.
남 멋지네. 그렇게 하자.

●●
brochure 소책자 **have a chance** 기회가 오다 **make a reservation** 예약하다 **special price** 특별가 **early bird** 일찍 오는 사람

18

M It's 3 o'clock in the morning. Cathy is lying in bed trying to go to sleep. However, she hears loud music coming from next door. She is trying to ignore the noise, but she can't. She has an important meeting tomorrow, so she needs to fall asleep right away. She has no more patience, and wants the neighbor to know that she is annoyed. In this situation, what would Cathy most likely say to the neighbor?

남 새벽 3시입니다. Cathy는 잠을 자기 위해 침대에 누워 있습니다. 그러나 그녀는 옆집에서 들려오는 큰 음악 소리를 듣습니다. 그녀는 그 소음을 무시하려 하지만, 그럴 수가 없습니다. 그녀는 내일 중요한 회의가 있어서 바로 잠들어야 합니다. 그녀는 더 이상 인내심을 가질 수 없고 자신이 화가 났음을 그 이웃사람이 알기를 원합니다. 이 상황에서 Cathy는 이웃에게 무엇이라고 말하겠습니까?

① 왜 제 말을 듣지 않으세요?
② 제가 중요한 회의가 있습니다. 행운을 빌어주세요.
③ 음악 소리가 너무 큽니다. 볼륨 좀 낮춰주십시오.
④ 아침 7시에 깨워주세요.
⑤ 이 음악이 좋습니다. 노래 제목이 무엇인가요?

●●
loud 시끄러운 **ignore** 무시하다 **noise** 소음 **fall asleep** 잠이 들다 **neighbor** 이웃 **be annoyed** 화가 나다

19

M What do you want to be when you grow up?
W I want to be a math teacher. Solving math problems helps to release my stress.
M Really? That sounds strange. Doesn't it give you more stress when you can't answer them?
W Not at all. I enjoy using processes for finding answers very much.
M Really? That sounds strange. I hate math.
W I hope you will like math one day.

남 너는 커서 무엇이 되고 싶니?
여 나는 수학 선생님이 되고 싶어. 수학 문제를 푸는 것은 스트레스 해소에 도움이 돼.
남 정말? 그거 이상하네. 문제를 풀지 못하면 스트레스를 더 받지 않니?
여 전혀. 나는 답을 찾는 과정을 이용하는 걸 매우 즐겨.
남 정말? 그거 이상하네. 나는 수학을 싫어해.
여 네가 언젠가는 수학을 좋아하길 바래.

① 나는 수학을 잘 못해.
② 네가 언젠가는 수학을 좋아하길 바래.
③ 왜 수학 선생님이 되고 싶니?
④ 수학 문제를 푸는 것은 내겐 너무 어려워.
⑤ 자, 수학 숙제 같이 하자.

●●
solve 풀다 **release stress** 스트레스를 해소하다 **strange** 이상한 **Not at all.** 전혀 아니다. **process** 과정 **hate** 싫어하다 **one day** 언젠가는

20

M I started working out this morning. I feel like I'm healthy already.
W Haha. Already? But why are you walking so slow?
M Honestly, my body aches all over. I think I worked out too hard.
W Oh, no. You shouldn't do that. Especially since today was your first day.
M I'm regretting it now. I don't know what I am supposed to do.
W Well, if you take a good rest, you will feel much better.

남 나 오늘 아침에 운동 시작했어. 난 이미 건강해진 느낌이야.
여 하하. 벌써? 그런데 왜 그렇게 천천히 걷고 있니?
남 솔직히 말하면, 내 몸 전체가 쑤셔. 너무 심하게 운동했나 봐.
여 오, 이런. 너 그렇게 하면 안돼. 특히 오늘은 첫 날이니까.
남 나는 지금 후회하고 있어. 어떻게 해야 할지 모르겠어.
여 만일 네가 잘 쉰다면, 훨씬 더 나아질 거야.

① 좋아. 가.
② 알았어, 신경 쓰지 마. 내가 알아서 할게.
③ 미안해. 나는 지금 체육관에 가야 해.
④ 나도 운동하는 것을 좋아해. 언젠가 나도 너랑 같이 해도 되니?
⑤ 만일 네가 잘 쉰다면, 훨씬 더 나아질 거야.

••
work out 운동하다 **honestly** 솔직하게 **ache** 아프다 **especially** 특히 **regret** 후회하다 **be supposed to-V** ~하기로 되어 있다

Further Study 정답

p. 64

1 She wants to go to the nearest post office.
2 He is going to buy her lunch because she didn't bring her purse.
3 She usually goes to the movies and sometimes goes to the library with her friends.
4 He is supposed to see the doctor this Thursday afternoon at 2.
5 It will cause sparks and might start a fire.
6 They are going to meet at the school gate in 10 minutes.
7 She wants to be a math teacher because solving math problems releases her stress.
8 The reason is that his body aches.

On Your Own 모범답안

p. 65

A

M Excuse me. How can I get to the nearest bank?
W (1)Go straight for one block and (2)turn right. You will see it (3)on your right. It's (4)next to the gift shop. You can't miss it.

가는 방법
(1) 한/두 블록 직진하기
(2) 오른쪽/왼쪽으로 돌기
(3) 오른편에/왼편에
(4) ~ 건너편에, ~ 옆에

남 실례합니다. 가장 가까운 은행은 어떻게 가야 하나요?
여 똑바로 한 블록 가서 오른쪽으로 도세요. 오른편에서 은행을 발견할 수 있을 거예요. 선물가게 옆에 있습니다. 찾기 쉬워요.

B

YOU ARE INVITED

You are invited to my 15th Birthday Party!
Please come and celebrate with me!!!

(1) Date:	June 23rd
(2) Time:	6 p.m.
(3) Theme (color):	Blue
(4) Place:	3245 Kings Avenue East, George Town
(5) Contact No.:	850-477-0007

I would like to invite you to my 15th birthday party. It will be on (1)June 23rd at (2)6 p.m. The theme color is (3)blue, so if you have anything in (3)blue, please wear or carry it with you. The place will be at (4)3245 Kings Avenue East, George Town. You can contact me on (5)850-477-0007. Please come and enjoy! I will be looking forward to seeing you.

초대합니다

나의 15번째 생일 파티에 초대할게.
와서 나와 함께 즐거운 시간을 보내자!!!

(1) 날짜: 6월 23일
(2) 시간: 오후 6시
(3) (테마) 색: 파란색
(4) 장소: 3245 Kings Avenue East, George Town
(5) 연락처: 850-477-0007

나의 15번째 생일 파티에 널 초대하고 싶어. 파티는 6월 23일 오후 6시야. 테마 색은 파란색이란다. 파란색으로 된 게 있으면 입거나 가져와. 장소는 George Town의 Kings Avenue East 3245번지야. 전화는 850-477-0007로 하면 돼. 와서 재미있게 보내자. 널 볼 수 있기를 고대할 거야.

07 Listening Test 정답

p. 70

01 ③	02 ②	03 ①	04 ①	05 ④
06 ③	07 ①	08 ②	09 ⑤	10 ④
11 ②	12 ⑤	13 ④	14 ③	15 ②
16 ③	17 ⑤	18 ③	19 ④	20 ②

01

W Good morning, Juliet Smith here with your weekend weather report. Right now, it is twenty degrees and clear. We're expecting the blue skies to last until late afternoon. However, from tonight, we'll see rain and a low of ten degrees. Tomorrow you can expect more rain throughout the day. Now, stay tuned for sports.

여 안녕하세요. 주말 일기 예보를 말씀드릴 Juliet Smith입니다. 지금은 20도이고 화창한 날씨입니다. 오후 늦게까지는 맑은 하늘이 지속될 것으로 기대됩니다. 하지만 오늘 밤부터는 비가 오겠고 기온은 10도까지 내려갈 것 같습니다. 내일은 하루 종일 더 많은 비가 올 것으로 예상됩니다. 이제 스포츠 뉴스를 계속 시청하시겠습니다.

weather report 일기예보 **degree** 도(℃) **clear** 화창한 **last** 지속되다 **however** 하지만 **stay tuned** 계속 시청하다

02

W What can I do for you?

M I'd like to buy a tie for a job interview.

W What color suit will you be wearing?

M A black suit with a white shirt.

W Then what about this red silk tie? Or this yellow one?

M I prefer the red tie to the yellow one. I think it will go well with my black suit.

여 무엇을 도와드릴까요?

남 취업 면접에 매고 갈 넥타이를 사고 싶어요.

여 어떤 색깔의 정장을 입으실 거예요?

남 검은색 정장에 흰색 셔츠를 입을 겁니다.

여 그러면 이 빨간색 실크 넥타이 어떠세요? 아니면 이 노란색 넥타이는요?

남 저는 노란색보다는 빨간색 넥타이가 더 마음에 드네요. 저의 검은색 정장에 잘 어울릴 것 같아요.

job interview 취업 면접 **suit** 정장 **prefer A to B** B보다 A를 더 좋아하다 **go with** ~와 잘 어울리다

03

M What are the seasons like in your hometown, Judy?

W You know I come from Australia. The seasons in Australia are opposite to those in Korea, so we have Christmas in the summer.

M Oh, that is very different. Do you celebrate Christmas?

W Yes, we celebrate it exactly the same as other people, only with different clothes.

M That's amazing. Christmas in summer!

남 너의 고향의 계절들은 어때, Judy?

여 너도 알다시피 나는 호주에서 왔어. 호주의 계절은 한국의 계절과는 정반대야. 그래서 크리스마스가 여름에 있지.

남 오, 정말 다르구나. 크리스마스를 기념하니?

여 응, 옷만 다르게 입지 다른 사람들과 똑같이 크리스마스를 기념해.

남 놀라워. 여름에 크리스마스라!

hometown 고향 **come from** ~출신이다 **be opposite to** ~와 정반대이다 **celebrate** 기념하다 **amazing** 놀라운

04

W Hello. Could you show me your passport and immigration card, please?

M Sure. Here you go.

W What is the purpose of your visit?

M I am here on business.

W How long are you planning to stay here?

M I'll be staying at Grand Hotel for two weeks.

W Okay, enjoy your stay!

여 안녕하세요. 당신의 여권과 입국 카드를 좀 보여주시겠습니까?

남 물론이죠. 여기 있습니다.
여 방문의 목적이 무엇입니까?
남 사업차 왔습니다.
여 얼마나 여기에 머무실 예정인가요?
남 Grand Hotel에서 2주간 머물 예정입니다.
여 네, 머무시는 동안 즐거운 시간 보내세요.

passport 여권 **immigration** 입국 **purpose** 목적 **on business** 사업차

05

M I'd like to buy some flowers for a close friend.
W Do you have anything special in mind?
M Not really. I just want something very beautiful.
W What about a dozen roses? We have some very nice roses today.
M That sounds good. Can you wrap two dozen roses for me, please?
W Yes, of course. Would you like a card to write a message on as well?

남 친한 친구에게 줄 꽃을 사고 싶습니다.
여 특별히 생각해두신 꽃 있으세요?
남 아뇨. 그냥 아주 아름다운 것으로 사고 싶어요.
여 장미 열두 송이 어떠세요? 오늘 장미가 아주 좋습니다.
남 좋네요. 장미 스물 네 송이를 제 대신 좀 포장해주시겠어요?
여 네, 물론이죠. 메시지를 쓸 카드도 필요하세요?

close 친한 **dozen** 열두 개 **wrap** 포장하다 **as well** 또한

06

M Do you want a pet that you can take care of? Before you decide to raise a pet, think about what it will mean to you to own a living animal. Remember that a pet cannot live without you. You have to feed it and clean its cage. If you are sure that you can take good care of an animal, then it is time to choose your pet.

남 당신이 보살필 수 있는 애완동물을 원하세요? 애완동물을 기르기로 결정하기 전에, 살아있는 동물을 가진다는 것이 당신에게 어떤 의미일지 생각해보세요. 애완동물은 당신 없이는 살 수 없다는 것을 기억하세요. 당신은 애완동물에게 먹이를 줘야 하고, 우리를 청소해야 합니다. 만약 당신이 동물을 잘 보살필 수 있다는 확신이 든다면 그때 애완동물을 선택하세요.

pet 애완동물 **take care of** ~를 돌보다 **decide** 결정하다 **raise** 기르다 **own** 소유하다 **feed** 먹이를 주다 **cage** 우리

07

W What did you do last weekend?
M On Saturday, I studied all day. Then, yesterday I helped my father wash his car. What about you?
W I visited my grandparents on Saturday. On Sunday, I wanted to do my English homework but couldn't find my textbook. I was looking for it all day.
M Really? I found an extra English book in my backpack. Is this yours?
W Oh, it's mine. Thank you so much.

여 지난 주말에 뭐 했니?
남 토요일에는 하루 종일 공부했어. 그러고 나서 어제는 아버지가 세차하시는 것을 도와드렸어. 너는 뭐 했어?
여 나는 토요일에는 할아버지 할머니 댁에 갔어. 일요일에는 영어 숙제를 하려고 했는데 교과서를 찾을 수가 없었어. 하루 종일 그걸 찾았어.
남 정말? 내 가방 안에 영어 교과서가 한 권 더 있더라고. 이거 네 거니?
여 오, 내 거야. 정말 고마워.

help+목적어+(to) 동사원형 ~가 …하도록 돕다 **textbook** 교과서 **extra** 여분의 **backpack** 배낭

08

[Telephone rings.]
M Hello, may I speak to Mina Kim, please?
W Speaking. Who's calling?
M I'm delivering a package to your address but there is nobody home right now.
W I'm sorry I'm out now. Can you leave the package in the security office at my apartment building?
M Yes, I can. If there is any problem, please call me at this number.
W Thanks, I appreciate your consideration.

[전화벨이 울린다.]

남 안녕하세요. Mina Kim 씨와 좀 통화할 수 있을까요?
여 전데요. 누구세요?
남 당신 주소로 온 소포를 배달하는 중인데 댁에 지금 아무도 안 계시네요.
여 죄송하지만 저 외출 중이에요. 제 아파트 경비실에 그 소포를 두시겠어요?
남 네, 그러죠. 무슨 문제가 있으면, 이 번호로 저에게 전화주세요.
여 감사합니다. 배려해주셔서 고맙습니다.

Speaking. (전화상에서) 저입니다. **Who's calling?** (전화상에서) 누구세요? **package** 소포, 꾸러미 **security office** 경비실 **appreciate** 감사하다 **consideration** 배려

09

① W What's wrong with you?
M I have a cold.
② W May I take your order?
M Yes. I want to have spaghetti.
③ W For here or to go?
M To go, please.
④ W What is in the bag?
M Some toy robots.
⑤ W These boxes are too heavy for me to carry.
M Can I give you my hand?

① 여 무슨 일이니?
남 감기에 걸렸어.
② 여 주문하시겠습니까?
남 네, 스파게티 주세요.
③ 여 여기서 드시나요, 가지고 가시나요?
남 가지고 갈 겁니다.
④ 여 상자 안에 무엇이 들어있나요?
남 장난감 로봇 몇 개요.
⑤ 여 이 상자는 너무 무거워서 내가 들 수가 없어.
남 도와줄까?

have a cold 감기에 걸리다 **order** 주문 **too + 형용사 + to-V** 너무 ~해서 …할 수 없다 **give ~ one's hand** ~에게 도움을 주다

10

M I heard you took a trip to Canada.
W Yes, I did.
M How did you like it?
W I loved it. I had a great time there.
M Where did you go in Canada?
W I visited many amazing places such as Niagara Falls and Banff National Park.
M How long did you stay there?
W For two weeks. I'm missing the beautiful scenery of Canada.

남 너 캐나다 여행 다녀왔다고 들었어.
여 응, 맞아.
남 어땠어?
여 너무 좋았어. 거기에서 즐거운 시간을 보냈어.
남 캐나다에서 어디를 갔었니?
여 나이아가라 폭포와 밴프 국립공원과 같은 많은 멋진 곳들을 갔었어.
남 거기서 얼마 동안 머물렀니?
여 2주 동안 있었어. 나는 캐나다의 멋진 풍경들이 그리워.

have a great time 즐거운 시간을 보내다 **fall** 폭포 **scenery** 경치

11

W Hey, Joe. What's up?
M Hi, Kaitlin. I'm looking for a book for my mom. Today is her birthday.
W I see. Does she like to read?
M Yes. She especially likes romance novels.
W Really? I like them, too. She has the same taste in books as me.
M That's good. Can you recommend one for me, then?
W Sure, why not?

여 야, Joe. 잘 지내니?
남 안녕, Kaitlin. 엄마께 사드릴 책을 찾고 있어. 오늘이 생신이시거든.
여 그렇구나. 엄마가 책 읽는 걸 좋아하셔?
남 응. 엄마는 특히 낭만 소설을 좋아하셔.
여 정말? 나도 그것들을 좋아해. 너의 엄마가 책에 대해선 나랑 같은 취향을 가지셨구나.
남 잘됐네. 그러면 한 권 추천해 줄래?
여 그래, 그러자.

look for ~을 찾다 **especially** 특히 **taste** 취향 **recommend** 추천하다

12

W Thank you for calling Eagle Airlines. If you would like to make a reservation, please press one. If you would like to cancel your reservation, please press two. If you would like to confirm your reservation, please press three. If you would like to talk to a representative, please press zero. To repeat this message, please press the pound sign.

여 Eagle 항공사에 전화 주셔서 감사합니다. 예약을 원하시면 1번을 눌러주세요. 예약 취소를 원하시면 2번을 눌러주세요. 예약 확인을 원하시면 3번을 눌러주세요. 상담원과의 통화를 원하시면 0번을 눌러주세요. 다시 듣기를 원하시면 우물정자를 눌러주세요.

cancel 취소하다 **confirm** 확인하다 **representative** 상담원; 대표자 **repeat** 반복하다 **pound sign** 파운드 (우물정자) 기호

13

W Hey, Han. Can you lend me your English book for a while?

M I'm sorry I can't.

W Please. I forgot to bring mine, and I have a class in 15 minutes.

M I can't lend it to you because I don't have it.

W Why?

M I already lent it to Jessie. She asked me for it right before you came.

W Oh, I'm sorry.

여 얘, Han. 네 영어책 좀 잠시 빌려줄래?

남 미안하지만 그럴 수가 없는데.

여 부탁이야. 잊고 안 가져왔는데 15분 후에 수업이 있어.

남 내가 가지고 있지 않아서 네게 빌려줄 수가 없어.

여 왜?

남 이미 Jessie에게 빌려줬거든. 네가 오기 바로 전에 걔가 그걸 좀 빌려 달라고 했어.

여 오, 미안해.

lend 빌려주다 **for a while** 잠시 동안 **already** 이미 **right before** 방금 전에

14

M Hello Mart is going to have a clearance sale. The sale will be on from May 1st to May 7th. All items will be on sale and there will be discounts of up to 80%. The store will open at 10 a.m. and close at midnight. Please note that no reward points are available during this period. Please come and enjoy shopping at the store.

재고 정리 세일!!

① 헬로우 마트

② 5월 1일에서 5월 7일까지

③ 최고 18% 가격 인하

④ 매장 영업시간: 오전 10시부터 자정까지

⑤ 해당 기간 동안 보상 포인트 없음

남 Hello Mart는 재고 정리 세일을 할 예정입니다. 세일은 5월 1일부터 5월 7일까지입니다. 모든 물품을 세일하며 최대 80%까지 할인이 있을 것입니다. 매장은 오전 10시에 문을 열어 자정에 닫을 것입니다. 이 기간 동안은 보상 포인트를 적립할 수 없음을 양해바랍니다. 오셔서 쇼핑을 즐기십시오.

clearance sale 재고 정리 세일 **from A to B** A부터 B까지 **up to** ~까지 **on sale** 세일 중인 **discount** 할인 **reward point** 보상 포인트 **during** ~ 동안

15

W Hi, Josh. I got two tickets for a soccer game. Will you go with me?

M When is it?

W Tomorrow at noon.

M Tomorrow? Don't you remember that you are supposed to be helping me move house, then?

W Oh, I'm so sorry. I will help you.

M How about the tickets? Will you sell them?

W No, I will give them to my parents or friends.

여 안녕 Josh. 나 축구 경기 표 2장이 생겼어. 나랑 같이 갈래?

남 언젠데?

여 내일 정오.

남 내일? 너 그럼 나 이사하는 것 도와주기로 한 것 잊었어?

여 오, 미안해. 도와줄게.

남 표는 어쩌고? 팔 거야?
여 아니, 부모님이나 친구들에게 줄 거야.

noon 정오 **remember** 기억하다 **be supposed to-V** ~하기로 되어 있다 **move** 이사하다

16

① W Are you ready to order?
M Yes. I will have seafood spaghetti, please.
② W How was your English test?
M It wasn't easy.
③ W Does this bus go to Dongdaemun?
M Yes. You can pay in cash.
④ W Why are you so nervous?
M I'll have a job interview tomorrow.
⑤ W How is your new school?
M It's pretty good.

① 여 주문하시겠습니까?
남 네. 해물 스파게티로 할게요.
② 여 영어 시험은 어땠니?
남 쉽지 않았어.
③ 여 이 버스가 동대문에 가나요?
남 네. 현금으로 지불하셔도 됩니다.
④ 여 왜 그렇게 불안해 하니?
남 내일 취업 면접이 있어서.
⑤ 여 새 학교는 어떠니?
남 꽤 괜찮아.

be ready to-V ~할 준비가 되다 **pay in cash** 현금으로 지불하다 **nervous** 불안한 **job interview** 취업 면접 **pretty** 꽤

17

[Telephone rings.]
M Hello. May I speak to Dr. Wilson, please?
W I'm sorry. He's not in yet. Who's on the line?
M This is Andy Kim. I am supposed to meet him at 5 o'clock this afternoon, but...
W Do you mean you can't come?
M I'm so sorry, but yes.
W Okay. I will leave a message. May I have your number?
M My number is 010-1243-1244. Thank you.

[전화벨이 울린다.]
남 여보세요. Wilson 선생님과 통화할 수 있을까요?
여 죄송합니다. 아직 안 오셨어요. 전화하신 분은 누구세요?
남 Andy Kim입니다. 오늘 오후 5시에 만나기로 되어있는데요...
여 못 오신다는 말씀이세요?
남 죄송하지만 그렇습니다.
여 알겠습니다. 메시지를 남겨드릴게요. 번호 알려주시겠어요?
남 제 번호는 010-1243-1244입니다. 감사합니다.

talk to ~와 이야기하다 **mean** 의미하다 **leave a message** 메시지를 남기다

18

W Tony was late again this morning. He said he stopped by the hospital because he had a fever. However, when the teacher called his mom, she said Tony just woke up late. Tony's teacher is really angry because Tony always gives her excuses for being late. Tony's teacher thinks she has to lecture Tony about his bad behavior. In this situation, what would the teacher most likely say to Tony?

여 Tony는 오늘 아침에 또 늦었다. 그는 열이 있어서 병원에 들렀다 왔다고 했다. 그러나 선생님이 그의 어머니께 전화했을 때, 어머니는 Tony는 단지 늦게 일어난 것이라고 했다. Tony의 선생님은 Tony가 늦는 것에 대해 늘 변명을 하는 것에 정말 화가 났다. Tony의 선생님은 Tony의 나쁜 행동들에 대해 훈계를 해야 한다고 생각한다. 이 상황에서 선생님은 Tony에게 무엇이라고 말하겠는가?

① 수업은 어땠니?
② 이 약을 먹어라.
③ 항상 진실을 말해야 한다.
④ 병원에 가는 게 어떻겠니?
⑤ 노력하지 않으면 좋은 성적을 얻을 수가 없어.

stop by ~에 들르다 **have a fever** 열이 나다 **angry** 화가 난 **give an excuse** 변명을 하다 **lecture** 훈계하다 **behavior** 행동

19

M Please have a seat. The class will start in a minute.
W Okay. I'm so excited to take Dr. Michael's class.

M Me, too. Is this your first time to take his class? He is one of the best professors in this school.

W I heard that. Is he strict? Does he give many pop quizzes?

M Not really. Let's listen carefully when he explains the course, though.

W Okay. Oh, he is coming now.

남 앉아. 곧 수업이 시작해.

여 알았어. Dr. Michael의 수업을 듣다니 정말 신나.

남 나도 그래. 그의 수업을 처음 듣는 거니? 그는 이 학교에서 가장 훌륭한 교수님들 중의 한 분이셔.

여 그 얘기 들었어. 엄격하시니? 깜짝 퀴즈도 많이 내시니?

남 꼭 그렇지는 않아. 그래도 강좌 설명하실 때 잘 들어보자.

여 알았어. 아, 지금 오신다.

① 강좌를 다시 설명해 주세요.
② Dr. Michael 수업을 신청하자.
③ 나는 깜짝 퀴즈를 잘 못 봤어.
④ 알았어. 아, 지금 오신다.
⑤ 나는 이번이 Dr. Michael의 수업을 두 번째 수강하는 거야.

have a seat 자리에 앉다 **in a minute** 곧 **one of the + 복수명사** ~들 중 하나 **strict** 엄격한 **pop quiz** 깜짝 퀴즈 **explain** 설명하다

20

M How was your trip to Jeju Island?

W I didn't enjoy it that much.

M Why? What happened?

W I mostly stayed at the hotel due to a typhoon. The heavy rain and the thunderstorms were quite scary.

M Oh, that's too bad. It's good that you came back without having an accident, though.

W I think so. I will go there again next holiday.

남 제주도 여행은 어땠니?

여 잘 즐기지 못했어.

남 왜? 무슨 일 있었어?

여 태풍 때문에 대부분 호텔에 있었어. 폭우와 심한 뇌우가 상당히 무서웠어.

남 오, 안됐다. 그래도 아무 사고 없이 돌아와서 다행이야.

여 나도 그렇게 생각해. 다음 휴가 때 다시 가려고.

① 나는 우산을 가져오지 않았어.
② 나도 그렇게 생각해. 다음 휴가 때 다시 가려고.
③ 자동차 사고 때문에 차가 많이 막혔어.
④ 나는 제주도에서 멋진 시간을 보냈어.
⑤ 비가 많이 오니 호텔에 머무는 것이 나을 거야.

mostly 대부분 **due to** ~ 때문에 **typhoon** 태풍 **heavy rain** 폭우 **thunderstorm** 심한 뇌우 **scary** 무서운 **without** ~ 없이

Further Study 정답

p. 74

1 He will be wearing a black suit with a white shirt.
2 She asks him to show her his passport and immigration card.
3 The reason was that she couldn't find her textbook.
4 She asks him to leave it in the security office at her apartment building.
5 She likes romance novels.
6 It opens at 10 a.m. and closes at midnight.
7 She is supposed to help the man move house.
8 The reason is that Tony always gives her excuses for being late.

On Your Own 모범답안

p. 75

A

Today will be (1)chilly with temperatures around ten degrees. We expect some (2)clouds this afternoon. Tonight we will see (3)rain and a low of 2 degrees. Tomorrow we're expecting (4)less rain and a high of 12 degrees. From the Korean Weather Center, I'm Minjun Jung.

오늘의 일기 예보	
(1) 추운 / 쌀쌀한 / 온화한 / 더운	(2) 맑은 날씨 / 구름 / 바람 / 안개
(3) 맑은 하늘 / 비 / 눈 / 폭풍우	(4) 눈이 더 내림 / 비가 덜 내림 / 눈이 덜 내림…

오늘 날씨는 쌀쌀하며 기온은 10도 정도가 될 것입니다. 오늘 오후에는 구름이 약간 몰려 올 것입니다. 오늘 밤에는 비가 오고 2도까지 떨어질

것입니다. 내일은 비가 오늘보다는 적게 오고 12도까지 오를 것 같습니다. 한국 기상센터에서, 정민준기자였습니다.

B

The Most Memorable Trip of My Life	
(1) Where and when did you go?	Paris, 2 years ago
(2) Who did you go with?	my family
(3) How long did you stay there?	for 15 days
(4) What did you do there?	visited the Eiffel Tower, Notre Dame Cathedral, and the Louvre Museum
(5) Why was that trip memorable?	① our first family trip ② spent most of our time together
(6) Would you like to visit again?	Yes

I'm going to talk about what is the most memorable trip of my life. I went to (1)Paris two years ago. I went there with (2)my family for (3)15 days. We (4)visited the Eiffel Tower, Notre Dame Cathedral, and the Louvre Museum. It was the most memorable trip of my life because ①it was our first family trip. Also, ②we spent most of our time together. That is why this trip is the most memorable trip of my life and I (6) would like to go there again.

내 생에 가장 기억에 남는 여행	
(1) 어디로, 언제 갔습니까?	파리, 2년 전
(2) 누구와 함께 갔습니까?	가족
(3) 그곳에서 얼마 동안 머물렀습니까?	15일 동안
(4) 그곳에서 무엇을 했습니까?	에펠 탑, 노트르담 대성당, 루브르 박물관 방문
(5) 왜 그 여행이 기억에 남습니까?	·첫 번째 가족여행 ·대부분의 시간을 함께 보냄
(6) 다시 가고 싶습니까?	예

저는 지금까지 살면서 가장 기억에 남는 여행에 대해 이야기할 것입니다. 저는 2년 전에 파리에 갔습니다. 저는 15일 동안 가족과 함께 그곳에 가서 지냈습니다. 우리는 에펠 탑과 노트르담 대성당, 그리고 루브르 박물관을 방문했습니다. 그것이 제게 가장 기억에 남는 이유는 처음으로 한 가족 여행이었기 때문입니다. 또한, 우리는 대부분의 시간을 함께 보냈습니다. 이것이 이 여행이 지금까지 살면서 제게 가장 기억에 남는 여행인 이유이며 또다시 그곳에 가고 싶습니다.

08 Listening Test 정답

p. 80

01 ①	02 ④	03 ②	04 ④	05 ①
06 ③	07 ③	08 ②	09 ③	10 ⑤
11 ⑤	12 ⑤	13 ④	14 ①	15 ④
16 ①	17 ④	18 ⑤	19 ①	20 ②

01

W Are you ready to play the game?
M Yes. What do we do?
W First, we look at each other's clothes. Then, we sit back to back and list what we remember.
M Okay, that's easy. I'm ready.
W What do you remember?
M You're wearing a polka-dot blouse and white shorts. Now it's your turn.
W You're wearing a striped shirt and black jeans.

여 게임 할 준비되었니?
남 응. 뭐 하면 돼?
여 먼저, 서로가 입은 옷을 보는 거야. 그리고 나서 등을 맞대고 앉아서 기억하는 것을 열거하는 거야.
남 그래, 쉽구나. 난 준비됐어.
여 너는 무엇을 기억하니?
남 너는 물방울 무늬 블라우스에 흰색 반바지를 입고 있어. 이제 너의 차례야.
여 너는 줄무늬 셔츠와 블랙진을 입고 있어.

be ready to-V ~할 준비가 되다 **back to back** 등을 맞대고
polka-dot 물방울 무늬의 **striped** 줄무늬의

02

M Hi. May I help you?
W Yes, please. What vegetables are good today?
M Everything is good, but the carrots and the lettuce are especially fresh.
W The lettuce looks great. I'll take two heads of lettuce, please.

M How about tomatoes? They just came in this morning.

W Okay, I'll take three. That's all for today. Thank you.

남 안녕하세요. 도와드릴까요?

여 네. 어떤 채소가 오늘 좋아요?

남 모든 것이 다 좋은데, 당근과 양상추가 특별히 신선합니다.

여 양상추가 좋아 보이네요. 양상추 두 포기 살게요.

남 토마토는 어떠세요? 바로 오늘 아침에 들어온 것들입니다.

여 좋아요. 세 개 주세요. 오늘은 그것만 살게요. 감사합니다.

lettuce 양상추 **a head of** 한 포기의 **look + 형용사** ~하게 보이다

03

W Here is a letter for you.

M Let me see. Mom, I got accepted. This is an acceptance letter from Stanford University.

W Are you sure?

M Yes, Stanford University accepted me!

W Oh, congratulations! I'm so happy for you.

M You know it is my dream school. I'm very excited that my dream has come true.

여 여기 너에게 온 편지야.

남 어디 봐요. 엄마, 저 합격했어요. 이 편지는 Stanford 대학교에서 온 합격통지서예요.

여 확실하니?

남 네, Stanford 대학교가 저를 합격시켜 줬어요.

여 오, 축하한다! 정말 행복하구나.

남 엄마도 아시듯이 거긴 제가 가고 싶어했던 학교잖아요. 제 꿈이 실현돼서 너무 신나요.

① 흥미 있는 ② 자랑스러운 ③ 후회하는
④ 안도한 ⑤ 짜증이 난

accept 받아들이다 **acceptance letter** 합격 통지서 **sure** 확실한 **come true** 실현되다

04

M Excuse me.

W Yes, sir. How can I help you?

M I have a terrible cold. I can't breathe very well or sleep. I need something strong.

W Why don't you take this cold medicine?

M Oh, I saw that on TV. How is it?

W It works really well.

M Then, I guess I'll try it.

남 실례합니다.

여 네. 어떻게 도와드릴까요?

남 심한 감기에 걸렸습니다. 숨을 잘 쉴 수도, 잠을 잘 수도 없어요. 뭔가 강한 약이 필요해요.

여 이 감기약 드셔보시는 것 어떠세요?

남 그거 TV에서 봤습니다. 어떤가요?

여 이 약은 참 잘 들어요.

남 그럼, 한 번 먹어 볼게요.

① 병원 ② 소방서 ③ 식료품점
④ 약국 ⑤ 전자제품 가게

have a cold 감기에 걸리다 **terrible** 심한 **breathe** 숨쉬다 **cold medicine** 감기약 **work well** (약이) 잘 듣다

05

W May I take your order?

M Yes, I'd like to have Happy Meal Set A, please.

W The set is a chicken burger, onion rings and a coke. Do you want anything else?

M No, that's all.

W Okay, that will be four dollars and fifty cents.

M Here is ten dollars.

W Here is your change. Enjoy your meal!

여 주문하시겠어요?

남 네, Happy Meal 세트 A 주세요.

여 그 세트는 치킨버거 하나, 양파링, 그리고 콜라 하나가 포함되어 있습니다. 그밖에 필요하신 것 있으세요?

남 아뇨, 그게 전부입니다.

여 네, 4달러 50센트입니다.

남 여기 10달러 있습니다.

여 잔돈 받으세요. 맛있게 드세요.

else 그 밖의 **That's all.** 그것이 전부입니다. **change** 잔돈, 거스름돈

06

M When you shop online, you have to make an ID and

a password. If you choose an easy password, your personal data can easily be exposed. Therefore, you should select a complex password to protect your data. For example, make a password with numbers, letters and special characters.

남 여러분은 온라인으로 물건을 살 때 아이디와 비밀번호를 만들어야 합니다. 만약 당신이 쉬운 비밀번호를 선택한다면, 당신의 개인정보는 쉽게 노출될 수 있습니다. 따라서, 당신의 개인정보를 보호하기 위해서 복잡한 비밀번호를 선택해야 합니다. 예를 들면, 숫자와 문자, 특수문자를 넣어 비밀번호를 만드세요.

shop online 인터넷 쇼핑하다 **password** 비밀번호 **personal data** 개인정보 **expose** 노출하다

07

W Dad, come over here quickly!

M Just a minute, Helen.

W Dad! The toilet is overflowing.

M Oh, my God. What did you do to it?

W I just put some food waste in it, but it was a small amount.

M Again? I told you not to do that. What a day!

여 아빠, 빨리 여기 좀 와주세요.

남 잠시만, Helen.

여 아빠! 변기에서 물이 넘쳐 흐르고 있어요.

남 오, 맙소사. 너 변기에다 뭘 한 거야?

여 그냥 음식물 쓰레기를 좀 넣었지만 작은 양이었어요.

남 또? 그렇게 하지 말라고 말했잖니. 정말 힘든 하루다!

toilet 변기 **overflow** 넘쳐 흐르다 **food waste** 음식물 쓰레기 **amount** 양 **What a day!** 정말 힘든 하루다!

08

M What do you want to major in?

W I'd like to major in history. How about you?

M I'm interested in science but my parents want me to be a doctor.

W So, are you going to let your parents decide your major for you?

M No, I want to be a science teacher and I plan to explain to them just how much I want it.

W I am sure they will understand.

남 너는 무엇을 전공하기를 원하니?

여 나는 역사를 전공하고 싶어. 너는 어떠니?

남 나는 과학에 관심이 있지만 부모님은 내가 의사가 되기를 원하셔.

여 그래서 네 대신 부모님이 네 전공을 결정하시도록 할 거야?

남 아니, 나는 과학 선생님이 되고 싶고, 부모님께 내가 얼마나 그렇게 되길 원하는지를 설명드릴 계획이야.

여 나는 그들이 이해해주실 거라고 확신해.

major in ~을 전공하다 **history** 역사 **be interested in** ~에 흥미가 있다 **explain** 설명하다

09

① M Do you have your library card?

W Yes, here it is.

② M May I try this shirt on?

W Yes. The fitting room is over there.

③ M Can you help me water the plants?

W No problem.

④ M How can I help you?

W I'd like to buy a cell phone.

⑤ M Excuse me. May I sit here?

W I'm sorry but that seat's taken.

① 남 도서관 카드 있으세요?

여 네, 여기 있습니다.

② 남 이 셔츠 입어봐도 되나요?

여 네, 탈의실은 저쪽에 있습니다.

③ 남 내가 식물에 물 주는 것 좀 도와 줄래요?

여 알았어요.

④ 남 어떻게 도와 드릴까요?

여 휴대전화를 사고 싶어요.

⑤ 남 실례합니다. 여기 앉아도 되나요?

여 죄송하지만 그 자린 임자가 있어요.

try on 입어보다 **fitting room** 탈의실 **water** 물을 주다 **plant** 식물

10

W I hate to do housework. It never ends.

M Let's do it together. Many hands make light work.

W Oh, really? Then, I'll wash the dishes and do the

laundry. Can you clean the refrigerator and do the vacuuming?

M Okay. Let's get started!

W You are the world's best husband.

M And you're a good wife. Why don't we go out for dinner after doing all these chores?

W That sounds wonderful!

여 집안일 하는 게 싫어요. 끝이 없어요.

남 함께 하자. 백지장도 맞들면 낫잖아.

여 오, 정말요? 그럼, 내가 설거지와 빨래를 할게요. 당신은 냉장고 청소와 진공청소기로 청소해줄래요?

남 좋아. 시작하자!

여 당신이 세계 최고의 남편이에요.

남 당신은 좋은 아내이고. 집안일 다 한 후에 저녁 먹으러 나가는 거 어때?

여 정말 좋아요.

housework 집안일 **wash the dishes** 설거지하다 **do the laundry** 빨래하다 **refrigerator** 냉장고 **do the vacuuming** 진공청소기로 청소하다 **chore** 허드렛일

11

W Long time no see. How are you doing?

M I'm good. It's great to see you.

W Me too. What are you doing here, anyway? Are you expecting a baby?

M Yes. My wife is going to give birth next month.

W Congratulations! Do you need any help?

M Yes. Can you recommend some things to buy for newborn babies to me?

W Sure.

여 오랜만이야. 어떻게 지내니?

남 잘 지내. 여기서 만나니 정말 반갑다.

여 나도 그래. 그런데 여기서 뭐 해? 아기가 태어날 예정이니?

남 응. 아내가 다음 달에 출산을 해.

여 축하해! 도움이 필요하니?

남 응. 신생아를 위해 살 물건들을 내게 추천해 줄 수 있니?

여 물론이지.

Long time no see. 오랜만이야. **expect a baby** 출산 예정이다 **give birth** 출산하다 **recommend** 추천하다 **newborn baby** 신생아

12

W What's the matter with you?

M I'm very nervous because I'm going to have a job interview tomorrow. Can you give me some advice?

W Why don't you draw up a list of common interview questions and practice answering them?

M OK. I will.

W You should stand in front of the mirror while practicing. Recording yourself is a good way, too.

M Oh, I see. Anything else?

W Well, wearing a suit will make you look neat and professional.

M Thank you.

여 무슨 일 있어?

남 내일 취업 면접이 있어서 너무 초조해. 나에게 조언 좀 해줄래?

여 일반적인 면접 질문들의 리스트를 작성해서 대답하는 걸 연습하는 게 어때?

남 알았어. 그럴게.

여 연습할 때는 거울 앞에 서서 해야 돼. 녹음하는 것도 좋은 방법이고.

남 오, 알았어. 다른 것은?

여 음. 정장을 입으면 깔끔하고 전문가처럼 보일 거야.

남 고마워.

nervous 불안한 **job interview** 취업 면접 **draw up** 작성하다 **in front of** ~ 앞에서 **while** ~하는 동안 **record** 녹음하다 **neat** 깔끔한

13

W Hello, Albert. What's up? Are you sick?

M No, I'm just really sleepy right now. I can't concentrate on anything.

W What did you do yesterday?

M I read an online novel called *Good-bye* until late at night. I think I am addicted to the Internet.

W Are you serious? You should stop doing that. It will not only ruin your health but also your studies.

M I know. I'm trying.

여 안녕, Albert. 무슨 일이야? 너 아프니?

남 아니. 그냥 지금 너무 졸려서. 아무것에도 집중할 수가 없어.

여 어제 뭐 했는데?
남 밤늦게까지 〈Good-bye〉라는 온라인 소설을 읽었어. 나 인터넷에 중독된 것 같아.
여 정말이야? 그거 당장 그만둬야 돼. 그건 네 건강을 해칠 뿐만 아니라 공부도 망쳐.
남 알아. 노력 중이야.

••
What's up? 잘 지내고 있니? **sleepy** 졸린 **concentrate on** ~에 집중하다 **novel** 소설 **addict** 중독되게 하다 **serious** 진지한 **ruin** 망치다

14

①W Evan is the youngest of the three.
②W Adam is older than Brandon.
③W Brandon is the smallest of the three.
④W Adam is younger than Evan.
⑤W Evan is taller than Adam.

이름	나이	키(cm)
Brandon	13	154
Adam	15	167
Evan	18	178

① 여 Evan은 세 명 중 가장 어리다.
② 여 Adam은 Brandon보다 더 나이가 많다.
③ 여 Brandon은 세 명 중 가장 작다.
④ 여 Adam은 Evan보다 더 어리다.
⑤ 여 Evan은 Adam보다 키가 더 크다.

15

M I heard that you are a good cook.
W Not really. But people seem to enjoy my food a lot.
M What kinds of food can you cook?
W Well... I can cook gimbab, bulgogi, galbi, and chapchae. But I can't make kimchi yet.
M Wow! When are you going to make some food? I'd like to try one of those dishes.
W Haha. Please come to my housewarming party this Saturday.
M Okay, I will.

남 네가 요리를 잘 한다고 들었어.
여 꼭 그렇진 않아. 그런데 사람들이 내가 한 음식을 많이 좋아하는 것 같아.
남 어떤 음식들을 할 수 있니?
여 글쎄… 김밥, 불고기, 갈비, 그리고 잡채를 할 수 있어. 그런데 아직 김치는 못 만들어.
남 우와! 음식 언제 만들 거니? 나도 그 음식들 중 하나를 먹어보고 싶어.
여 하하. 이번 주 토요일 내 집들이에 와.
남 그래. 알았어.

••
dish 음식; 접시 **housewarming party** 집들이

16

① W What time did you get up this morning?
M I went to bed at 8 o'clock.
② W How do you go to school?
M On foot.
③ W When is the due date?
M This coming Friday.
④ W Long time no see.
M Yes. Nice to see you again.
⑤ W Where did you lose your bag?
M I think I left it on the bus.

① 여 오늘 아침에 몇 시에 일어났니?
남 8시에 잠자리에 들었어.
② 여 학교에 어떻게 가니?
남 걸어서.
③ 여 마감 기한이 언제야?
남 이번 주 금요일이야.
④ 여 오랜만이구나.
남 응. 다시 만나서 반가워.
⑤ 여 네 가방을 어디서 잃어 버렸니?
남 버스에 놔둔 것 같아.

••
go to bed 잠자리에 들다 **on foot** 걸어서 **due date** 마감 기한 **lose** 잃어버리다

17

W David, you don't look good. What's the matter with you?
M I got a C on my math test.
W You can do better next time. Cheer up!
M Thank you. But I'm afraid of my parents seeing my

report card. They will be really angry.

W I understand. But if you did your best, they won't be upset.

M I hope so. I will tell them I will try harder next time.

여 David, 너 안 좋아 보이네. 무슨 일이니?

남 수학 시험에서 C를 받았어.

여 다음에 더 잘하면 되지. 힘내!

남 고마워. 그런데 부모님께서 내 성적표 받아보시는 게 두려워. 정말 화나실 거야.

여 이해해. 그런데 네가 최선을 다했다면, 화내지 않으실 거야.

남 그러길 바라. 다음 번에 더 노력하겠다고 말씀드려야겠어.

Cheer up! 힘내! **afraid** 두려워하는 **report card** 성적표 **do one's best** 최선을 다하다

18

M Mina is walking on the street with her best friend. While she is walking, she sees a man standing in front of her drop his wallet onto the ground. The man doesn't know that he has dropped it. So she picks up the wallet and wants to give it back to the man. In this situation, what would Mina most likely say to him?

남 Mina는 단짝 친구와 길을 걷고 있다. 걷는 동안 그녀는 그녀의 앞에 서 있는 남자가 땅에 지갑을 떨어뜨리는 것을 본다. 그 남자는 자신이 그것을 떨어뜨린 것을 알지 못한다. 그래서 그녀는 지갑을 주워 그 남자에게 돌려 주려고 한다. 이 상황에서 Mina는 그 남자에게 무어라 이야기하겠는가?

① 실례합니다. 지갑이 얼마입니까?
② 네 지갑 좋은데, 어디서 샀니?
③ 남성용 지갑이 어디 있는지 아세요?
④ 이거 네 거야. 생일 축하해!
⑤ 실례합니다. 지갑을 떨어뜨리셨네요.

in front of ~의 앞에 **drop** 떨어뜨리다 **wallet** 지갑 **ground** 땅 **pick up** 줍다

19

M Wow! Look at this picture. That bridge is so beautiful.

W I think so too. I took the photo in London and I'd like to go there again.

M Did you see the bridge open?

W Of course I did. Look at the next picture. You can see it opening.

M My goodness! I can't believe my eyes.

W Yeah, it was fantastic!

남 우와! 이 사진을 봐. 다리가 정말 아름답다.

여 나도 그렇게 생각해. 런던에서 찍은 사진이야. 다시 그곳에 가고 싶어.

남 다리가 열리는 것을 봤니?

여 물론이지. 다음 사진을 봐. 그게 열리는 것을 볼 수 있어.

남 오 이런! 내 눈을 믿을 수가 없어.

여 맞아, 환상적이었어!

① 맞아, 환상적이었어!
② 걱정 마. 난 널 믿어.
③ 내 사진 한 장 찍어줘.
④ 난 파리에 가본 적이 없어. 네가 부러워.
⑤ 다리는 저녁 7시에 문이 닫혀.

bridge 다리 **of course** 물론 **believe** 믿다

20

M What are you doing, Ava?

W I'm searching the web to buy a pair of sneakers.

M A pair of sneakers? Again? You just bought your new pair last week.

W I know. This time they are for my younger brother. His birthday is coming soon.

M I see. What a great sister! Do you want to buy a pair for your sister, too?

W I'd love to, but I'm broke.

남 Ava, 너 뭐 하니?

여 운동화 한 켤레 사려고 인터넷을 검색하고 있어.

남 운동화 한 켤레? 또? 지난 주에 새로 한 켤레 샀잖아.

여 알아. 이번에는 내 남동생 거야. 곧 그 애 생일이거든.

남 알았어. 정말 좋은 누나네! 너 여동생한테도 한 켤레 사주고 싶니?

여 그러고 싶은데 난 빈털터리야.

① 네 신발 사이즈가 뭐니?
② 그러고 싶은데 난 빈털터리야.
③ 함께 쇼핑 가자.

④ 네 남동생 생일이 언제니?
⑤ 네 남동생에게 생일 축하 한다고 전해줘.

••
search 검색하다 **a pair of** ~ 한 켤레 **sneakers** 운동화 **I'm broke.** 난 빈털터리야.

Further Study 정답

p. 84

1 He is wearing a striped shirt and black jeans.
2 He can't breathe very well or sleep.
3 A chicken burger, onion rings and a coke are included.
4 We have to make a password with numbers, letters and special characters.
5 He is going to have a job interview.
6 It is this Saturday.
7 She is walking with her best friend.
8 She is searching the web to buy a pair of sneakers.

On Your Own 모범답안

p. 85

A

My Favorite Painting			
(1) Title	(2) Painter	(3) Description	(4) Reasons I like
Starry Night	Vincent van Gogh	a scene of a town on a starry night, the sky bright with stars, contrasting with the silent village below	vivid colors, the beauty of a night with stars

My favorite painting is (1)the *Starry Night* by (2)Vincent van Gogh. The painting describes (3)a scene of a town on a starry night. In the picture, (3)the sky is bright with stars and it contrasts with the silent village below. I love this painting because (4)the colors are very vivid and it shows the beauty of a night with stars.

내가 가장 좋아하는 그림			
(1) 제목	(2) 화가	(3) 그림 설명	(4) 좋아하는 이유
별이 빛나는 밤	빈센트 반 고흐	별이 빛나는 밤의 마을 풍경, 별들로 환한 하늘, 아래에 있는 고요한 마을과 대조를 이룸	생기있는 색, 별이 빛나는 밤의 아름다움

내가 가장 좋아하는 그림은 빈센트 반 고흐가 그린 〈별이 빛나는 밤〉입니다. 그 그림은 별이 빛나는 밤의 한 마을의 풍경을 묘사하고 있습니다. 그림에서 하늘은 별들로 환한데 이것은 아래에 있는 고요한 마을과 대조를 이룹니다. 나는 사용된 색들이 아주 생기있고 그림이 별이 빛나는 밤의 아름다움을 보여주기 때문에 이 그림을 좋아합니다.

B

My Favorite Food	
(1) Name of the food	tuna sandwich
(2) Ingredients	canned tuna, bread, mayonnaise
(3) How to make	① drain the oil from the canned tuna ② mix the tuna with the mayonnaise ③ put the tuna and mayonnaise on a slice of bread ④ place another slice of the bread on top

I'm going to talk about my favorite food. My favorite food is (1)a tuna sandwich. The ingredients are (2)canned tuna, bread, and mayonnaise. I will tell you how to make it. First, ①drain the oil from the canned tuna. Second, ②mix the tuna with the mayonnaise. Third, ③put the tuna and mayonnaise on a slice of bread. Lastly, ④place another slice of bread on top and enjoy. Please try to cook it. It will be a lot of fun!

내가 가장 좋아하는 음식	
(1) 음식명	참치 샌드위치
(2) 재료	캔 참치, 식빵, 마요네즈
(3) 만드는 법	① 참치 캔의 기름 따라 버리기 ② 참치와 마요네즈 섞기 ③ 참치와 마요네즈 섞은 것을 식빵 위에 올리기 ④ 그 위에 또 다른 식빵 한 쪽 올리기

저는 제가 가장 좋아하는 음식에 대해 이야기할 것입니다. 제가 가장 좋아하는 음식은 참치 샌드위치입니다. 준비할 재료들은 캔 참치, 식빵, 그리고 마요네즈입니다. 어떻게 만드는지 말씀해드리겠습니다. 첫 번째로, 참치 캔에서 기름을 따라 버립니다. 두 번째로, 참치를 마요네즈와 함께

섞습니다. 세 번째로, 참치와 마요네즈 섞은 것을 식빵 위에 올립니다. 마지막으로 또 다른 빵 한 쪽을 그 위에 올린 후 먹으면 됩니다. 한번 만들어 보세요. 아주 재미있을 것입니다!

01 ②	02 ④	03 ②	04 ①	05 ④
06 ③	07 ②	08 ⑤	09 ②	10 ①
11 ②	12 ④	13 ⑤	14 ⑤	15 ⑤
16 ③	17 ④	18 ④	19 ③	20 ④

01

M Look at this old photo. My mom sent it to me.
W Oh, is this you?
M Yes, with my little brother and friends. We would go on picnics together.
W You were cute. Which one is your brother?
M He is wearing a striped T-shirt and a cap.
W I need more hints. Which row is he in?
M He is in the second row.

남 이 오래된 사진 좀 봐. 엄마가 보내 주셨어.
여 오, 이 사람이 너야?
남 응, 내 동생이랑 친구들과 같이 찍은 거야. 우린 함께 소풍을 가곤 했거든.
여 너 귀여웠다. 네 동생은 누구야?
남 줄무늬 티셔츠에 야구모자를 쓰고 있어.
여 나 힌트가 더 필요해. 몇 번째 줄에 있어?
남 두 번째 줄에 있어.

photo 사진 **go on a picnic** 소풍 가다 **row** 줄

02

W Did you have a good vacation?
M Yes, I traveled around the country with my family.
W Oh! That sounds interesting. How did you travel?
M We went in my father's car. We hiked in the mountains a lot.
W What else did you do on your trip?
M We visited hot springs, picked plums and slept in a tent. I had a really exciting time.

여 방학 즐겁게 보냈어?
남 응, 가족들과 함께 전국을 여행했어.
여 오! 재미있었겠다. 여행은 어떻게 했니?
남 아빠 차로 다녔어. 우리는 산행을 많이 했어.
여 그 외엔 여행에서 무엇을 했어?
남 온천도 갔고, 자두도 따고, 텐트에서 잠도 잤어. 정말 신나는 시간이었어.

travel 여행하다 **in a + 교통수단** ~을 타고 **hike** 도보여행을 하다 **hot spring** 온천 **plum** 자두

03

M I am sick and tired of my girlfriend.
W Why? What's wrong with you guys?
M She likes shopping too much and I hate it. Yesterday she shopped all day long.
W Most girls like shopping, but she seems a little bit too serious about it.
M Yes, also she often asks me to give her expensive gifts.
W I don't think she is the right person for you.

남 나는 내 여자친구에게 완전 질려버렸어.
여 왜? 너희들 무슨 일 있니?
남 그녀는 쇼핑을 너무 좋아하고 나는 쇼핑을 싫어해. 어제 그녀는 하루 종일 쇼핑했어.
여 대부분의 여자들이 쇼핑을 좋아하지만 그녀는 조금 너무 심한 것 같네.
남 응, 또 종종 나에게 비싼 선물을 사달라고 요구해.
여 내 생각에 그녀는 너에게 적당한 사람이 아닌 거 같아.

① 무서워하는 ② 짜증이 난 ③ 불안한
④ 편안한 ⑤ 만족하는

be sick of ~에 진절머리가 나다 **all day long** 하루 종일 **serious** 심각한 **expensive** 비싼 **right** 적절한

04

W Good morning. I'd like to have this coat cleaned.

M Okay, let me look at it. There is a stain on the sleeve. Do you know that?

W Yes, it is a coffee stain. Can you remove it?

M I'll do my best. Do you want me to deliver it?

W Yes, please. How soon can I get it back?

M It will be ready by tomorrow.

여 안녕하세요. 이 코트 세탁하고 싶어요.

남 네, 한 번 볼게요. 소매에 얼룩이 있네요. 알고 계세요?

여 네, 커피 얼룩이에요. 제거할 수 있나요?

남 최선을 다할게요. 배달해 드릴까요?

여 네, 해주세요. 언제 받을 수 있나요?

남 내일까지면 가능할 것 같아요.

① 세탁소 ② 옷 가게 ③ 커피숍
④ 미용실 ⑤ 빵 가게

stain 얼룩 **sleeve** 소매 **remove** 제거하다 **do one's best** 최선을 다하다 **deliver** 배달하다 **by tomorrow** 내일까지

05

M Good morning, I would like to book a room for my wife and me.

W Good morning, sir. We have a room available for two people next week.

M Oh, that's fine with me. How much is the room?

W It is 90 dollars a night plus ten percent tax.

M Okay, I'd like to stay for 3 nights.

W Can I have your name and phone number, please?

남 안녕하세요. 제 아내와 제가 쓸 방을 예약하고 싶어요.

여 안녕하세요. 두 사람이 쓸 수 있는 방은 다음 주에 사용 가능합니다.

남 오, 좋아요. 그 방은 얼마입니까?

여 일박 90달러에 10퍼센트 세금이 더 붙습니다.

남 좋아요. 3일 밤 머물겠습니다.

여 그러면, 이름과 전화번호를 좀 말씀해주시겠어요?

book 예약하다 **available** 이용 가능한 **tax** 세금

06

W This is an important item in our lives. Nowadays this is the best device to use to communicate with others, as it is easy to carry from one place to another. Also, this has various functions, such as taking photos, listening to music, and transferring data. Besides, parents are able to keep track of their kids using this.

여 이것은 우리의 삶에서 중요한 물품입니다. 오늘날 이것은 이곳 저곳으로 가지고 다니기 쉽기 때문에 타인과 의사소통을 하기 위해 사용할 최고의 장치입니다. 또한, 이것은 사진 찍기, 음악 듣기, 자료 전송 등 다양한 기능이 있습니다. 게다가 부모들은 이것을 사용하여 자녀들이 어디에 있는지 파악할 수 있습니다.

item 물품 **device** 장치 **communicate** 의사소통하다 **various** 다양한 **function** 기능 **transfer** 옮기다 **data** 자료 **be able to-V** ~할 수 있다 **keep track of** ~을 추적하다

07

M What do you think of Tom?

W He's awful. I think he is boring.

M Is he? Why do you think that?

W He talks about himself all the time. He's only interested in one thing, and that's Tom himself.

M Don't you think he is funny?

W No, I don't. He is a real bore.

남 Tom에 대해서 어떻게 생각하니?

여 그는 끔찍해. 나는 그가 재미없는 사람이라고 생각해.

남 그가? 왜 그렇게 생각해?

여 그는 언제나 자신에 대해서만 이야기해. 그는 오직 한 가지에만 관심이 있는데 그건 바로 Tom 자신이야.

남 그가 재미있다고 생각되지 않니?

여 아니. 나는 그렇게 생각 안 해. 그는 정말 따분한 사람이야.

What do you think of ~? ~에 대해서 어떻게 생각하니? **awful** 끔찍한 **boring** 따분한 **be interested in** ~에 흥미가 있다 **bore** 따분한 사람

08

W Dinner will be ready in ten minutes. Are you hungry?

M Yes, I am. What have you cooked?

W I have cooked bulgogi, chapchae and some side dishes.

M Oh, they smell really delicious. Is somebody coming to dinner?

W Yes, Kevin is having a bite to eat with us and I know he likes those dishes. Would you mind setting the table?

M Of course not. Where are the placemats?

여 저녁은 10분 후에 다 준비돼요. 배 고파요?
남 응. 무엇을 요리했어?
여 불고기, 잡채, 그리고 반찬 몇 가지 했어요.
남 오, 정말 맛있는 냄새 난다. 저녁식사에 누가 와?
여 네, Kevin이 우리와 같이 밥 먹기로 했는데 그가 저 음식들을 좋아할 거예요. 식탁 좀 차려 줄래요?
남 물론이지. 식탁 매트는 어디에 있어?

side dish 반찬 **have a bite to eat** (가벼운) 식사를 하다 **mind -ing** ~하는 것을 꺼리다 **set the table** 식탁을 차리다 **placemat** 식탁용 매트

09

① M Mom, I can't sleep.
W Why don't you drink some warm milk?

② M Which floor are you going to?
W My button is already pressed. Thanks.

③ M Can I have the bill?
W Sure. Here it is.

④ M Can I pay for this by card?
W Of course you can.

⑤ M Let's take the elevator!
W That is not a very good idea. Let's take the stairs.

① 남 엄마, 잠이 안 와요.
여 따뜻한 우유를 좀 마셔보는 게 어때?
② 남 몇 층 가세요?
여 이미 눌러져 있네요. 감사합니다.
③ 남 계산서 주시겠어요?
여 네, 여기 있습니다.
④ 남 카드로 지불해도 되나요?
여 물론이죠.
⑤ 남 엘리베이터 타자!
여 별로 좋은 생각이 아니야. 계단을 이용하자.

press 누르다 **bill** 계산서 **stairs** 계단

10

M Hello, can you wrap this? The salesclerk said to come over to this counter.

W That's right, we do it here. This is a pretty doll.

M It is for my granddaughter. I have seven grandsons. Now, finally I have a granddaughter.

W Congratulations! Which style of wrapping paper would you prefer?

M I'll take that one with the puppies on it.

W Good choice. And a pink ribbon?

M Yes, please.

남 안녕하세요. 이것 좀 포장해주시겠어요? 판매원이 이 계산대로 가라고 말하더군요.
여 맞습니다. 여기서 합니다. 귀여운 인형이네요.
남 그것은 제 손녀를 위한 것이에요. 저에게는 7명의 손자가 있어요. 이제 드디어 손녀가 생겼지요.
여 축하 드려요. 어떤 스타일의 포장지가 좋으세요?
남 저기 강아지 그림이 있는 포장지로 할게요.
여 훌륭한 선택입니다. 그리고 분홍색 리본도 사용할까요?
남 네, 그렇게 해주세요.

salesclerk 판매원 **counter** 계산대 **grandson** 손자 **granddaughter** 손녀 **wrapping paper** 포장지 **puppy** 강아지

11

W Did you see the Korea-Japan soccer match last night?

M Of course. It was the best match I've ever seen.

W I wish I had seen it. Who won the game?

M Obviously, Korea won. Why don't you watch the rerun?

W Oh, can I? Tell me when it is on, please.

M I don't know. Let me check.

여 너 어젯밤에 일본과 한국 축구 경기 봤니?
남 물론이지. 내가 본 경기들 중 최고였어.
여 나도 봤으면 좋을 텐데. 누가 이겼니?
남 물론 한국이 이겼지. 재방송을 보지 그래?
여 오, 볼 수 있어? 언제 하는지 말해줘.
남 몰라. 확인해볼게.

match 경기 **wish** 소망하다 **obviously** 확실히 **Why don't you ~?** ~하는 게 어때? **rerun** 재상영

12

W Could you please tell me how to make a photocopy of this book?

M Sure. First, you have to turn on the copy machine and wait for it to warm up.

W And then?

M Place the book on the scanning surface after opening the cover. Press the numbers to select the amount of copies.

W Is that all?

M Lastly, close the cover and press the start button.

W Thanks.

여 이 책을 어떻게 복사하는지 알려줄래?
남 물론이지. 첫 번째로, 복사기를 켜고 예열할 때까지 잠시 기다려.
여 그리고?
남 뚜껑을 열고 스캔하는 곳 표면에 책을 올려놔. 번호를 눌러 복사 수량을 선택해.
여 그게 다야?
남 마지막으로 뚜껑을 닫고 시작 버튼을 누르면 돼.
여 고마워.

make a photocopy 복사를 하다 **turn on** 켜다 **warm up** 예열하다 **scan** 스캔하다 **surface** 표면 **lastly** 마지막으로

13

M Welcome to Western Inn. Can I help you?

W Yes. I have a reservation and I'd like to check in.

M Okay. Please give me your name.

W It's Mary Simpson.

M I'm sorry ma'am. I can't find your name on the reservation list.

W Are you sure? I made a reservation a month ago. Please check it again.

M All right. Please spell your last name for me.

남 Western Inn에 오신 것을 환영합니다. 무엇을 도와드릴까요?
여 네. 예약을 했는데요, 체크인을 하고 싶습니다.
남 알겠습니다. 성함을 알려주세요.
여 Mary Simpson입니다.
남 부인, 죄송합니다. 예약자 명단에서 당신의 이름을 찾을 수가 없군요.
여 확실해요? 한 달 전에 예약했는데요. 다시 확인해 주세요.
남 알겠습니다. 성의 철자를 좀 말씀해주세요.

Welcome to ~. ~에 온 것을 환영합니다. **check in** 체크인하다, 투숙하다 **reservation list** 예약자 명단 **spell** 철자를 말하다 **last name** 성

14

① M The party is for Sandy.
② M The party is on December 2nd.
③ M The party will be at a restaurant.
④ M The contact number is 651-7788-9999.
⑤ M Any questions will be answered by Sandy.

Sandy를 위한 깜짝 파티
날짜: 12월 2일, 오후 7시
장소: Jake's Steak House
연락처: Julia, 651-7788-9999

① 남 파티는 Sandy를 위한 것이다.
② 남 파티는 12월 2일이다.
③ 남 파티는 식당에서 열린다.
④ 남 연락처는 651-7788-9999번이다.
⑤ 남 궁금한 사항은 Sandy가 답해줄 것이다.

December 12월 **contact** 연락, 접촉

15

W Sweetie, can you buy me some eggs, please? There aren't any in the refrigerator.

M I'm doing work on the computer now, though. You also asked me to clean the living room.

W I'm sorry. But I have to make sandwiches, so I

can't go out.

M Well, if I help you do that, then, can I play computer games tonight?

W Okay. You can play computer games for an hour tonight.

M Hooray! I love you, mom.

여 얘야, 계란 좀 사다 줄래? 냉장고에 계란이 없네.
남 난 지금 컴퓨터로 작업을 하고 있는데요. 거실도 치우라고 하셨잖아요.
여 미안해. 그런데 내가 샌드위치를 만들고 있어서 밖에 나갈 수가 없어.
남 음, 제가 만일 도와드린다면 오늘 밤에 컴퓨터 게임 해도 되나요?
여 알았어. 오늘 밤에 한 시간 동안 컴퓨터 게임 해도 돼.
남 야호! 사랑해요 엄마.

refrigerator 냉장고 **living room** 거실

16

① W Can I go out now?
M No, you have to finish cleaning your room first.

② W How are you?
M I'm good.

③ W Can you speak Chinese?
M Yes. I am Korean.

④ W My mom is sick in bed.
M I'm sorry to hear that.

⑤ W I'm starving.
M Me too. Let's grab a sandwich.

① 여 저 지금 나갈 수 있어요?
남 아니. 네 방 먼저 치워라.
② 여 어떻게 지내?
남 잘 지내.
③ 여 중국어 할 수 있니?
남 응. 나는 한국 사람이야.
④ 여 엄마가 몸져누우셨어.
남 안됐구나.
⑤ 여 나 너무 배고파.
남 나도 그래. 샌드위치 먹자.

sick in bed 몸져누운 **starve** 굶주리다 **grab** 움켜쥐다

17

W Welcome to ACE Computer Shop. May I help you?

M Yes. I'm looking for a laptop computer. Can you recommend one for me?

W Sure. How about this? It has a 14-inch LCD monitor and it only weighs 1.1kg.

M How much is it?

W It is actually 190 dollars, but I will give you a 15% discount.

M Good. What colors are available?

W We have white, black, and pink in stock.

여 ACE 컴퓨터 가게에 오신 것을 환영합니다. 무엇을 도와드릴까요?
남 네. 노트북 컴퓨터를 찾고 있습니다. 하나 추천해 주시겠어요?
여 물론입니다. 이거 어떠세요? 14인치 LCD 모니터에 무게는 1.1kg밖에 안됩니다.
남 얼마인가요?
여 원래는 190달러이지만 15% 할인해 드릴게요.
남 좋아요. 어떤 색상이 있죠?
여 흰색, 검정색, 그리고 분홍색이 있습니다.

weigh (무게가) ~이다 **actually** 실제로 **available** 구할 수 있는 **in stock** 재고가 있는

18

W Jessica is working as a receptionist in a dental clinic. Suddenly, an old man comes into the clinic and tries to go directly into the dentist's room. He says that he has a terrible toothache and can't stand the pain. It seems that he is a walk-in, so he doesn't have an appointment. In this situation, what would she most probably say to the man?

여 Jessica는 치과에서 접수 담당자로 일하고 있다. 갑자기, 한 나이든 남자가 들어와서 곧장 진료실로 들어가려고 한다. 그는 이가 너무 아프다며 고통을 참을 수 없다고 한다. 그는 불쑥 찾아온 환자로 보이며 약속이 잡혀있지 않다. 이 상황에서 그녀는 필시 그 남자에게 무엇이라 말하겠는가?

① 죄송합니다. 진료 끝났습니다.
② 더 일찍 오셨으면 좋았을 텐데요.
③ 왜 진료 받기를 원하십니까?

④ 번호표 뽑으시고 순서가 될 때까지 기다려주세요.
⑤ 의사선생님이 지금 안 계십니다. 잠시만 기다려 주십시오.

●●
receptionist 접수 담당자 **dental clinic** 치과 **directly** 곧바로 **dentist** 치과의사 **toothache** 치통 **stand** 참다 **walk-in** 불쑥 찾아온 방문자

19

W Hi, Henry. What are you going to do this weekend?
M I have no plans yet. I might stay at home and take a good rest. Why?
W I was wondering if you would like to see a movie with me. I'd like to see *The Face Reader*.
M Okay. I heard that it is very interesting.
W Perfect! When and where shall we meet?
M Let's meet at 5 o'clock at BLG cinema.

여 안녕, Henry. 너 이번 주말에 뭐 할 거니?
남 아직 계획 없어. 집에 있으면서 푹 쉴지도 모르지. 왜?
여 나랑 같이 영화 보러 갈 생각이 있을까 해서. 나 〈관상〉을 보고 싶어.
남 좋아. 그 영화 정말 재미있다고 하더라고.
여 좋았어! 언제 어디서 만날까?
남 BLG 극장에서 5시에 만나자.

① 지금 몇 시니?
② 나 이미 그 영화 봤어.
③ BLG 극장에서 5시에 만나자.
④ 미안해. 다음 번에 가자.
⑤ 난 극장이 어디 있는지 몰라.

●●
have no plan 계획이 없다 **stay at** ~에 머무르다 **take a rest** 휴식을 취하다 **perfect** 완벽한

20

W Did you know that Jinho has come back from the U.S.?
M Are you serious? When?
W He called me up last night and said he had just arrived at the airport.
M Really? I will call him. I have really missed him.
W He said that too. He asked me how you are doing. He also said that he will call you today.
M Nice! Let's have a welcome home party for him.

여 너 진호가 미국에서 돌아온 것 알고 있었니?
남 정말? 언제?
여 어젯밤에 내게 전화해서 방금 공항에 도착했다고 말했어.
남 정말? 내가 전화해 봐야겠다. 난 걔가 정말 보고 싶어.
여 걔도 그렇게 말했어. 네가 어떻게 지내는지 물어보더라. 그리고 오늘 네게 전화한다고도 말했어.
남 좋았어! 그를 위한 환영 파티를 하자.

① 공항에 가자.
② 넌 참 착하구나.
③ 나는 해외에서 공부하기 싫어.
④ 좋았어! 그를 위한 환영 파티를 하자.
⑤ 너 진호가 언제 한국에 오는지 알고 있니?

●●
arrive 도착하다 **airport** 공항 **miss** 그리워하다 **welcome party** 환영 파티

Further Study 정답

p. 94

1 He traveled around the country with his family in his father's car.
2 He will be staying there for 3 nights with his wife.
3 She asks him to set the table.
4 He chooses the one with the puppies on it.
5 The last step of making a photocopy is closing the cover and pressing the start button.
6 It is on December 2nd.
7 White, black, and pink are available.
8 She asks the man to go to see a movie with her.

On Your Own 모범답안

p. 95

A

The Place I Visited during Summer Vacation		
(1) The place I visited	(2) How I went there (Transportation)	(3) Things I did

Haenam	in my father's car	① hiked in the mountains ② learned how to milk a cow ③ picked spinach ④ watched the stars at night

During my summer vacation, I visited (1)Haenam with my family. We got there (2)in my father's car. We ①hiked in the mountains, ②learned how to milk a cow, and ③picked spinach there. We also ④watched the stars at night and it was the best. We had a great time there.

여름방학 동안 내가 방문했던 곳		
(1) 장소	(2) 교통 수단	(3) 한 일들
해남	아버지 차로	① 산행함 ② 젖소 우유 짜는 방법을 배움 ③ 시금치를 캠 ④ 밤에 별을 관찰함

여름방학 동안 나는 가족과 함께 해남에 갔다. 우리는 아버지 차로 거기에 갔다. 거기에서 산행도 했고, 젖소 우유 짜는 방법도 배웠고, 시금치도 캤다. 우리는 또한 밤에 별을 관찰했는데 최고였다. 우리는 거기에서 아주 즐거운 시간을 보냈다.

B

Making a Reservation for a Hotel Room	
(1) When do you want to stay?	on January 1st
(2) How many days are you going to stay?	5 days
(3) How many people are going to stay?	3 people
(4) Would you like a(n) ocean/city view?	an ocean view
(5) Would you like a twin/double bed?	a double bed
(6) Your name and contact number	Yujin Han, 010-0101-0202

I would like to make a reservation for a hotel room. I'd like to stay there on (1)January 1st. I want to stay for (2)5 days. (3)Three people are going to stay, including me. If possible, please give me a room with an (4)ocean view. Lastly, I'd like a (5)double bed rather than a (5)twin bed. My name is (6)Yujin Han and my contact number is (6)010-0101-0202. Thank you.

호텔 방 예약하기	
(1) 언제 투숙하고 싶습니까?	1월 1일
(2) 며칠 동안 머물 예정입니까?	5일
(3) 몇 사람이 머물 예정입니까?	3명
(4) 바다가 보이는 방을 원하세요, 시내가 보이는 방을 원하세요?	바다가 보이는 방
(5) 트윈 침대를 원하세요, 더블 침대를 원하세요?	더블 침대
(6) 당신의 이름과 연락처	한유진, 010-0101-0202

호텔 방을 예약하고 싶습니다. 저는 1월 1일에 거기서 머물려고 합니다. 저는 5일 동안 머물고 싶습니다. 저를 포함한 세 명이 머물 것입니다. 만일 가능하다면, 바다가 보이는 방으로 해주세요. 마지막으로, 저는 트윈 침대보다는 더블 침대가 더 좋습니다. 제 이름은 한유진이며, 연락처는 010-0101-0202번입니다. 감사합니다.

10 Listening Test 정답

중학영어듣기 모의고사 10회

p. 100

01 ②	02 ①	03 ①	04 ③	05 ⑤
06 ⑤	07 ④	08 ①	09 ②	10 ④
11 ⑤	12 ①	13 ⑤	14 ②	15 ③
16 ④	17 ④	18 ⑤	19 ②	20 ③

01

W Let's have sandwiches for lunch.

M That's a good idea, Mom.

W What would you like on your sandwich?

M What is there?

W We have ham, lettuce, tomato, cheese, tuna, cucumber, and onion.

M Could I have some lettuce, tomato, cheese and ham?

W You bet. Here you go.

여 점심으로 샌드위치 먹자.
남 좋은 생각이에요, 엄마.
여 샌드위치에 무엇을 넣고 싶니?
남 뭐가 있어요?
여 햄, 양상추, 토마토, 치즈, 참치, 오이 그리고 양파가 있어.
남 양상추, 토마토, 치즈, 그리고 햄을 넣어 주실래요?
여 물론이지. 여기 있단다.

cucumber 오이 **You bet.** 물론이지. **Here you go.** 여기 있다.

02

M How many bedrooms are in your house?
W We have three bedrooms: one for my parents, one for my elder sister, and one for me.
M Tell me about your room.
W It is in the center of the second floor.
M Is your house a two-story building?
W Yes it is, but it is not all that big.
M I envy you. I live in the apartment where I have to share a bedroom with my brother.

남 너의 집에는 방이 몇 개 있니?
여 부모님 방, 언니 방, 그리고 내 방 이렇게 세 개가 있어.
남 너의 방에 대해서 말해줘.
여 내 방은 이층 가운데에 있어.
남 너의 집은 이층 건물이니?
여 응, 하지만 그렇게 크지 않아.
남 네가 부러워. 나는 내 남동생과 침실을 같이 써야 하는 아파트에서 살아.

elder sister 언니, 누나 **center** 중앙 **two-story** 이층의 **share** 함께 쓰다

03

W Good afternoon, sir.
M Hello. My name is Michael Lee. My secretary made a reservation under my name.
W Ah, yes, Mr. Lee. A single room for three nights?
M That's right.
W Here's your key, Room 514. It is on the fifth floor.
M Where is the elevator?
W It's just behind you. Have a nice evening.

여 안녕하세요.
남 안녕하세요. 제 이름은 Michael Lee입니다. 제 비서가 제 이름으로 예약을 했습니다.
여 아 네, 이 선생님. 1인용 객실로 3일밤인가요?
남 맞아요.
여 여기 514호 열쇠 있습니다. 방은 5층에 있습니다.
남 엘리베이터가 어디 있습니까?
여 바로 손님 뒤에 있습니다. 편안한 저녁 되세요.

① 호텔 접수원 ② 비서 ③ 여행 가이드
④ 경찰관 ⑤ 수리공

secretary 비서 **single** 1인용의 **floor** 층 **behind** ~ 뒤에

04

M What is your favorite sport?
W My favorite sport is baseball.
M Do you prefer watching or playing baseball?
W I like watching it better than playing it.
M Why don't you like to play it?
W I sweat so much during exercise and it makes me embarrassed.
M If you think that is serious, why don't you talk to a doctor about it?

남 네가 가장 좋아하는 스포츠는 뭐니?
여 내가 가장 좋아하는 스포츠는 야구야.
남 너는 야구를 보는 것과 하는 것 중 어떤 것을 더 좋아하니?
여 나는 야구를 하는 것보다 보는 것을 더 좋아해.
남 왜 야구하는 것은 안 좋아하니?
여 나는 운동하는 동안 땀이 너무 많이 나고 그 점이 나를 당황스럽게 해.
남 그것이 심각하다고 생각되면 의사한테 말해 보는 것이 어때?

play baseball 야구 하다 **sweat** 땀 흘리다 **embarrassed** 당황한

05

W What time is it, daddy?
M It's seven thirty.
W How long does it take to go back home?
M Why? Did you forget something?

W Yes. I think I left my notebook with all my homework in it there.

M Well, it'll only take ten minutes. But it will take another thirty minutes to get to your school from home.

W Can we go back home, daddy?

여 아빠 몇 시예요?
남 7시 30분이다.
여 집으로 다시 돌아가는 데 얼마나 걸려요?
남 왜? 뭐 잊어버렸니?
여 네. 숙제가 다 들어있는 노트를 집에 두고 온 것 같아요.
남 글쎄, 10분 정도 걸릴 거야. 하지만 집에서 학교까지 가는 데 다시 30분이 더 걸릴 거야.
여 아빠, 집에 가주시겠어요?

forget 잊다 **leave** 두고 오다

06

M When it becomes hot, everybody likes to be in or around the water. Going to the swimming pool or the beach on a hot day is a great way to beat the heat. As long as there are safeguards, most people don't think much about water safety. However, a lot of people die because of drowning. So we have to know and follow safety rules in water before we go swimming.

남 더워지면, 모든 사람들은 물가에 있거나 물에 들어가는 것을 좋아한다. 더운 날에 수영장이나 해변에 가는 것은 더위를 이길 수 있는 훌륭한 방법이다. 안전요원이 있는 한, 대부분의 사람들은 수상 안전에 대해서 많이 생각하지 않는다. 하지만, 많은 사람들이 물에 빠짐으로써 죽는다. 그래서 우리는 수영하기 전에 물에서 지켜야 할 안전 규칙에 대해서 알고 지켜야 한다.

beat 이기다 **as long as** ~하는 한 **safeguard** 안전요원 **because of** ~ 때문에 **drown** 익사하다 **safety rule** 안전 규칙

07

W Are you interested in traveling?

M Yes, I really like it. I've been to lots of places.

W Have you ever traveled abroad?

M Yes. I have been to Japan, China and the States.

W What about Thailand?

M Yes, I've been there, too. It's a place of wonders.

W Which country do you recommend that I visit during this summer vacation?

여 너 여행하는 것에 관심이 있니?
남 응, 여행 정말 좋아해. 많은 곳들을 다녀왔어.
여 해외 여행 한 적 있니?
남 응. 나는 일본, 중국 그리고 미국을 다녀왔어.
여 태국은 어때?
남 응. 거기도 다녀왔어. 거기는 아주 멋진 곳이야.
여 너는 여름 방학에 내가 방문할 곳으로 어떤 나라를 추천해주겠니?

be interested in ~에 관심이 있다 **abroad** 해외로, 해외에서 **the States** 미국 **Thailand** 태국 **wonder** 경이로움 **recommend** 추천하다

08

M What did you do yesterday?

W Oh, a lot. In the morning I went to a movie theater with my friend. It was quite good.

M Where did you have lunch?

W I had lunch at my favorite Chinese restaurant.

M Sounds great. What did you do in the evening?

W I went to Erin's housewarming party.

M Wow! What a busy day you had!

남 어제 뭐 했니?
여 오, 많은 것을 했지. 아침에는 친구와 영화 보러 갔었어. 꽤 괜찮았지.
남 점심은 어디서 먹었니?
여 내가 아주 좋아하는 중국음식점에서 먹었어.
남 좋았겠다. 저녁에는 뭐 했니?
여 Erin의 집들이에 갔었어.
남 우와! 진짜 바쁜 하루였구나!

movie theater 극장 **housewarming party** 집들이

09

① M What are you doing?
W I'm doing my homework.

② M Why don't you eat some more?

W No thanks. I'm full.

③ M Excuse me. How can I get to City Hall?

W I beg your pardon?

④ M Can I see the menu?

W Yes, here it is.

⑤ M Are you going to borrow all these books?

W Yes. I love reading books.

① 남 뭐 하고 있니?

여 숙제 하는 중이야.

② 남 좀 더 먹지 그래?

여 아니. 배불러.

③ 남 실례합니다. 시청에 어떻게 가나요?

여 다시 말씀해주시겠어요?

④ 남 메뉴 좀 볼 수 있을까요?

여 네, 여기 있습니다.

⑤ 남 이 책들 전부 다 빌릴 거야?

여 응. 나는 책 읽는 것을 무척 좋아해.

full 배가 부른 **I beg your pardon?** 뭐라고요? **borrow** 빌리다

10

W Can you turn down the volume on TV, please?

M Oh, I'm sorry. I didn't know you were here.

W That's fine. Anyway are you all done with cleaning?

M No, I still need to clean the bedrooms and the bathroom.

W I think you are watching too much TV. You're wasting your time.

M Come on. It has been just twenty minutes since I started watching TV. I'm just taking a short rest.

여 TV 볼륨 좀 줄여줄래?

남 오, 미안해, 네가 여기에 있는 줄 몰랐어.

여 괜찮아. 그나저나 청소는 다 했어?

남 아니, 침실과 화장실은 여전히 청소해야 해.

여 나는 네가 TV를 너무 많이 본다고 생각해. 시간을 낭비하는 거야.

남 아냐. TV 보기 시작한 지 20분밖에 되지 않았어. 난 그냥 잠깐 쉬고 있는 거야.

turn down 줄이다 **still** 여전히 **waste** 낭비하다 **take a rest** 휴식을 취하다

11

W My goodness. Look! It's Girls' Generation.

M Girls' Generation? Where? Where? I'm a big fan of them.

W Why don't you go and get their autograph, then?

M I'd like to, but I'm too shy. Can you do that for me?

W What? Come on. Be brave.

M Oh, please. I shall never forget your kindness.

W Okay. I will try.

여 맙소사. 봐! 소녀시대야.

남 소녀시대? 어디? 어디? 나 그들의 광 팬이야.

여 그러면 가서 사인 받지 그래?

남 그러고 싶은데 너무 부끄러워서. 네가 나 대신 받아줄래?

여 뭐라고? 왜 이래. 용감해져 봐.

남 오, 제발. 너의 친절함은 절대 잊지 않을게.

여 알았어. 해볼게.

My goodness! 맙소사! **autograph** 사인, 서명 **shy** 수줍은 **brave** 용감한 **kindness** 친절

12

W In public restrooms, this is installed near the washstand. You use this after washing your hands. If you place your hands under the air hole, the hot air will blow out automatically and dry your wet hands. If you rub your hands together, they will dry faster and easier. It also turns off automatically when you walk away.

여 공중 화장실에서 이것은 세면대 가까이에 설치되어 있습니다. 당신은 손을 씻은 후에 이것을 사용합니다. 만일 당신이 바람 구멍 아래에 손을 놓으면 뜨거운 바람이 자동으로 나와서 젖은 손을 말려 줍니다. 만일 당신이 손을 비빈다면 더 빠르고 쉽게 마를 수 있습니다. 그것은 당신이 떠나면 자동적으로 꺼지기도 합니다.

public restroom 공중 화장실 **install** 설치하다 **washstand** 세면대 **place** 놓다 **blow out** 불다 **automatically** 자동적으로 **rub** 비비다 **turn off** 꺼지다

13

W Charles, I'm going to change the wall paper in your room.

M Really? I'm happy to hear that. What color do you have in mind?

W I'm thinking of sky blue or green. Is there any color you'd like to have?

M Green is my favorite color. It makes me feel calm and warm.

W Green also makes people's eyes relaxed.

M Please change it soon. I am very excited about it.

여 Charles, 네 방의 벽지를 바꿀 거야.

남 정말요? 반가운 얘기네요. 어떤 색을 고려하고 계세요?

여 하늘색이나 녹색을 생각하고 있어. 네가 원하는 색이 있니?

남 녹색이 제가 가장 좋아하는 색이에요. 녹색은 저를 차분하고 따뜻하게 느끼게 해줘요.

여 녹색은 또한 사람들의 눈을 편안하게도 해주지.

남 빨리 바꿔주세요. 그거 정말 신나요.

wall paper 벽지 **think of** ~에 대해 생각하다 **sky blue** 하늘색 **calm** 차분한 **warm** 따뜻한 **relax** 편하게 하다

14

① M Students study English 20 hours a week.

② M Students study Language Arts the most.

③ M Students study Math more than Language Arts.

④ M Students study Math less than English.

⑤ M Students study Science the least.

학생들의 주간 공부 시간

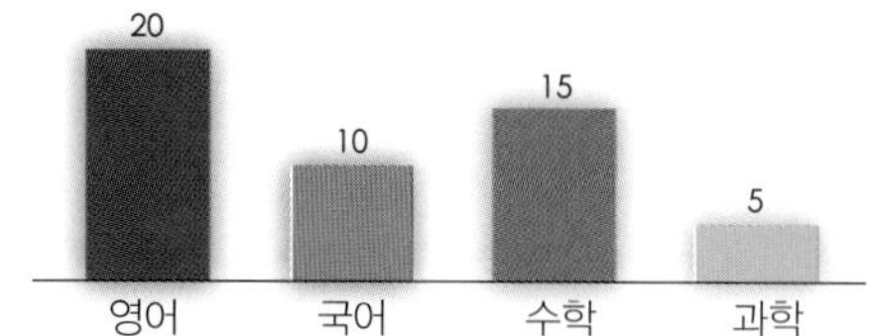

① 남 학생들은 일주일에 영어를 20시간 공부한다.

② 남 학생들은 국어를 가장 많이 공부한다.

③ 남 학생들은 국어보다 수학을 더 많이 공부한다.

④ 남 학생들은 영어보다 수학을 더 적게 공부한다.

⑤ 남 학생들은 과학을 가장 적게 공부한다.

in a week 일주일에 **Language Arts** (과목) 언어, 국어 **more than** ~보다 더 많이 **less than** ~보다 더 적게 **least** 가장 적게

15

M Oh, I'm late for the conference. I've got to take a taxi.

W I heard on the news that traffic is terrible this morning due to the heavy rain.

M What should I do, then?

W You'd better take public transportation like a bus or the subway.

M I see. By the way, would you drop me off at the subway station? I think that's the fastest way.

W Okay, I will.

남 오, 회의에 늦었네. 택시를 타야겠어.

여 폭우 때문에 오늘 아침 차가 많이 막힌다고 뉴스에서 들었어요.

남 그러면 어떻게 해야 하지?

여 버스나 지하철 같은 대중교통을 이용하는 게 더 나아요.

남 알았어. 그런데, 지하철역까지 태워다 줄래? 내 생각에는 그게 가장 빠를 것 같은데.

여 알겠어요. 그럴게요.

conference 회의 **take a taxi** 택시를 타다 **due to** ~ 때문에 **heavy rain** 폭우 **had better + 동사원형** ~하는 게 더 낫다 **public transportation** 대중교통

16

① W How was your holiday?

M I really had fun.

② W Can I borrow your pen?

M Sure. Here it is.

③ W Do you have a bigger size?

M Yes. I will get it for you.

④ W When does the subway arrive?

M I will take line number 2.

⑤ W What do you want to eat?

M I will have a hamburger.

① 여 휴가 어땠어?

남 정말 재미있었어.

② 여 네 펜 좀 빌려도 될까?
남 물론이지. 여기 있어.
③ 여 더 큰 사이즈 있나요?
남 네. 가져다 드릴게요.
④ 여 지하철이 언제 도착하나요?
남 저는 2호선을 탈 겁니다.
⑤ 여 무엇을 먹고 싶니?
남 햄버거 먹을게.

holiday 휴가 **get** 가져다 주다 **line** 노선

17

W Did you hear about Youngsoo?

M No. Why?

W I heard that he had a car accident on the way to school this morning.

M I'm sorry to hear that. Is he hurt bad?

W Unfortunately, yes. He broke his arm and leg, so he's in the hospital now.

M Oh, no. How long does he have to stay in the hospital?

W At least two weeks.

여 영수 얘기 들었니?
남 아니. 왜?
여 오늘 아침에 학교로 오는 길에 차 사고가 났다고 들었어.
남 안됐구나. 심하게 다쳤니?
여 불행하게도 그래. 팔과 다리가 부러졌대. 그래서 지금 병원에 있다고 해.
남 오, 이런. 병원에 얼마나 있어야 한대?
여 최소 2주.

car accident 차 사고 **on the way to** ~로 가는 길에 **bad** 심하게 **unfortunately** 불행하게도 **at least** 최소한

18

W Alice is absent from school for three days because of a bad cold. Unfortunately, on the day she goes back to school, she will have a Social Studies test. Dennis feels bad about it, so he wants to offer to share his notes with Alice. In this situation, what would Dennis most probably say to Alice?

여 Alice는 독감으로 인해 3일 동안 학교에 결석했다. 불행하게도, Alice가 학교로 돌아오는 날 사회 시험을 치를 것이다. Dennis는 Alice가 안돼서 그의 공책을 함께 보자고 그녀에게 제안하고자 한다. 이 상황에서 Dennis는 Alice에게 필시 무엇이라고 말하겠는가?

① 내 공책을 찾을 수가 없어.
② 네 공책을 빌릴 수 있을까?
③ 나는 사회 과목을 안 좋아해.
④ 수업시간에 늦지 않게 좀 와.
⑤ 네가 원한다면 내 공책을 빌려줄게.

be absent from ~에 결석하다 **bad cold** 독감 **Social Studies** (과목) 사회 **offer** 제안하다

19

W I'd like to enroll in the cooking class. Can you show me a timetable?

M Sure. Here it is. If you have any questions, please let me know.

W Okay. Thanks. [pause] Is the Wednesday class still available?

M Would you like to take a morning class or an evening class?

W I would prefer an evening class.

M Good. We have only one place left.

여 요리 수업을 등록하고 싶습니다. 시간표 좀 보여주시겠어요?
남 물론이죠. 여기 있습니다. 질문이 있으시면 말씀해 주세요.
여 네. 고맙습니다. 수요일 수업 자리가 아직 남아 있나요?
남 오전 수업을 원하세요, 저녁 수업을 원하세요?
여 저녁 수업이 더 좋아요.
남 잘 됐네요. 딱 한 자리 남았어요.

① 어떤 수업에 관심이 있으세요?
② 잘 됐네요. 딱 한 자리 남았어요.
③ 좋아요. 시간표 보여드릴게요.
④ 저녁 수업에도 등록하고 싶어요.
⑤ 우와. 나는 당신이 요리에 관심이 있는 줄 몰랐네요.

enroll in ~에 등록하다 **timetable** 시간표 **Wednesday** 수요일 **available** 이용 가능한 **prefer** 더 좋아하다

20

W I'd like to buy tickets to Busan. When is the soonest I can leave?
M Let me check. There is a bus in an hour.
W In an hour? Isn't there an earlier one?
M I'm sorry. That's the fastest.
W I have no choice then I suppose. Please give me two adult tickets. How much are they?
M It's 18,000 won per person.

여 부산 가는 표를 구입하고 싶습니다. 제가 떠날 수 있는 가장 빠른 시간이 언제인가요?
남 확인해 볼게요. 한 시간 후에 버스가 있네요.
여 한 시간 후에요? 더 빠른 것은 없나요?
남 죄송합니다. 그게 가장 빠른 거예요.
여 그러면 선택의 여지가 없겠군요. 성인 두 장 주세요. 얼마인가요?
남 1인 18,000원입니다.

① 한 시간 후에 떠납니다.
② 일찍 오신 분이군요.
③ 1인 18,000원입니다.
④ 부산에 왜 가시나요?
⑤ 카드로 결제해도 되나요?

in an hour 한 시간 후에 **have no choice** 선택의 여지가 없다
suppose 생각하다 **adult** 성인

Further Study 정답

p. 104

1 There are four people in her family: her parents, her elder sister and her.
2 He advises her to talk to a doctor about her sweating if she thinks that is serious.
3 The reason is that she left her notebook with all her homework in it there.
4 The reason is that he is watching TV, even though he hasn't finished cleaning the bedrooms and the bathroom.
5 He said green makes him feel calm and warm.
6 The reason is that there is heavy rain.
7 Yes. He broke his arm and leg.
8 She was absent from school for three days.

On Your Own 모범답안

p. 105

A

My Favorite Book				
(1) Title	(2) Writer	(3) Main character	(4) What he/she does	(5) Why I like the book
Harry Potter	J. K. Rowling	Harry Potter	goes to Hogwarts School to become a wizard and has many adventures	① fun and interesting ② learned about the importance of friendship

I'd like to introduce my favorite book, (1)*Harry Potter*. It was written by (2)J. K. Rowling. In the story, (3)Harry Potter (4)goes to Hogwarts School to become a wizard and has many adventures. I like the book because ①its story is so fun and interesting. Also, ②I learned about the importance of friendship. I think you will all like it, too.

내가 가장 좋아하는 책				
(1) 제목	(2) 작가	(3) 주인공	(4) 그/그녀가 한 일	(5) 책을 좋아하는 이유
해리 포터	J.K. Rowling	Harry Potter	마법사가 되기 위해서 Hogwarts 학교에 가서 많은 모험들을 한다	① 재미있고 흥미로움 ② 우정의 중요성에 대해 배웠음

나는 내가 가장 좋아하는 책인 〈해리포터〉를 여러분에게 소개하고 싶습니다. 그것은 J. K. Rowling이 썼습니다. 이야기에서 해리포터는 마법사가 되기 위해서 Hogwarts 학교에 가고 많은 모험들을 경험하게 됩니다. 저는 이야기가 무척 재미있고 흥미롭기 때문에 이 책을 좋아합니다. 또한 저는 우정의 중요성에 대해서도 배웠습니다. 여러분 모두도 좋아할 것이라고 생각합니다.

B

My Favorite Color	
(1) What is your favorite color?	red
(2) Why do you like the color?	passion, love
(3) What are 3 typical things in the color?	rose, apple, fire engine
(4) What items do you have in the color?	bag, scarf, mouse pad

I like the color (1)red because it (2)represents passion and love. (3)Roses, apples, and fire engines are all (1)red. I have (4)a bag, a scarf and a mouse pad in (1)red. What is your favorite color? Do you like the color (1)red, too? If so, please share your things with me.

내가 가장 좋아하는 색	
(1) 가장 좋아하는 색은?	빨간색
(2) 그 색을 좋아하는 이유는?	열정, 사랑
(3) 그 색으로 된 전형적인 것 3가지는?	장미, 사과, 소방차
(4) 갖고 있는 물건들 중 그 색으로 되어 있는 것은?	가방, 스카프, 마우스 패드

나는 빨간색을 좋아합니다. 왜냐하면 그것은 열정과 사랑을 나타내기 때문입니다. 장미, 사과, 그리고 소방차가 모두 빨간색입니다. 나는 빨간색으로 된 가방, 스카프, 그리고 마우스 패드를 가지고 있습니다. 여러분이 가장 좋아하는 색깔은 무엇입니까? 여러분도 빨간색을 좋아하나요? 만일 그렇다면, 나와 함께 그 물건들에 대해 이야기 나누어요.

11 Listening Test 정답

p. 110

01 ②	02 ③	03 ①	04 ⑤	05 ④
06 ④	07 ①	08 ②	09 ③	10 ④
11 ⑤	12 ⑤	13 ④	14 ②	15 ①
16 ①	17 ③	18 ②	19 ②	20 ⑤

01

M It is time to close the book. Now, what do you remember about the picture?

W First, at the top of the picture there are some clouds in the sky.

M What about at the bottom of the picture?

W Two children are flying kites.

M How about the sun? Where is it?

W It is in the top left-hand corner.

M That's right. You remembered everything. Good job!

남 책을 덮을 시간이야. 자, 그림에서 기억나는 게 뭐가 있니?
여 먼저, 그림의 윗부분에는 하늘에 구름이 좀 있어요.
남 그림의 밑부분은 어떠니?
여 두 명의 어린이들이 연을 날리고 있는 중이에요.
남 태양은 어때? 어디에 있니?
여 그것은 왼쪽 맨 윗부분에 있어요.
남 맞아. 전부 다 기억하는구나. 잘 했어!

top 꼭대기 **bottom** 바닥 **kite** 연 **left-hand** 왼쪽의 **Good job!** 잘 했어!

02

W Dad, look at that road sign. The man is walking on the keys of a piano.

M Oh, that is actually a crosswalk. The man is walking across a crosswalk.

W What does the sign mean?

M It means we are coming up to a crosswalk.

W Are we going to cross the street?

M Yes, we are. Remember to be careful and look left and right before we cross.

여 아빠, 저 도로표지판 좀 보세요. 남자가 피아노 건반 위에서 걷고 있어요.
남 오, 그것은 사실 횡단보도란다. 그 남자는 횡단보도에서 걷고 있는 거지.
여 그 표지판은 무슨 의미예요?
남 우리가 횡단보도로 다가가고 있다는 의미야.
여 우리 길 건너요?
남 그래, 맞아. 길을 건너기 전에 조심해서 오른쪽, 왼쪽을 잘 살펴야 한다는 점을 잊지 마라.

road sign 도로표지판 **keys of a piano** 피아노 건반 **crosswalk** 횡단보도

03

W Do you know what happened yesterday?

M No, what happened?

W I looked out the window and saw our new neighbor holding a knife with blood on his shirt!

M What? He might have killed somebody! Did you call the police?

W Yes! The police came quickly!

M So did they find a dead body? Did he kill someone?

W No! It turned out he was just a make-up artist!

여 너 어제 무슨 일이 있었는지 아니?

남 아니. 무슨 일이 있었는데?

여 내가 창문 밖을 보다가 새로 온 이웃 사람이 셔츠에 피를 묻힌 채 칼을 들고 있는 걸 보게 됐어.

남 뭐라고? 그는 누군가를 죽였을지도 몰라. 경찰에 전화했어?

여 그럼! 경찰도 빨리 왔지!

남 그래서 그들이 시체를 발견했어? 그가 누굴 죽였던 거야?

여 아니! 그는 그냥 분장사로 판명되었어!

① 안도하는 ② 충격을 받은 ③ 신나는
④ 지루한 ⑤ 무서운

neighbor 이웃 사람 **blood** 피 **dead** 죽은 **make-up artist** 분장사

04

M Where would you like to go for dinner?

W What do you think of that French restaurant we went to last month? It's a nice place, isn't it?

M I don't think so. We waited for an hour to get the table there.

W Of course, we forgot to book a table.

M Let's go to a Korean restaurant.

W Okay, if you want.

남 저녁 식사 하러 어디로 가고 싶어?

여 지난 달에 갔던 프랑스 음식점 어떻게 생각해? 멋진 곳이잖아, 안 그래?

남 나는 그렇게 생각하지 않아. 지난번에 갔을 때 자리를 잡기까지 한 시간이나 기다렸어.

여 그건 물론 우리가 자리를 예약하는 것을 잊어버려서 그랬지.

남 한국 음식점에 가자.

여 그래, 네가 원한다면 그렇게 하자.

French 프랑스의 **book** 예약하다

05

M Good morning ma'am, I'd like five tickets for the Picasso exhibition.

W Of course, and if you have a student card, you can get a student discount.

M Here it is.

W That will be three dollars per person. Do you need a guide? It only costs an additional two dollars for all of the people in a single group.

M That would be convenient. May I pay by credit card?

W Sure. Thanks, here is your receipt.

남 안녕하세요. 피카소 전시회 입장권을 다섯 장 사고 싶어요.

여 네, 학생증이 있으면, 학생 할인을 받으실 수 있습니다.

남 여기 있습니다.

여 그럼 1인당 3달러입니다. 안내인이 필요하세요? 한 단체에 속해있는 모든 사람에 대해 2달러만 추가로 내시면 됩니다.

남 그게 좋겠네요. 신용카드로 지불해도 될까요?

여 물론이죠. 감사합니다. 여기 영수증 있습니다.

exhibition 전시회 **additional** 추가의 **convenient** 편리한 **receipt** 영수증

06

W This is one of the greatest inventions in human history. Before it was invented, mail was the main method of communication. Also, people had to go to one another and talk to in person. Thanks to this invention, people no longer had to talk face to face. It has played a major role in making the world a global village.

여 이것은 인류 역사상 가장 위대한 발명품 중 하나이다. 그것이 발명되기 전에는 우편이 의사소통을 위한 주된 방법이었다. 또한 사람들은 직접 서로에게 가서 이야기해야 했다. 이 발명품 덕분에 사람들은 더 이상 얼굴을 맞대고 이야기할 필요가 없어졌다. 그것은 세계가 지구촌화되는 데 중요한 역할을 했다.

① 라디오　② 프린터　③ TV
④ 전화　⑤ 사진기

invention 발명품 **method** 방법 **communication** 의사소통 **in person** 직접 **play a major role in** ~에 중요한 역할을 하다 **global** 지구의

07

M　Do you want to ride your bike with me?
W　Okay, I'll ride with you. Where are we going?
M　Let's go to the lake.
W　Sounds good. By the way, do you have a bike pump? One of my tires is flat.
M　I don't have one. How about leaving your bike at home and using my brother's bike?
W　That's nice of you.

남　너 나와 함께 자전거 타러 갈래?
여　좋아. 같이 타러 갈게. 어디 갈 거야?
남　호수에 가자.
여　좋아. 그런데 너 자전거 펌프 있니? 자전거 바퀴 하나가 바람이 빠졌어.
남　난 펌프 없는데. 집에 네 자전거를 놔두고 내 동생 자전거를 타고 가는 거 어때?
여　고마워.

ride 타다 **lake** 호수 **by the way** 그런데 **flat** 공기가 빠진 **That's nice of you.** 너 참 착하구나.

08

W　May I talk to Jenny, please? It is Sumi here.
M　Sorry, she's out right now. Would you like to leave a message?
W　Yes, please tell her to call me back this afternoon. My number is 720-3671.
M　Okay, let me repeat that: Sumi, 720-3617. Please call tonight.
W　Actually, it's 3671 and I would like her to call me this afternoon.
M　I'm sorry.
W　That's okay. Thank you.

여　Jenny와 통화할 수 있을까요? 저는 수미예요.
남　미안하지만 걘 외출 중이란다. 전할 말을 남기겠니?
여　네, Jenny에게 오늘 오후에 제게 전화해달라고 말해주세요. 제 전화번호는 720-3671번이에요.
남　그래, 내가 다시 말해볼게. 수미이고, 720-3617번, 오늘밤에 전화해달라는 거지.
여　사실은 3671번이고, 오늘 오후에 제게 전화해 주길 바랍니다.
남　미안하구나.
여　괜찮아요. 감사합니다.

① 수미 / 720-3617 / "오늘 오후에 전화할 것"
② 수미 / 720-3671 / "오늘 오후에 전화할 것"
③ Jenny / 725-3671 / "오늘 밤에 전화할 것"
④ Jenny / 725-3671 / "오늘 오후에 전화할 것"
⑤ 수미 / 720-3617 / "오늘 밤에 전화할 것"

be out 외출 중이다 **leave a message** 메시지를 남기다 **repeat** 반복하다

09

① W　Did you feed the dog?
M　I think I did.
② W　May I help you?
M　Yes, can I bring this coffee into the library?
③ W　Can you help me choose a book for my son?
M　Sure. How about this one?
④ W　Can you open the door?
M　Sure, I can.
⑤ W　Thanks for driving me to school.
M　Don't mention it.

① 여　개에게 먹이 줬니?
남　그런 것 같아요.
② 여　도와드릴까요?
남　네, 도서관으로 이 커피를 가지고 들어가도 되나요?
③ 여　내 아들을 위한 책을 고르는 것을 도와주시겠어요?
남　물론이죠. 이 책은 어떠세요?
④ 여　문 좀 열어주시겠어요?
남　물론이죠.
⑤ 여　학교까지 데려다 주셔서 감사합니다.
남　천만에.

feed 먹이를 주다 **bring** 가지고 오다 **Don't mention it.** 천만에.

10

M What kind of neighborhood do you live in?
W It's a very quiet neighborhood. It has quiet streets with lots of trees and parks.
M How long have you lived there for?
W I've lived there since I was five years old. How about yours?
M I live in a very active area. There are lots of stores, cars, and apartments.
W Have you lived there for a long time?
M No, I only moved there last month.

남 너는 어떤 지역에서 살고 있니?
여 매우 조용한 지역이야. 많은 나무와 공원들이 있는 조용한 거리들이 있어.
남 얼마나 오랫동안 거기서 살았니?
여 다섯 살 때부터 죽 거기서 살고 있어. 네가 사는 곳은 어때?
남 나는 활기찬 지역에서 살아. 많은 상점들, 차들 그리고 아파트들이 있어.
여 거기서 오랫동안 살았니?
남 아니, 겨우 지난 달에 이사 왔어.

neighborhood 사는 지역 **quiet** 조용한 **area** 지역 **apartment** 아파트

11

W Excuse me. Can you show me your passport?
M Okay. Here you are.
W What is the purpose of the visit?
M I am taking a vacation.
W Did you fill out the immigration declaration form?
M No, not yet. Can you help me out with it, please? I don't understand some of the English words.
W Okay. But next time, you have to fill it out in the plane.

여 실례합니다. 여권 좀 보여주시겠어요?
남 네. 여기 있습니다.
여 방문 목적이 무엇인가요?
남 휴가 중에 있습니다.
여 입국 신고서는 작성하셨나요?
남 아니오, 아직요. 저 좀 도와주시겠습니까? 몇몇 영어 단어 뜻을 잘 몰라서요.
여 네. 하지만 다음부터는 비행기 안에서 작성하셔야 합니다.

passport 여권 **immigration** 입국 **declaration** 신고 **help out** 도와주다 **fill out** 작성하다

12

M Did you hear the news that a boy died from the flu this morning?
W Really? I can't believe that flu can cause death.
M Hard to believe, right? It happens though. We need to wash our hands more often.
W Okay. I heard that is the best way to prevent flu. What else can we do, anyway?
M Wearing a mask and brushing your teeth are also helpful.
W I see. Thank you.

남 오늘 아침에 한 소년이 독감으로 사망했다는 뉴스 들었니?
여 정말? 독감이 죽음의 원인이 된다니 믿을 수 없어.
남 정말 믿기 어렵지? 하지만 일어나는 일이지. 우리는 손을 더 자주 씻어야 해.
여 알았어. 그것이 독감을 예방하는 최고의 방법이라고 들었어. 그런데 다른 것들로는 어떤 것을 할 수 있을까?
남 마스크를 착용하고 양치를 하는 것도 도움이 돼.
여 알았어. 고마워.

die from ~로 사망하다 **cause** 야기하다 **death** 사망 **prevent** 예방하다 **mask** 마스크 **brush one's teeth** 양치하다

13

W Can I ask you something?
M Sure. What is it?
W Someone took my wallet out of my bag while I was choosing a T-shirt on the display stand.
M Oh, no. Where was the display stand?
W It was on the second floor next to the escalator.
M I see.
W Since there is a special discount being offered there, the area was full of people.
M I will check the CCTV coverage of that area. I'm so

sorry for the trouble.

여 뭐 좀 물어봐도 될까요?
남 물론이죠. 뭔데요?
여 판매용 전시대 위에 있는 티셔츠를 고르는 동안 누군가가 제 가방 안에 있는 지갑을 꺼내갔어요.
남 오, 저런. 판매대가 어디 있었나요?
여 2층 에스컬레이터 옆에 있었습니다.
남 알겠습니다.
여 특별 할인을 하고 있어서 그 구역은 사람들이 가득 찼었어요.
남 그 구역 CCTV에 촬영된 것을 확인해 보겠습니다. 폐를 끼쳐드려 죄송합니다.

out of ~에서 **escalator** 에스컬레이터 **special discount** 특별 할인 **be full of** ~로 가득 차다 **coverage** 촬영한 것 **trouble** 고통

14

① M The zoo opens from 9:00 a.m. to 6:00 p.m. all year round.
② M The entrance fee is free for children and the elderly only.
③ M If not accompanied by an adult, children under the age of 10 may not be admitted.
④ M People should not scare the animals.
⑤ M People are not allowed to feed the animals.

사파리 월드에 오신 것을 환영합니다.	
개장	오전 9:00부터 오후 6:00까지 연중 무휴
입장료	$10 7세 미만 어린이 무료 노인과 장애인 무료
어린이 입장	10세 미만의 어린이는 성인을 동반해야 합니다.
경고	동물들에게 겁을 주거나 먹이를 주지 마세요.

① 남 동물원은 일년 내내 오전 9시부터 오후 6시까지 개장합니다.
② 남 입장료는 어린이들과 노인들에게만 무료입니다.
③ 남 어른을 동반하지 않으면 10세 미만의 어린이들은 입장이 허용되지 않습니다.
④ 남 사람들은 동물들을 겁주어서는 안됩니다.
⑤ 남 사람들은 동물들에게 먹이를 줄 수 없습니다.

all year round 일년 내내 **entrance fee** 입장료 **free** 무료의 **elderly** 노인의 **be accompanied by** ~을 동반하다 **admit** (입장을) 허용하다 **scare** 겁주다 **be allowed to-V** ~하는 것이 허용되다

15

[Telephone rings.]
M Hello. Can I talk to Mary?
W Hello, Mary speaking. Who's this?
M It's me, Justin. Would you like to go to see a baseball game this weekend?
W Really? Were you able to get tickets? I heard that all tickets were sold out within 10 minutes.
M Fortunately, I got a couple of them. I'm so excited.
W Thanks for asking me. I really wanted to see the game.

[전화벨이 울린다.]
남 여보세요. Mary와 통화할 수 있을까요?
여 여보세요. 전데요. 전화 거신 분은 누구세요?
남 나 Justin이야. 이번 주말에 야구 경기 보러 갈래?
여 정말? 표 구할 수 있었어? 10분 만에 표가 다 매진됐다던데.
남 운 좋게도 두 장 구했어. 정말 신나.
여 내게 물어봐 줘서 고마워. 그 경기 정말 보고 싶었어.

~ speaking. 제가 ~인데요. **Who's this?** (전화 거신 분은) 누구세요? **be sold out** 매진되다 **within** ~ 안에 **fortunately** 운 좋게도

16

① W Are you coming home late tonight?
M Yes. My mom got angry because I came home late.
② W Where is Steve?
M I saw him in the hallway.
③ W Do you like meat?
M Yes, I do.
④ W What do you think of this dress?
M It's very pretty.
⑤ W How was the food?
M I enjoyed it a lot.

① 여 너 오늘 밤에 늦게 오니?
남 응. 엄마가 내가 집에 늦게 가서 화내셨어.
② 여 Steve는 어디 있니?

남 복도에서 봤는데.
③ 여 너 육식 좋아하니?
남 응.
④ 여 이 드레스 어때?
남 정말 예쁘다.
⑤ 여 음식 어땠어?
남 정말 맛있었어.

••
get angry 화가 나다 **hallway** 복도 **meat** 육류

17

W Are you okay? I heard that you fell off your bicycle.
M Yes. I hurt my elbows and knees. But I'm okay.
W You should be more careful when you're riding your bike next time.
M Thank you for your concern. By the way, are you ready for the test?
W Well. I think so. But I'm going to look through it one more time.
M You're a good student.

여 너 괜찮니? 자전거에서 떨어졌다고 들었어.
남 응, 팔꿈치랑 무릎을 다쳤어. 그런데 괜찮아.
여 다음에 자전거를 탈 때는 더 조심해.
남 걱정해줘서 고마워. 그런데 너 시험 준비 다 됐니?
여 글쎄, 그런 것 같아. 그런데 한 번 더 훑어볼 거야.
남 넌 훌륭한 학생이네.

••
fall off ~에서 떨어지다 **hurt** 다치게 하다 **elbow** 팔꿈치 **knee** 무릎 **concern** 걱정 **be ready for** ~에 준비가 되어 있다 **look through** ~을 철저히 검토하다 **one more time** 한 번 더

18

W There was a boy named Hudson. He wanted to buy a new cell phone, but he didn't have enough money to buy one. So, he decided to save his money by not buying unnecessary things. He saved his money for several months, and one day he was able to buy a new cell phone. What proverb do you think matches the story?

여 Hudson이란 이름을 가진 소년이 있었다. 그는 새 휴대전화를 구입하길 원했다. 그러나 그는 그것을 사기에 충분한 돈을 가지고 있지 않았다. 그래서 그는 불필요한 물건들을 사지 않음으로써 돈을 모으기로 결심했다. 그는 몇 달 동안 돈을 모았고 어느 날 새로운 휴대전화를 살 수 있게 되었다. 당신은 어떤 속담이 이 이야기와 잘 맞는다고 생각하는가?

① 하지 않는 것보다는 늦더라도 하는 것이 낫다.
② 티끌 모아 태산.
③ 백지장도 맞들면 낫다.
④ 일찍 일어나는 새가 먹이를 잡는다.
⑤ 로마에선 로마의 법을 따라라.

••
enough 충분한 **decide to-V** ~할 것을 결심하다 **save** 저금하다 **unnecessary** 불필요한 **several** 몇몇의 **be able to-V** ~할 수 있다 **proverb** 속담

19

W It's been raining for five days. I want to see clear skies.
M I've got good news for you then. I heard that the rain will stop this afternoon on the radio this morning.
W Really? I'm so happy.
M What do you want to do when the rain stops?
W Shall we go on a picnic tomorrow?
M That sounds great!

여 5일 동안 비가 오네. 맑은 하늘을 보고 싶다.
남 그러면 좋은 소식이 있어. 오늘 아침에 라디오를 들었는데 오늘 오후에 비가 그친대.
여 정말? 정말 기뻐.
남 비가 그치면 무얼 하고 싶니?
여 내일 소풍 갈까?
남 좋은 생각이야!

① 나 너무 배고파.
② 좋은 생각이야!
③ 나는 맑은 날을 더 좋아해.
④ 좋아, 집에 가자.
⑤ 난 매일 아침 라디오를 들어.

••
clear (날씨가) 맑은 **go on a picnic** 소풍 가다

20

W What are you doing? Aren't you going to dress up for Camilla's birthday party?

M Oh, I'm afraid I can't attend the party.

W Why? What's the matter with you?

M You know my grandmother is 101 years old. She is sick and in the hospital so I have to visit her.

W That's too bad. Does she have a serious illness?

M No, she's just not feeling very well today.

여 너 뭐 하고 있니? Camilla의 생일파티인데 옷 안 차려 입어?
남 아, 나 그 파티에 참석 못할 것 같아.
여 왜? 무슨 일인데?
남 너도 알다시피 할머니께서 101세시잖아. 편찮으셔서 병원에 계시는데 찾아가 뵈어야 해.
여 저런. 심각한 병이니?
남 아니, 그냥 오늘 몸이 별로 안 좋으시대.

① 응, 곧 나으실 거야.
② 나 대신 안부 전해드려.
③ 병원에 같이 가자.
④ 할머니 연세가 어떻게 되시니?
⑤ 아니, 그냥 오늘 몸이 별로 안 좋으시대.

dress up 옷을 차려 입다 **I'm afraid that** 유감스럽지만 ~이다 **attend** ~에 참석하다 **serious** 심각한 **illness** 질병

Further Study 정답

p. 114

1 He is a make-up artist.
2 They did not book a table so they had to wait for an hour to get one.
3 One of the tires on her bike is flat and they don't have a pump for it.
4 He has lived there just for one month, moving there last month.
5 ① Washing my hands / ② Wearing a mask / ③ Brushing my teeth
6 The reason was that he wants to ask her to go to see a baseball game with him this weekend.
7 He didn't buy unnecessary things.
8 She wants to go on a picnic.

On Your Own 모범답안

p. 115

A

I'd like to introduce my dream house. It is a (1)two-story house located in (2)the country. It has (3)five bedrooms, three bathrooms, and one study. Also, it has (3)a big kitchen as well as a living room. Most of all, there are (4)fancy gardens in the backyard. In (4) the gardens, there are lots of flowers and trees. I wish I could live in my dream house now.

내가 살고 싶은 집			
(1) 집 종류	(2) 위치	(3) 방	(4) 기타 시설
아파트 일층집 이층집	도시 시골	침실, 욕실, 부엌, 거실, 서재, 세탁실	수영장, 정원, 바비큐장

나는 나의 꿈의 집을 소개하고 싶습니다. 그것은 시골에 위치한 이층집입니다. 그 집에는 침실 5개, 욕실 3개와 서재 1개가 있습니다. 또한 거실뿐 아니라 큰 부엌도 하나 있습니다. 무엇보다도 멋진 정원이 뒷마당에 있습니다. 정원에는 많은 꽃과 나무가 있습니다. 나는 지금 나의 꿈의 집에서 살고 있으면 좋겠습니다.

B

Lost-and-Found Center	
(1) What did you lose?	shoulder bag
(2) Where did you lose it?	on subway line 5
(3) When did you lose it?	this morning on my way to school
(4) What does it look like?	a rugby ball
(5) What color is it?	black
(6) Your contact number	010-5566-7788

I want to tell you about something that I lost. I lost (1)my shoulder bag. I think I lost it (2)on subway line 5. If my memory is right, I lost it (3)this morning on my way to school. It looks like (4)a rugby ball. It is (5)black. My contact number is (6)010-5566-7788. Thank you.

분실물 센터	
(1) 무엇을 잃어버렸나요?	어깨에 매는 가방
(2) 어디서 잃어버렸나요?	지하철 5호선
(3) 언제 잃어버렸나요?	오늘 아침 학교 가는 길에
(4) 어떻게 생겼나요?	럭비공 모양
(5) 무슨 색인가요?	검정색
(6) 연락 가능한 전화번호	010-5566-7788

저는 제가 잃어버린 것에 대해 이야기하고자 합니다. 저는 숄더백을 잃어버렸습니다. 지하철 5호선에서 그것을 잃어버린 것 같습니다. 제 기억이 맞는다면, 오늘 아침 학교에 가는 길에 잃어버렸습니다. 그것은 럭비공처럼 생겼습니다. 색은 검정색입니다. 제 연락처는 010-5566-7788번입니다. 감사합니다.

12 Listening Test 정답

p. 120

01 ⑤	02 ②	03 ⑤	04 ②	05 ③
06 ①	07 ①	08 ④	09 ⑤	10 ④
11 ④	12 ①	13 ④	14 ③	15 ①
16 ②	17 ⑤	18 ②	19 ③	20 ③

01

W We had a yard sale last spring.

M Really? What did you sell?

W My brother's old books, my old dolls and some of my mom's old clothes. So many things!

M Did you sell all of them?

W No. Things like my mom's old handbag and my old sneakers weren't sold.

M What were the hot selling items, then?

W We sold all of my little brother's stuff: his old caps, pants, shorts, and even his old socks.

여 우리는 지난 봄에 마당에서 물건을 팔았어.

남 정말? 뭘 팔았니?

여 오빠 책들, 내 오래된 인형, 그리고 우리 엄마의 오래된 옷들을 팔았어. 정말 많은 물건들이었지.

남 전부 다 팔았니?

여 아니. 엄마의 옛 핸드백과 내 옛 운동화는 안 팔렸어.

남 그럼 어떤 게 잘 팔린 품목들이야?

여 내 남동생 물건들은 다 팔았어. 모자, 바지, 반바지 그리고 양말까지 말이야.

yard sale 야드 세일(주택 마당에서 사용하던 물건을 파는 것) **hot** 인기 있는 **item** 품목 **stuff** 물건 **shorts** 반바지

02

M What is your bedroom like?

W I share it with my sister.

M What furniture do you have in your room?

W We each have a bed and a desk, but we share a dresser, drawers and a closet.

M Do you have a computer?

W No. Our family computer is in the living room.

M I don't have the computer in my bedroom, either.

남 네 방은 어떻게 되어 있어?

여 나는 내 여동생과 방을 같이 써.

남 방에는 어떤 가구들이 있니?

여 침대와 책상은 각자 하나씩 있지만 화장대, 서랍장 그리고 옷장은 같이 사용해.

남 컴퓨터 있니?

여 아니. 가족이 함께 쓰는 컴퓨터는 거실에 있어.

남 나도 내 방에 컴퓨터가 없어.

What is ~ like? ~는 (성격, 모양이) 어때? **furniture** 가구 **each** 각각 **dresser** 화장대 **drawers** 서랍장 **closet** 옷장

03

W Good morning, officer. My car was stolen this morning. I want to make a statement.

M All right. What kind of car is it?

W It is a black Kia K5 with a leather interior.

M What is the registration number?

W It's 10A 2435. It was parked in front of my house.

M Can I see your ID and your car registration please?

W Here they are.

여 안녕하세요. 오늘 아침에 제 차를 도난 당했어요. 진술서를 작성하고 싶어요.

남 네. 차종이 어떻게 되세요?

여 내부가 가죽으로 된 검은색 기아 K5입니다.

남 차 번호가 어떻게 되나요?

여 10A 2435입니다. 제 집 앞에 주차되어 있었어요.

남 신분증과 자동차 등록증 좀 보여주시겠어요?

여 여기 있습니다.

① 기자 ② 소방관 ③ 경비원
④ 안전요원 ⑤ 경찰관

statement 진술 **leather** 가죽 **registration** 등록 **interior** 내부 **park** 주차하다

04

M So you're finally here. You are two hours late!

W I'm sorry Mr. Park. It will not happen again.

M I hope not. The meeting was at seven thirty. Did you forget?

W I knew what time it was, but I had a terrible stomachache.

M Whenever you are late, I hear the same old excuse. What should I do?

W I understand how you feel. I'm really sorry.

M Okay, this is your last chance. Don't let it happen again.

남 마침내 왔군. 당신은 두 시간 지각이오.

여 죄송합니다, Mr. Park. 다시는 이런 일 없을 거예요.

남 나도 그러길 바라지. 회의는 7시 30분이었어요. 잊어버렸소?

여 알고 있었지만 배가 몹시 아팠습니다.

남 당신이 지각할 때마다 난 늘 같은 변명을 듣는군. 내가 어떻게 해야 할까?

여 어떤 기분이신지 이해합니다. 정말 죄송합니다.

남 좋아요, 이번이 마지막 기회요. 다시는 이런 일이 생기지 않게 하세요.

have a stomachache 배가 아프다 **terrible** 지독한 **whenever** ~할 때마다 **excuse** 변명

05

W Do you have any plans for tomorrow?

M I'm going to visit the National Museum. Do you want to join me?

W Sure. Where shall we meet?

M Let's meet in front of our school at 1 o'clock.

W Why don't we meet thirty minutes early and eat lunch together?

M Sounds great. What do you want to eat for lunch?

여 너는 내일 무슨 계획 있니?

남 나는 국립 박물관에 갈 예정이야. 같이 갈래?

여 좋아. 어디서 만날까?

남 학교 앞에서 1시에 만나자.

여 30분 일찍 만나서 점심 같이 먹는 것 어때?

남 좋아. 뭘 먹고 싶니?

national museum 국립 박물관 **early** 일찍

06

M It is fun to make musical instruments from things you can easily find in your home. You can turn a comb into a harmonica or water glasses into a xylophone. Does this sound interesting? If so, follow the following directions and in no time you will be playing your own instrument!

남 집에서 쉽게 찾을 수 있는 물건으로 악기를 만드는 것은 재미있습니다. 당신은 빗으로 하모니카를 만들거나 물이 담긴 유리잔으로 실로폰도 만들 수 있습니다. 재미있게 들리십니까? 만약 그렇다면, 다음의 지시사항을 따라 해 보세요. 그러면 즉시 당신은 당신만의 악기를 연주할 것입니다.

musical instrument 악기 **turn A into B** A를 B로 바꾸다 **comb** 빗 **xylophone** 실로폰

07

W Frank, wake up. You're going to be late for school.

M I don't feel well, mom. I can't go to school today.

W What's wrong?

M I feel sick. I can't stop coughing.

W Well, you need to go see a doctor and get a shot to cure your cold.

M No, mom. I think I'm okay now. But can you tell my teacher that I was so sick that I couldn't do my homework?

W That's why you don't want to go to school. No way!

여 Frank, 일어나라. 학교에 지각하겠다.

남 엄마 몸이 안 좋아요. 오늘 학교에 못 갈 것 같아요.

여 무슨 일이니?

남 저 아파요. 기침이 멈추질 않아요.

여 그래, 그럼 감기를 치료하려면 진찰 받고 주사 좀 맞자.

남 아니에요, 엄마. 저 괜찮은 것 같아요. 하지만 선생님께 제가 너무 아파서 숙제를 할 수 없었다고 말씀해주시겠어요?

여 그것이 바로 네가 오늘 학교에 가고 싶지 않은 이유이구나. 절대 안돼!

feel well 건강이 좋다 **feel sick** 아프다 **shot** 주사 **cure** 치료하다 **cold** 감기 **No way!** 절대 안돼!

08

M I have serious problems with my roommate.

W Why? Is he mean to you?

M No. He is quite a nice guy, but he listens to loud music all the time.

W Have you talked to him about it?

M No, I haven't. I am getting along fine with him; I just can't stand his loud music anymore.

W Well, then, why don't you just tell him about how you feel?

M I'll try, but what if I feel awkward after telling him?

남 나는 내 룸메이트와 심각한 문제가 있어.

여 왜? 그가 너에게 못되게 구니?

남 아니. 그는 꽤 착한 친구지만 항상 시끄러운 음악을 들어.

여 그에게 그 점에 관해서 이야기해 봤니?

남 아니. 나는 지금 그와 사이가 아주 좋아. 단지 더 이상 그의 시끄러운 음악을 견딜 수가 없을 뿐이야.

여 음, 그럼 그에게 네 기분이 어떤지 말해보는 게 어때?

남 한 번 해보겠지만 만약 그에게 말한 후 어색해지면 어떻게 해?

be mean to ~에게 못되게 굴다 **loud** 시끄러운 **get along with** ~와 친하게 지내다 **stand** 참다 **not ~ anymore** 더 이상 ~할 수 없는 **awkward** 어색한

09

① W There is an upside-down triangle with two small circles in it.

② W A girl is playing with two dolls.

③ W There is an elephant eating a carrot with its trunk.

④ W A round shaped clock is on the wall.

⑤ W There is a man holding one rose in his hand.

① 여 두 개의 작은 원이 들어 있는 거꾸로 된 삼각형이 있다.

② 여 한 소녀가 인형 두 개를 가지고 놀고 있다.

③ 여 코를 사용해서 당근을 먹고 있는 코끼리 한 마리가 있다.

④ 여 벽에 둥근 모양의 시계 하나가 있다.

⑤ 여 장미 한 송이를 들고 있는 한 남자가 있다.

upside-down 거꾸로 된 **triangle** 삼각형 **circle** 원형 **trunk** (코끼리의) 코

10

M It's nice to see you again, Helen.

W Max! I haven't seen you all winter vacation.

M Wow! You look so slender and healthy.

W Thanks. I've exercised a lot. You look like you gained a little weight.

M I did. I just studied, slept and ate all vacation. I didn't exercise at all.

W When are you going to start exercising again?

M I'm going to start tomorrow. I'm planning on jogging in the morning.

W Sounds great. If you need a companion, just ask me.

남 Helen, 다시 만나서 반가워.

여 Max! 겨울방학 내내 너를 못 봤었는데.

남 우와! 너 정말 날씬하고 건강해 보인다.

여 고마워. 운동을 많이 했거든. 너는 살이 좀 찐 것 같다.

남 그래. 방학 내내 나는 공부하고, 잠자고 먹기만 했거든. 운동은 전혀 안 했어.

여 언제부터 다시 운동을 시작할 거야?

남 내일부터 시작할 거야. 아침에 조깅할 계획이야.

여 좋아. 동행이 필요하면 나한테 부탁해.

slender 날씬한 **healthy** 건강한 **gain weight** 몸무게가 늘다 **jog** 천

천히 달리다, 조깅하다 **companion** 동행(인)

11

W Do you want to go to the night market with me?

M When?

W At ten. If you are going, I will pick you up at your house.

M That's quite late for me. I will pass this time.

W Oh, come on. Let's go. There will be lots of things to enjoy. Moreover, tomorrow is Sunday. You can take a rest.

M Alright. Give me a call before you come to pick me up, though.

여 나랑 같이 야시장에 갈래?

남 언제?

여 10시에. 만일 네가 간다면, 내가 너를 너의 집에서 태워 갈게.

남 나한테는 꽤 늦은 시간이네. 이번에는 넘어갈래.

여 오, 왜 그래. 가자. 즐길 거리가 많이 있을 거야. 게다가 내일은 일요일이야. 쉴 수 있잖아.

남 알았어. 그래도 나 태우러 오기 전에 전화해 줘.

night market 야시장 **quite** 꽤 **moreover** 게다가 **take a rest** 휴식을 취하다

12

W How do you go to school?

M I used to walk to school when I was in elementary school, but now I take a school bus.

W I see. How long does it take to get there?

M It usually takes about 15 minutes. It depends on the traffic though.

W Have you ever tried to take public transportation, like a bus or the subway?

M Yes, I have. But it takes much longer.

여 너는 어떻게 학교에 가니?

남 초등학교 때는 걸어서 다녔는데 이제는 스쿨버스를 타.

여 그렇구나. 거기 가는 데 시간이 얼마나 걸리니?

남 보통 약 15분 정도 걸려. 교통상황에 따라 다르기는 해.

여 버스나 지하철 같은 대중교통을 타본 적은 있니?

남 응, 있어. 그런데 훨씬 더 오래 걸려.

elementary school 초등학교 **depend on** ~에 달려있다 **traffic** 교통(량) **Have you ever + p.p.?** ~해본 적이 있니? **public transportation** 대중교통

13

[Telephone rings.]

M Hello, Emma. This is Jacob.

W Hi, Jacob. What's up?

M I'm sorry to tell you that I can't make it to our appointment. My sister is sick.

W Why? What's wrong with her?

M She has a high fever. I think I will have to take her to the hospital.

W That's too bad. Do you want me to go with you?

M I would appreciate your help if you could do so. Thank you.

[전화벨이 울린다.]

남 안녕, Emma. 나 Jacob이야.

여 안녕, Jacob. 무슨 일이야?

남 미안하지만 오늘 약속 못 지킬 것 같다고 말하려고. 여동생이 아파.

여 왜? 무슨 일이야?

남 고열이 있어. 병원에 데려가야 할 것 같아.

여 저런. 같이 가줄까?

남 그렇게 해줄 수 있다면 나야 고맙지. 고마워.

What's up? 무슨 일이니? **make it to** ~ 시간에 대다 **appointment** 약속 **high fever** 고열 **appreciate** 고마워하다

14

① M Sujin studies English three times a week.

② M Sujin has P.E. class on Thursday afternoon.

③ M Sujin has Science classes every Wednesday and Friday.

④ M Sujin has Art class on Wednesday morning.

⑤ M Sujin's Language Arts classes are both in the evening.

수진이의 주간 수업 시간표					
	월	화	수	목	금
오전	영어	수학	미술	과학	영어
오후	수학	역사	사회	체육	과학
저녁	국어	영어	음악	국어	역사

① 남 수진이는 일주일에 세 번 영어를 공부한다.
② 남 수진이는 목요일 오후에 체육 수업이 있다.
③ 남 수진이는 매주 수요일과 금요일에 과학 수업이 있다.
④ 남 수진이는 수요일 오전에 미술 수업이 있다.
⑤ 남 수진이의 국어 수업은 둘 다 저녁에 있다.

●●
three times 세 번 **P.E. (Physical Education)** 체육

15

W Honey, did you check the mail in the living room?
M Not yet. Why? Is there an important letter?
W In a way, yes.
M What is it?
W It is a notice that says we didn't pay our gas bill last month, so we have to pay a penalty fee.
M What?
W Besides, if we don't pay the bill by today, the gas company will cut off the gas.
M Oh, no. I will do an account transfer right away.

여 여보, 거실에 있는 우편물 확인했어요?
남 아직. 왜? 중요한 편지라도 있어?
여 한 편으로는 맞아요.
남 뭔데?
여 우리가 지난 달에 가스 요금을 내지 않아서 벌금을 내야 한다는 통지예요.
남 뭐라고?
여 게다가 오늘까지 요금을 내지 않으면 가스 회사에서 가스를 차단할 거래요.
남 오, 안돼. 당장 계좌이체 할게.

●●
mail 우편물 **in a way** 한편으로는 **penalty** 벌 **fee** 요금 **bill** 청구서
cut off 중단하다 **account transfer** 계좌 이체

16

① W Do you need any help?
M Yes, please.
② W How's the weather today?
M I hate the cold.
③ W Do you know how to drive a car?
M Of course. I'm a good driver.
④ W Why don't we play a computer game?
M I'd love to but I can't.
⑤ W Where are you going?
M I'm going to the supermarket.

① 여 도와드릴까요?
남 네.
② 여 오늘 날씨 어때?
남 나는 추운 것이 싫어.
③ 여 너 운전할 줄 아니?
남 물론이지. 나는 훌륭한 운전사야.
④ 여 컴퓨터 게임을 하는 거 어때?
남 그러고 싶지만 안돼.
⑤ 여 너 어디 가니?
남 슈퍼마켓에 가고 있어.

●●
how to-V ~하는 방법 **drive** 운전하다

17

W Do you have a pet?
M Yes. I have a pet snake.
W My goodness! A pet snake? Isn't it scary?
M Not at all. If you touch its skin, it is very cold and smooth. Would you like to touch it?
W No. No. No. I'm very scared of it. It is terrifying to me. I'm also afraid it might bite me.
M Haha. No, it won't.

여 너 애완동물 있니?
남 응. 애완용 뱀이 있어.
여 맙소사! 애완용 뱀? 무섭지 않니?
남 전혀 안 그래. 가죽을 만지면 아주 차갑고 부드러워. 만져볼래?
여 아니. 아니. 아니. 나는 너무 무서워. 내게는 무서워. 나를 물까 겁도 나고.
남 하하. 안 그럴 거야.

●●
pet 애완동물 **scary** 무서운 **smooth** 부드러운 **terrifying** 무서운 **bite** 물다

18

W Jane got a C on her English test in the final exam. Her grade is quite far below average. She is disappointed because her grade is as bad as her midterm grade. However, her classmate Brandon failed his midterm exam but got a perfect score on the final exam. Jane asked him what his secret was and he said that he just studied really hard. He memorized at least 20 words every day. He told Jane that "No one can beat a hard worker." What proverb do you think matches this story?

여 Jane은 기말고사 영어시험에서 C를 받았다. 그녀의 점수는 평균을 한참 밑돈다. 그녀는 점수가 중간고사 때만큼이나 나빠서 실망했다. 그런데, 그녀의 학급 친구인 Brandon은 중간고사 때는 낙제했지만 기말고사에서는 만점을 받았다. Jane은 그에게 비법을 물어봤고, 그는 그냥 열심히 공부했을 뿐이라고 말했다. 그는 매일 최소한 20개 단어씩 외웠다. 그는 Jane에게 "열심히 공부하는 사람은 아무도 이길 수 없다"고 말했다. 어떤 속담이 이 이야기와 맞는다고 생각하는가?

① 쇠뿔도 단 김에 빼라.
② 노력이 완벽을 만든다.
③ 남의 떡이 더 커 보인다.
④ 높이 나는 새가 멀리 본다.
⑤ 백지장도 맞들면 낫다.

final exam 기말고사 **grade** 점수 **average** 평균 **be disappointed** 실망하다 **as + 형용사 + as ~** ~만큼 …한 **midterm exam** 중간고사 **beat** 이기다

19

W Did you go to the Italian restaurant that I told you about?
M Yes. I had lunch there with my mom last week.
W How was the food? Was it tasty?
M It was awesome. I shared seafood spaghetti and Gorgonzola cheese pizza with my mom. I ate every last bite.
W Did your mom enjoy the food, too?
M Yes. She liked it very much.

여 내가 이전에 말했던 이탈리아 음식점에 갔었니?
남 응. 지난 주에 거기서 엄마와 점심을 먹었어.
여 음식 어땠어? 맛있었니?
남 끝내줬어. 나는 해물 스파게티와 고르곤졸라 치즈 피자를 엄마와 함께 먹었어. 난 마지막 한 입까지 다 먹었어.
여 엄마도 그 음식을 좋아하셨니?
남 응. 아주 좋아하셨어.

① 안됐구나.
② 주문하시겠습니까?
③ 응. 아주 좋아하셨어.
④ 응, 우리 엄마는 요리하는 걸 아주 즐기셔.
⑤ 아니, 난 네가 무슨 말을 하는지 이해가 안돼.

tasty 맛있는 **awesome** 끝내주는

20

W May I help you?
M I'm looking for a scarf for my mom.
W We have various choices here. What about this floral pattern one? It is popular among women.
M I see. How about this striped one? It looks quite fashionable.
W It is also nice. Are you going to buy it?
M Yes. Please wrap it for me.

여 무엇을 도와드릴까요?
남 엄마께 드릴 스카프를 찾고 있습니다.
여 저희 매장엔 다양한 스카프가 있어요. 꽃 무늬가 있는 이것은 어떠세요? 여성들 사이에서 인기입니다.
남 그렇군요. 이 줄무늬는요? 꽤 멋있어 보이는데.
여 그것도 좋아요. 그것으로 하시겠습니까?
남 네. 포장해주세요.

① 많이 드세요.
② 아니, 신경 쓰지 마세요.
③ 네. 포장해주세요.
④ 재미있겠는데요.
⑤ 탈의실이 어디인가요?

look for ~을 찾다 **various** 다양한 **floral** 꽃의 **pattern** 무늬 **among** (셋 이상) ~ 사이에 **striped** 줄무늬의

Further Study 정답

p. 124

1 She has two beds, two desks, a dresser, drawers and a closet. However, she doesn't have a computer in her bedroom.
2 She arrived at work at 9:30, two hours late, and she said the reason was that she had a terrible stomachache.
3 He asks her to tell his teacher that he was too sick to do his homework.
4 His roommate listens to loud music all the time and the man can't stand it anymore.
5 They are going to go to a night market.
6 He walked to school.
7 She said it was terrifying to her.
8 The reason is that her grade is as bad as her midterm grade.

On Your Own 모범답안

p. 125

A

I'd like to introduce the way to make your own musical instrument, (1)a water glass xylophone. There are several steps to make it. First, (2)line up seven or more water glasses that are the same size. Second, (3)put some water in the first glass. Third, (4)put a little more water in each of the other glasses. Finally, (5)carefully tap the water glasses with a spoon. Now, you can make beautiful sound with them.

나만의 악기	
(1) 악기	유리잔 실로폰
(2) 1단계	같은 크기로 일곱 개 이상의 유리잔을 일렬로 배열
(3) 2단계	첫 번째 잔에 물 담기
(4) 3단계	각각의 다른 잔에 물을 조금씩 더 담기
(5) 4단계	숟가락으로 조심스럽게 물잔을 두드림

나는 당신만의 악기인 유리잔 실로폰을 만드는 방법을 소개하고 싶습니다. 그것을 만드는 데는 몇 단계가 있습니다. 첫 번째로, 같은 크기의 일곱 개 이상의 물잔을 일렬로 배열합니다. 두 번째로, 첫 번째 잔에 물을 담습니다. 세 번째로, 각각의 다른 잔에 물을 조금씩 더 담습니다. 마지막으로 숟가락으로 조심스럽게 물잔을 두드립니다. 이제 당신은 그것들로 아름다운 소리를 만들 수 있습니다.

B

My Pet	
(1) What do you (want to) have as a pet?	a puppy
(2) What do you like about it?	cute, loyal, sweet
(3) What does it look like?	brown fur, long ears, long legs, pretty eyes
(4) Where did/can you get it?	my uncle gave it to me
(5) What do you (want to) do with it?	walk together, play Frisbee in the park

I have a (1)puppy as a pet. I think it is (2)cute, loyal, and sweet. It (3)has brown fur with long ears and long legs. Also, it (3)has pretty eyes. I got it (4)from my uncle. I (5)usually walk together or play Frisbee in the park with it.

나의 애완동물	
(1) 갖고 있는[싶은] 애완동물은?	강아지
(2) 그것에 대해 어떻게 생각합니까?	귀엽고, 순종적이며, 다정함
(3) 어떻게 생겼습니까?	갈색 털, 긴 귀, 긴 다리, 예쁜 눈
(4) 어디서 구했습니까[구할 수 있습니까]?	삼촌이 주심
(5) 함께 무엇을 합니까[하고 싶습니까]?	함께 산책, 공원에서 원반던지기를 함

저는 애완동물로 강아지를 키우고 있습니다. 저는 그 강아지가 귀엽고, 순종적이고, 다정하다고 생각합니다. 강아지는 갈색 털에 긴 귀와 긴 다리를 가지고 있습니다. 또한, 예쁜 눈도 가지고 있습니다. 그 강아지는 저의 삼촌으로부터 얻은 것입니다. 저는 대개 강아지와 함께 걷거나 공원에서 원반던지기 놀이를 합니다.

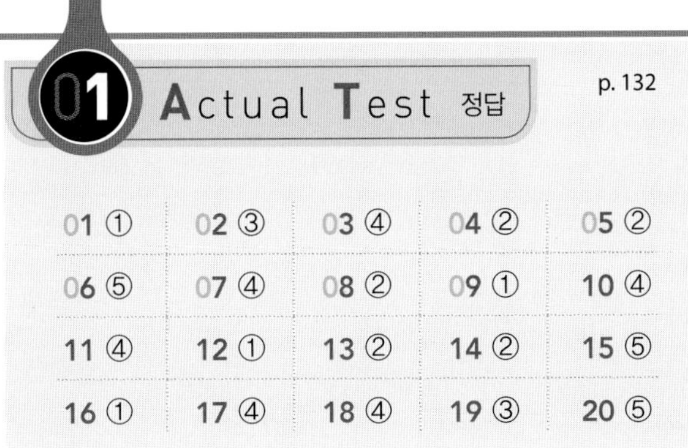

01 Actual Test 정답

p. 132

01 ①	02 ③	03 ④	04 ②	05 ②
06 ⑤	07 ④	08 ②	09 ①	10 ④
11 ④	12 ①	13 ②	14 ②	15 ⑤
16 ①	17 ④	18 ④	19 ③	20 ⑤

01

M There are lots of people coming to this party.
W Yes. Is your new roommate here, as well?
M Of course, he's right over there.
W Which one is he?
M He is standing next to the window.
W The guy with the beard?
M No, the one with the shaved head.

남 이 파티에 많은 사람들이 왔어.
여 응. 너의 새로운 룸메이트도 여기에 있니?
남 물론이지, 그는 바로 저기에 있어.
여 어떤 사람이 그야?
남 그는 창문 옆에 서 있는 남자야.
여 턱수염이 있는 남자?
남 아니, 머리를 면도한 남자.

next to ~의 옆에 **beard** 턱수염 **shave** 면도하다

02

W Did you finish feeding the dog?
M Yes, I did. And I watered the flowers as well. Do you want me to do more?
W Sounds good. Can you milk the cow?
M But mom, I am not very good at it.
W Then, what about picking some apples?
M Okay. That is a piece of cake. How many apples should I pick?

여 개 밥 다 줬어?
남 네, 그리고 꽃에 물도 줬어요. 더 도와드릴까요?
여 잘됐다. 우유 좀 짜주겠니?
남 하지만 엄마, 저는 우유 짜는 건 잘 못해요.
여 그러면 사과 좀 따주겠니?
남 좋아요. 그건 식은 죽 먹기죠. 사과 몇 개나 딸까요?

finish -ing ~하는 것을 끝내다 **water** 물을 주다 **milk a cow** 우유를 짜다 **a piece of cake** 아주 쉬운 일

03

M How was your first day of work?
W Oh, it was just awful. It was really embarrassing.
M I'm sorry to hear that. Tell me about it.
W The job is wonderful and the people there are really nice to me.
M Sounds good. So what went wrong?
W When I walked into the welcome meeting, I tripped on the doorway. On my first day at work, I fell over!

남 첫날 근무 어땠어?
여 오, 아주 안 좋았어. 정말 난처했지.
남 안됐다. 한 번 이야기해봐.
여 일은 아주 좋고, 거기 사람들도 나한테 아주 잘 대해줘.
남 잘됐네. 그럼 뭐가 잘못됐던 거야?
여 환영 모임장으로 걸어 들어갈 때 문턱에 발이 걸려 넘어졌어. 첫 날 직장에서, 벌렁 나자빠졌다고!

① 자신만만한 ② 기쁜 ③ 고마워하는
④ 부끄러운 ⑤ 지루한

awful 몹시 나쁜 **embarrassing** 곤란한 **go wrong** 잘못되다 **be nice to** ~에게 친절하게 대하다 **trip on** ~에 걸려 넘어지다 **fall over** 벌렁 나자빠지다

04

W What's wrong with this? It doesn't work.
M Are you having trouble?
W Oh, do you know about computers? Can you help me?
M Sure! What is the problem?
W After downloading some files, my computer isn't working at all.

M Let me take a look. Well... It looks like your computer is infected with a virus.
W What shall I do?

여 뭐가 잘못된 거지? 전혀 작동을 안 하네.
남 문제가 있니?
여 오, 너 컴퓨터에 대해 아니? 나 좀 도와줄래?
남 물론이지! 뭐가 문제야?
여 어떤 파일을 다운로드 한 후에 내 컴퓨터가 전혀 작동을 안 해.
남 한번 볼게. 그게… 네 컴퓨터는 바이러스에 감염된 것 같아.
여 그럼 어떻게 해야 돼?

take a look 훑어보다 **infect** 감염시키다

05

M Let's have a break, shall we?
W No. Our term paper is due on next Monday.
M We already finished two pages of it.
W We need a ten page term paper, though! And today is Thursday.
M Don't worry about it. We can put lots of pictures in it. They will take up three or four pages.
W We can't use pictures. We have to write the remaining eight pages.

남 좀 쉬자, 응?
여 안돼. 우리 학기말 리포트가 다음 주 월요일이 마감일이야.
남 우리는 이미 두 페이지 썼어.
여 하지만 우리는 열 장을 써야 해. 그리고 오늘이 목요일이야.
남 걱정하지 마. 사진을 많이 넣으면 돼. 3쪽에서 4쪽은 차지할 거야.
여 그림은 사용하지 못해. 남은 8쪽을 다 글로 써야만 해.

break 잠시의 휴식 **term paper** 학기말 리포트[보고서] **due** 마감이 ~까지인 **take up** 차지하다 **remaining** 남아 있는

06

W This lives in the sea. It doesn't have any backbone and it has a soft body. There are two main ways for it to protect itself. One is to shoot out black ink from its body. The other is for it to change its color according to its surroundings. It has two eyes and several arms. What is it?

여 이것은 바다에 삽니다. 그것은 등뼈가 없고 부드러운 몸체를 가지고 있습니다. 자신을 보호하는 주된 두 가지 방법이 있습니다. 하나는 몸에서 검은색 잉크를 쏘는 것입니다. 다른 방법은 주위 환경에 따라 자신의 색깔을 변화시키는 것입니다. 그것은 두 개의 눈과 여러 개의 팔을 가지고 있습니다. 이것은 무엇일까요?

backbone 등뼈 **protect** 보호하다 **shoot out** 쏘다 **according to** ~에 따라서 **surroundings** 주위 환경 **several** 몇몇의

07

M The Bucheon Film Festival is looking for volunteers.
W I know, but I can't apply.
M Why not? You want to be a film director.
W That's right, but I'm not very good at speaking English.
M Come on, your English is fine. It'll also be a good chance to practice it.
W I guess you're right. I'll apply for it right now.
M Good luck to you!

남 부천 영화제가 자원봉사자를 모집하고 있는 중이래.
여 알고 있지만, 나는 지원 못해.
남 왜 못해? 너는 영화감독이 되기를 원하잖아.
여 맞아, 하지만 나는 영어를 잘 못해.
남 이봐, 너의 영어 실력은 괜찮아. 또한 영어를 연습할 좋은 기회가 될 거야.
여 네가 맞는 것 같아. 지금 당장 지원할 거야.
남 행운을 빌어!

volunteer 자원봉사자 **apply for** ~에 지원하다 **film director** 영화감독 **be good at** ~를 잘하다

08

W I just got a new job.
M Congratulations! What are you doing at the new company?
W I'm a secretary. I organize and file documents.
M Great! I'm so proud of you.
W Well, I don't have enough suits to wear to work and I'm broke until I get paid. Would you mind lending me some money?

M Of course not. Do you want to go shopping together?

W That would be wonderful. Thanks.

여 나 막 취직했어.
남 축하해. 거기서 무슨 일을 하고 있니?
여 난 비서야. 문서를 정리정돈 해.
남 잘됐다! 나는 네가 너무 자랑스러워.
여 하지만 나는 일하러 갈 때 입을 정장이 충분하지 않고 월급을 받을 때까진 돈이 하나도 없어. 돈 좀 빌려줄래?
남 물론이지. 같이 쇼핑 가고 싶니?
여 좋아. 고마워.

secretary 비서 **organize** 정리하다 **file documents** 서류를 철하다 **suit** 정장 **mind -ing** ~하는 것을 꺼리다 **lend** 빌려주다

09

① M It is time to take a test. Put everything into your backpack.
W What about my pencil and eraser?
② M How many roses do you want?
W A dozen, please.
③ M Which class do you want to take?
W I want to enroll in the swimming class.
④ M May I help you?
W I'm looking for comfortable walking shoes.
⑤ M Would you like some milk?
W Yes, please.

① 남 시험 칠 시간이에요. 가방 안에 모든 것을 다 넣으세요.
여 연필과 지우개는 어떻게 해요?
② 남 장미 몇 송이 사실 거예요?
여 열두 송이 주세요.
③ 남 어떤 수업을 듣고 싶으세요?
여 수영 수업에 등록하고 싶어요.
④ 남 도와드릴까요?
여 편한 워킹화를 사고 싶어요.
⑤ 남 우유 좀 마시겠습니까?
여 네, 주세요.

take a test 시험을 보다 **backpack** 배낭 **eraser** 지우개 **dozen** 열 두 개 **enroll in** ~에 등록하다 **comfortable** 편안한

10

W Good afternoon. May I take your order?
M It's hard to choose. What can you recommend?
W Why don't you try today's special?
M The meatball spaghetti?
W Yes, we will also serve you a fresh salad and some corn soup.
M Sounds great! I'll have that.
W OK! I'll be right back with your meal.

여 안녕하세요. 주문하시겠습니까?
남 선택하기가 너무 어렵네요. 뭘 추천해주실 수 있나요?
여 오늘의 특별요리 어떠세요?
남 미트볼 스파게티요?
여 네, 신선한 샐러드와 옥수수 수프도 같이 제공됩니다.
남 좋아요! 그것으로 할게요.
여 알겠습니다. 곧 식사 가져다 드리겠습니다.

take an order 주문을 받다 **recommend** 추천하다 **serve** (음식을) 차려내다 **be back** 돌아오다

11

W Hey, what's up?
M Oh, I'm just doing some online shopping. A lot of websites are having Christmas sales. You can save up to 80% on some items.
W Really? That's a big saving. What are you looking for?
M Well, I'm looking for a Christmas present for my girlfriend. I think I will get her a necklace.
W I see.
M Can you recommend a nice necklace for me?
W Sure.

여 얘, 너 뭐 하니?
남 아, 온라인 쇼핑 좀 하고 있어. 많은 사이트에서 크리스마스 세일을 해. 어떤 물품에 대해선 최대 80%까지 절약할 수가 있어.
여 정말? 돈 많이 절약하겠다. 넌 뭘 찾고 있는데?
남 음, 내 여자친구에게 줄 크리스마스 선물을 보고 있어. 목걸이를 사줄 생각이야.
여 그렇구나.
남 괜찮은 목걸이 추천해 줄 수 있겠니?

여 물론이지.

●●
online shopping 온라인 쇼핑 **save** 절약하다 **up to** 최대 ~까지 **present** 선물 **necklace** 목걸이

12

W Wow! I like your new shoes. They look very expensive.

M You're right. I had to save money for several months to get them.

W Really? What did you do?

M I mostly did house chores. I did the dishes, cleaned my room, and polished my parents' shoes.

W They don't sound easy. I don't think I could do those things.

M I wanted the shoes a lot. I even separated the recyclables.

여 우와! 네 새 신발 멋지다. 무척 비싸 보이는데.

남 맞아. 이 신발을 사기 위해 몇 달 동안 저축해야 했어.

여 정말? 무엇을 했는데?

남 나는 대개 집안일을 했어. 설거지, 방 치우기, 그리고 부모님 신발 닦아 드리기를 했어.

여 쉽지 않아 보이네. 나는 그런 일들을 못할 것 같아.

남 내가 그만큼 그 신발을 갖고 싶었던 거지. 난 재활용 쓰레기 분리도 했어.

●●
save money 저축하다 **chore** 허드렛일 **polish one's shoes** ~의 신발을 닦다 **separate** 분리하다 **recyclable** 재활용품

13

M Chloe, why are you humming songs?

W Because I feel good today.

M What makes you feel so good?

W I saw my favorite actor in a coffee shop this afternoon. When I was walking out, he was walking in.

M Really? Did you get his autograph?

W Of course I did. I even took a picture with him and shook his hand.

M Wow! Good for you!

남 Chloe, 왜 노래를 흥얼거리고 있니?

여 왜냐하면 오늘 기분이 좋아서.

남 왜 그렇게 기분이 좋은데?

여 오늘 오후에 커피숍에서 내가 아주 좋아하는 배우를 봤거든. 내가 밖으로 나가는데 그가 들어오는 거야.

남 정말? 사인 받았어?

여 물론이지. 사진도 찍고 악수도 했는 걸.

남 우와! 잘됐다!

●●
hum (노래를) 흥얼거리다 **actor** 배우 **walk out** (걸어) 나가다 **walk in** (걸어) 들어오다 **autograph** 서명, 사인 **shake one's hand** ~와 악수하다

14

M ACE Mart is looking for salesclerks. The working hours are flexible, but you have to work at least 7 hours a day. Applicants should have at least 1 year of experience. E-mail your resume to apply@jobsearch.com. If you have any questions, please call Robert Wilson on 210-231-3456. We look forward to hearing from you.

에이스 마트 취업 기회

① 모집 부문: 판매 사원
② 근무 시간: 1일 8시간 (근무 시간대 조절 가능)
③ 자격 조건: 최소 1년의 경력
④ 연락처: Robert Wilson ☎ 210-231-3456
⑤ 이메일: apply@jobsearch.com

남 ACE Mart는 판매 직원을 구하고 있습니다. 근무 시간은 조절 가능하나 하루에 최소 7시간을 근무해야 합니다. 지원자는 최소 1년의 경력이 있어야 합니다. apply@jobsearch.com으로 당신의 이력서를 보내주세요. 궁금하신 사항이 있으면 Robert Wilson, 210-231-3456번으로 전화 주세요. 당신의 연락을 기다립니다.

●●
salesclerk 판매 사원 **working hours** 근무 시간 **flexible** 융통성 있는 **at least** 최소한 **applicant** 지원자 **experience** 경험 **look forward to -ing** ~하는 것을 고대하다

15

M Do you know that Kevin is really mad at you?

W Yes. But there's nothing I can do.

M Why don't you call him? He has no class now.

W I tried several times but he isn't answering my phone calls and text messages.

M That's too bad. I think you'd better go see him and apologize. I saw him in the cafeteria a while ago.

W Thank you for your advice.

남 너 Kevin이 너한테 정말 화난 것 알고 있어?
여 응. 그런데 내가 할 수 있는 일이 아무것도 없어.
남 그에게 전화를 하지 그래? 그 애 지금 수업 없어.
여 나 여러 번 시도했었는데 내 전화나 문자 메시지를 받지 않아.
남 안됐구나. 그에게 가서 사과하는 것이 좋겠어. 조금 전에 구내 식당에서 그를 봤어.
여 충고 고마워.

mad 화난 **several** 몇몇의 **text message** 문자 메시지 **apologize** 사과하다 **cafeteria** 구내식당 **a while ago** 조금 전에 **advice** 충고

16

① **W** Please show me your new bag.
M I know it is very expensive.

② **W** Watch your step.
M Oh, thank you.

③ **W** What's up?
M Nothing much. I just feel tired.

④ **W** Please pass me the pepper and the salt.
M Sure. Here they are.

⑤ **W** What's your favorite subject?
M I like English best.

① 여 새 가방을 보여줘.
남 그것이 매우 비싼 걸 알아.
② 여 발 조심해.
남 오, 고마워.
③ 여 괜찮아?
남 별일 아니야. 그냥 좀 피곤해.
④ 여 후추와 소금 좀 건네줘.
남 물론이지. 여기 있어.
⑤ 여 네가 가장 좋아하는 과목은 무엇이니?
남 나는 영어를 가장 좋아해.

expensive 비싼 **Watch your step.** 발 조심해. **feel tired** 피곤하다 **pepper** 후추 **salt** 소금 **subject** 과목

17

W It's very cloudy, today. Did you see today's weather report?

M Yes. There is a chance of rain tonight. You'd better take an umbrella with you.

W Thanks. How about tomorrow? Will it rain?

M No, the weatherman said that tomorrow will be a perfect day for outdoor activities.

W Wonderful! I am going to ride my bike with my friends in the park then.

M Have fun!

여 오늘 구름이 많네. 오늘 날씨 예보 봤니?
남 응. 오늘 밤 비 올 확률이 있대. 우산을 가져가는 것이 좋겠어.
여 고마워. 내일은? 비 온대?
남 아니. 날씨 예보에 의하면 내일은 야외활동 하기에 최적의 날이 될 거래.
여 좋았어! 그럼 공원에서 친구들과 자전거 탈 거야.
남 재미있는 시간 보내!

chance 가능성 **take an umbrella** 우산을 가져가다 **weatherman** 일기 예보자 **outdoor activity** 야외 활동

18

W Your best friend Lisa looks worried. She is waiting for a call from her younger brother. He was supposed to call her 30 minutes ago, but he hasn't called her yet. Lisa calls her brother's cellular phone, but it is turned off. After a while, her brother calls her on his friend's phone and tells her that his phone has a dead battery. You think that Lisa cares about her brother too much and gets nervous too easily. What proverb do you think Lisa should keep in mind?

여 당신의 단짝 친구 Lisa가 걱정이 있어 보인다. 그녀는 남동생 전화를 기다리고 있다. 그는 30분 전에 그녀에게 전화를 해야 했지만 아직까지 안 했다. Lisa는 남동생의 휴대전화로 전화하지만 전원이 꺼져있다. 얼마 후에 그녀의 남동생이 친구 전화로 전화를 걸어 그의 휴대전화 배터리가 나간 상태라고 말한다. 당신은 Lisa가 동생을 너무 신경 쓰고 너무 쉽게 불안해 한다고 생각한다. Lisa가 명심해야 할 속담은 무엇이라고 생각하는가?

① 고생이 없으면 얻는 것도 없다.
② 돌다리도 두드려 보고 건너라.
③ 자만은 추락을 낳는다.
④ 무소식이 희소식이다.
⑤ 소 귀에 경 읽기.

••
be supposed to-V ~하기로 되어 있다 **have a dead battery** 배터리가 나가다 **get nervous** 불안해하다

19

W Excuse me. Are you ready to order?
M Yes. We will have beef noodle soup and pineapple fried rice.
W How about drinks?
M Just water, please. [pause]
W Your order is ready. Enjoy your meal.
M Thanks. Wow! It smells so good! My mouth is watering.
W I hope you like the food.

여 실례합니다. 주문 하시겠습니까?
남 네. 소고기 국수와 파인애플 볶음밥 주세요.
여 음료는요?
남 그냥 물 주세요.
여 주문하신 것 나왔습니다. 맛있게 드세요.
남 감사합니다. 우와! 냄새가 정말 좋네요. 입에 군침이 도네요.
여 맛있게 드시기 바랍니다.

① 여기서 드실 건가요, 가져가실 건가요?
② 총 얼마예요?
③ 맛있게 드시기 바랍니다.
④ 금연석으로 주세요.
⑤ 이런, 다시 요리해 드릴게요.

••
order 주문하다 **beef** 쇠고기 **fried rice** 볶음밥 **meal** 식사 **smell** ~한 냄새가 나다 **water** 침을 흘리다

20

W Are you done with your homework?
M Yes. I just finished it. How about you?
W I have three more math problems to solve. If you don't mind, could you please explain them to me?
M Sure, I will. Please show me the questions.
W Here they are. I envy you a lot. I wish I was as good at math as you.
M You're good at English. I envy you.
W I think everyone has his or her own talent.

여 너 숙제 다 했니?
남 응. 방금 끝냈어. 너는?
여 수학문제 3개만 더 풀면 돼. 괜찮다면, 그 문제들을 내게 설명해 줄래?
남 당연히 해줄게. 문제를 보여줘 봐.
여 여기 있어. 나는 네가 많이 부럽다. 나도 너처럼 수학을 잘하면 좋겠어.
남 너는 영어를 잘하잖아. 나는 네가 부러워.
여 사람들에겐 저마다의 재능이 있는 것 같아.

① 좋겠다!
② 영어는 정말 재미있어.
③ 이제 숙제 시작하자.
④ 너 숙제 언제 끝낼 수 있니?
⑤ 사람들에겐 저마다의 재능이 있는 것 같아.

••
be done with ~을 끝내다 **solve** 풀다 **explain** 설명하다 **envy** 부러워하다 **be good at** ~을 잘하다 **talent** 재능

02 Actual Test 정답

p. 140

01 ⑤	02 ②	03 ②	04 ③	05 ④
06 ③	07 ⑤	08 ①	09 ②	10 ③
11 ①	12 ①	13 ④	14 ③	15 ③
16 ①	17 ⑤	18 ①	19 ④	20 ④

01

W Are you ready for your trip to Mexico?
M Yes, but I still have a lot of things to prepare.
W Have you paid for your rental car yet?

M Not yet. I'll search for one on the Internet.

W What about sunglasses?

M Yes, I packed them with my clothes, underwear and swimsuit.

W Don't forget to take your passport as well!

여 멕시코로 여행 갈 준비 되었니?

남 응, 하지만 여전히 준비해야 할 게 많이 있어.

여 렌터카 대금은 지불했니?

남 아직. 인터넷으로 찾아 볼 거야.

여 그럼 선글라스는 챙겼니?

남 응, 옷, 속옷, 수영복과 함께 챙겼어.

여 여권 챙기는 것도 잊지 마.

rental car 렌터카 **search for** ~을 찾다 **pack** 짐을 싸다 **passport** 여권 **as well** 역시

02

M Do you have a favorite pair of shoes?

W I sure do. They are flat red shoes with white ribbons.

M Who bought them for you?

W My grandfather did on my birthday. What about you?

M These new ones that I'm wearing now. All black sneakers with white stars on them.

W Oh, you bought them! They look cool!

남 너는 아주 좋아하는 신발이 있니?

여 물론 있지. 하얀색 리본이 있는 빨간색 플랫슈즈야.

남 누가 사줬어?

여 할아버지가 내 생일에 사주셨어. 너는 어때?

남 내가 지금 신고 있는 이 새 신발이야. 까만색에 하얀색 별이 있는 운동화지.

여 오! 네가 산 신발이구나! 멋지다!

flat 납작한 **sneakers** 운동화 **cool** 멋진

03

W I hate Julia. I will never forgive her!

M What's wrong with her?

W She wanted to use my laptop so I let her.

M Did she lose it?

W No, but she deleted all my music files. I tried to restore them but nothing worked.

M Have you talked to her about it?

W Yes, she just said, "Sorry!" That was it.

여 나는 Julia가 미워. 그녀를 결코 용서 안 할 거야.

남 그녀에게 무슨 문제가 있니?

여 그녀는 내 노트북을 사용하길 원했고 난 그렇게 하도록 해줬어.

남 그녀가 그것을 잃어버렸니?

여 아니, 하지만 나의 음악 파일을 다 지웠어. 내가 복구하려고 애썼지만 안되더라고.

남 그녀에게 이것에 관해서 말했어?

여 응, 그냥 "미안!" 이라고만 하더라고. 그게 다였어.

① 긴장한 ② 화가 난 ③ 슬픈
④ 괴로운 ⑤ 혼란스러운

delete 지우다 **restore** 복구하다 **That's it.** 그게 다야.

04

M Hello, how may I help you?

W My hair is getting very long. I'd like to have it cut.

M How much do you want me to cut?

W Maybe two inches off the ends? I want it to look neat.

M All right. And would you like to dye your hair?

W No, I want to keep my natural color.

M Okay, I see.

남 안녕하세요. 어떻게 도와드릴까요?

여 제 머리가 점점 길어져서요. 머리를 자르고 싶어요.

남 얼마나 잘라 드릴까요?

여 아마도 끝에서 2인치 정도? 깔끔하게 보이고 싶어요.

남 알겠습니다. 그리고 염색하시겠어요?

여 아니요. 저는 원래 제 머리 색을 유지하고 싶어요.

남 네, 알겠습니다.

① 기술자 ② 편집자 ③ 미용사
④ 요리사 ⑤ 예술가

neat 깔끔한 **dye** 염색하다 **natural** 타고난, 자연스러운

05

W Hello. Can I see that pair of shoes in size 7?

M Yes, we also have different colors: red, black, brown, and pink.

W Then, can you show me the ones in black and brown?

M Of course. Here they are.

W How much are they?

M They are 70 dollars a pair.

W I want to take both pairs, please. Can I pay by credit card?

여 안녕하세요. 저 신발, 사이즈 7짜리로 좀 볼 수 있을까요?

남 네, 색깔도 다양하게 있습니다. 빨간색, 검은색, 갈색, 그리고 분홍색요.

여 그럼 검은색과 갈색 좀 보여주시겠어요?

남 물론이죠. 여기 있습니다.

여 얼마인가요?

남 한 켤레에 70달러입니다.

여 그럼 두 켤레 다 살게요. 신용카드로 지불해도 되나요?

••
different 다른 **both** 둘 다 **pay by credit card** 신용카드로 지불하다

06

M In a picture book, the pictures help you to understand the story. They show you what the people and the places look like, and what is happening. The pictures also show the story's tone or mood. The pictures tell you if a story is funny, scary or sad. Pictures may help you catch the feeling of poems, too.

남 그림책에서 그림은 당신이 이야기를 이해하는 데 도움을 준다. 그것들은 사람이나 장소가 어떤 모습인지를, 그리고 무슨 일이 일어나고 있는지를 보여준다. 그림들은 또한 이야기의 분위기나 기분을 보여준다. 그림들은 당신에게 이야기가 재미있는지, 무서운지, 또는 슬픈지를 말해준다. 그림들은 시의 느낌을 이해하는 것에도 도움을 줄 수도 있다.

••
happen 일어나다 **tone** 분위기 **mood** 기분 **poem** 시

07

W Are you looking for something?

M Yes, I'm lost here.

W Where do you want to go?

M I'm supposed to get a chest X-ray.

W The X-ray room is right there, next to the eye clinic.

M Yes, there is the sign. Thank you so much.

여 무언가 찾고 계세요?

남 네, 여기서 길을 잃어버렸어요.

여 어디를 가고 싶으세요?

남 가슴 X레이 사진을 촬영하기로 되어 있습니다.

여 X레이실은 바로 저기, 안과 옆에 있어요.

남 네, 간판이 있네요. 대단히 감사합니다.

① 백화점 ② 헬스클럽 ③ 공항
④ 버스터미널 ⑤ 병원

••
be lost 길을 잃다 **chest** 흉부 **eye clinic** 안과

08

M This camping trip is great. It is so relaxing to be out here.

W I agree. This was a great idea. Look at the beautiful colors in the sky.

M It's getting a bit cold though. I'll gather some wood to make a fire.

W Okay, do you need my help?

M Not really. I can do it alone.

W Then I'm going to make instant noodles.

M Sounds perfect!

남 이 캠핑 여행은 아주 좋아. 여기 야외에 있으니까 아주 기분이 느긋해져.

여 나도 그렇게 생각해. 이건 훌륭한 생각이었어. 저 아름다운 하늘 색깔 좀 봐.

남 그런데 좀 추워진다. 나는 불을 피울 나무를 좀 모을게.

여 좋아. 내 도움이 필요하니?

남 별로. 나 혼자 할 수 있어.

여 그럼, 나는 라면을 끓일게.

남 완벽해!

●●
relaxing 마음을 느긋하게 해주는 **agree** 동의하다 **make a fire** 불을 피우다 **alone** 혼자 **instant noodle** 즉석 면, 라면

09

① M Do you have the time?
W Yes, it is 6 o'clock.
② M Can I buy two tickets for the 7 o'clock concert?
W I'm sorry we don't have any seats available.
③ M Can I speak to Carl, please?
W I think you have the wrong number.
④ M I'd like to rent a car for a week.
W Okay, what kind of car do you want to rent?
⑤ M Good morning, front desk.
W I'd like to check out this morning, please.

① 남 몇 시인가요?
여 네, 6시예요.
② 남 7시 콘서트 표 두 장 살 수 있나요?
여 죄송하지만 자리가 없습니다.
③ 남 Carl과 통화할 수 있을까요?
여 전화 잘못 거셨어요.
④ 남 일주일 동안 차를 빌리고 싶습니다.
여 네, 어떤 종류의 차를 빌리고 싶으세요?
⑤ 남 안녕하세요. 프런트데스크입니다.
여 오늘 아침에 체크아웃 하고 싶습니다.

●●
Do you have the time? 몇 시예요? **have the wrong number** 전화 잘못 걸다 **rent** 빌리다

10

M You look like you are gaining some weight.
W Yes, I am. I gained 5kgs. I am really out of shape.
M I swim three times a week. It helps me stay in shape.
W That's why you look so healthy. I'm planning to take an aerobics class from next week.
M It is important to warm up before you exercise. You should also exercise regularly.
W Thank you for your advice. I'll keep it in mind.

남 너 체중이 좀 느는 것 같이 보여.
여 맞아. 5킬로 불었어. 몸이 정말 안 좋아.
남 나는 일주일에 세 번 수영해. 그것은 건강을 유지하는 데 도움을 줘.
여 그래서 네가 그렇게 건강해 보이는 거구나. 나는 다음 주부터 에어로빅 수업을 받을 계획이야.
남 운동 전에 준비운동하는 것이 중요해. 그리고 규칙적으로 운동해야 하고.
여 충고 고마워. 꼭 명심할게.

●●
out of shape 몸 상태가 나쁜 **in shape** 몸 상태가 좋은 **healthy** 건강한 **warm up** 준비운동을 하다 **regularly** 규칙적으로

11

W Edison, where are you going?
M I'm on the way to the library.
W Why? Do you have something to return?
M No. I'm going to check out some books for my report.
W I see. Can you do me a favor?
M Sure. What is it?
W Can you please return this book for me? I'm late for class.
M No problem.

여 Edison, 너 어디 가니?
남 도서관에 가는 길이야.
여 왜? 반납할 거 있니?
남 아니. 나는 보고서에 쓸 책을 대여할 거야.
여 그렇구나. 내 부탁 좀 들어줄래?
남 물론이지. 뭔데?
여 이 책 좀 나 대신 반납해 줄 수 있니? 내가 수업에 늦었거든.
남 알았어.

●●
on the way to ~로 가는 길에 **return** 반납하다 **check out** (절차를 밟고) 빌리다 **do ~ a favor** ~의 부탁을 들어주다

12

W Luke, can you tell me how to make kimchi fried rice?
M Okay. Prepare a frying pan, kimchi, cooked rice, oil, and ham.
W What should I do then?
M First, chop the kimchi and cube the ham. Second,

heat the pan and add some oil.

W Okay, that's easy.

M Now put all the ingredients together in the pan, except for the rice. Mix them. Then put the rice in the pan, and mix them again.

W It doesn't sound hard. I will try to make it. Thanks.

여 Luke, 김치볶음밥 만드는 법 좀 알려줄 수 있니?
남 좋아. 프라이팬, 김치, 밥, 식용유, 그리고 햄을 준비해.
여 그런 다음에 무엇을 해야 해?
남 먼저 김치를 다지고 햄을 네모나게 잘라. 두 번째로, 팬을 달구어서 기름을 둘러.
여 응, 쉽네.
남 이제 팬에 밥을 제외한 모든 재료들을 함께 넣고 섞어. 그런 다음 팬에 밥을 넣고, 다시 잘 섞어.
여 어렵지 않네. 해봐야겠다. 고마워.

prepare 준비하다 **chop** 다지다 **cube** 네모로 자르다 **heat** 가열하다 **ingredient** 재료 **except for** ~을 제외하고 **mix** 섞다

13

W Hi, Gabriel. Long time no see. I'm glad to see you.

M I'm glad to see you, too. How have you been?

W I'm good. And you?

M I'm fine. By the way, do you still practice the oboe every Sunday?

W Yes, but not this Sunday. I have a makeup class in math and English. The midterm exams are starting next week.

M I see. Good luck on your exams.

여 안녕, Gabriel. 오랜만이야. 만나서 반가워.
남 나도 만나서 반가워. 어떻게 지냈어?
여 잘 지냈어. 너는?
남 나도 잘 지내. 그런데 너 아직도 매주 일요일마다 오보에 연습하니?
여 응. 그런데 이번 주 일요일은 안 해. 수학이랑 영어 보충수업이 있어. 중간고사가 다음 주에 시작하거든.
남 그렇구나. 시험 잘 봐.

be glad to-V ~하게 되어 기쁘다 **by the way** 그런데 **practice** 연습하다 **oboe** (악기) 오보에 **makeup class** 보충수업 **midterm** 중간의

14

① W Victoria reads the most among the students.

② W Olivia reads more than Natalie.

③ W Andrew reads more than Joshua.

④ W Natalie reads less than Olivia.

⑤ W Joshua reads five books a month.

학생들이 한 달간 읽는 책 수

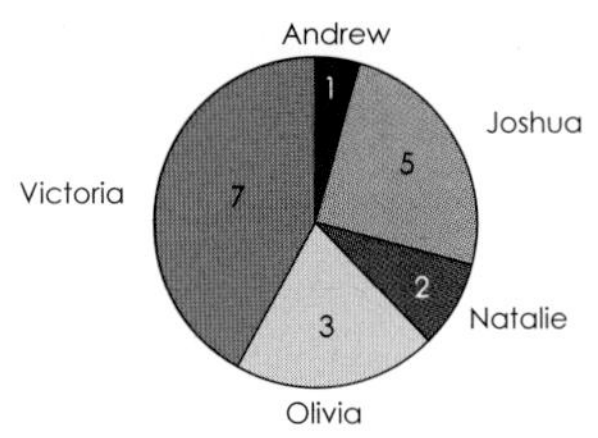

① 여 Victoria는 학생들 중에서 가장 많이 읽는다.
② 여 Olivia는 Natalie보다 더 많이 읽는다.
③ 여 Andrew는 Joshua보다 더 많이 읽는다.
④ 여 Natalie는 Olivia보다 더 적게 읽는다.
⑤ 여 Joshua는 한 달에 5권의 책을 읽는다.

15

M Please tell me my afternoon schedule.

W You have a meeting with Dr. Costner at 3 o'clock.

M What about my meeting with Professor Herrington?

W He's scheduled for 5:40 this afternoon. I sent you the copies of the contracts you will need to sign via email.

M Thank you. Can you prepare some drinks and snacks for my guests, please?

W Sure. I'll do that now.

M Okay. I'll be checking my email, then.

남 나의 오후 일정을 말해줘요.
여 Costner 교수님과 3시에 회의가 있습니다.
남 Herrington 교수님과의 회의는요?
여 그 분과는 오늘 오후 5시 40분에 일정이 잡혀 있습니다. 서명하기 위해 필요한 계약서 사본을 이메일로 보내드렸습니다.
남 고마워요. 손님들을 위한 음료와 간식 거리를 좀 준비해줄 수 있나요?
여 네. 지금 하겠습니다.

남 좋아요. 난 그럼 내 이메일을 확인해야겠어요.

●●
be scheduled for ~로 일정이 잡히다 **contract** 계약서 **via** ~을 거쳐 **prepare** 준비하다 **guest** 손님

16

① W Are you married?
M Yes. I'm going to get married next month.
② W Where are you from?
M I'm from Chicago.
③ W How do you go to school?
M My dad takes me to school.
④ W Let's go to the movies.
M Sounds great!
⑤ W How much is that vase?
M It is 3 dollars.

① 여 너 결혼했니?
남 응. 다음 달에 결혼해.
② 여 너 어디 출신이니?
남 나는 Chicago에서 왔어.
③ 여 학교에 어떻게 가니?
남 아빠가 데려다 주셔.
④ 여 영화 보러 가자.
남 좋아!
⑤ 여 이 꽃병 얼마예요?
남 3달러입니다.

●●
get married 결혼하다 **be from** ~ 출신이다 **take A to B** A를 B로 데려가다 **vase** 꽃병

17

M Did you sign up for a club?
W No. I don't even know how many and what kinds of clubs there are in this school.
M There are 15 clubs. Since it is mandatory, you should join at least one.
W I know. Which one do you belong to?
M I belong to the dancing club.
W That sounds like fun. I think I'll join up, too.

남 너 동호회에 가입했니?
여 아니. 나는 이 학교에 얼마나 많이, 또 어떤 종류의 클럽들이 있는지도 모르는 걸.
남 15개가 있어. 의무사항이라 최소 하나는 꼭 가입해야 해.
여 알아. 너는 어디 소속이야?
남 나는 댄스 동아리에 속해 있어.
여 재미있겠다. 나도 가입해야겠어.

●●
sign up for ~에 가입하다 **club** 클럽, 동호회 **even** ~조차 **mandatory** 의무적인 **belong to** ~에 속해 있다

18

M Carol is a flight attendant. She is announcing that passengers must turn off electric devices like mp3 players, laptops, and cell phones. It is because their signals may interfere with the plane's navigation system. At that time, she sees a man take his mp3 player out and try to turn it on. In this situation, what would Carol most likely say to the man?

남 Carol은 비행기 승무원이다. 그녀는 승객들에게 mp3 플레이어, 노트북 컴퓨터, 그리고 휴대전화와 같은 전자기기는 꺼야 한다고 방송으로 알리고 있다. 왜냐하면 그것들의 신호가 비행기의 운항 체계를 방해할 수 있기 때문이다. 그때, 그녀는 한 남자가 mp3 플레이어를 꺼내어 켜려고 하는 것을 본다. 이 상황에서 Carol은 그 남자에게 무어라 말하겠는가?

① 실례합니다. 그것 좀 꺼주세요.
② 좋은 mp3 플레이어를 가지고 계시네요.
③ 지금 듣고 계시는 노래가 무엇인가요?
④ 당신의 mp3 플레이어를 좀 빌릴 수 있을까요?
⑤ 소리 좀 줄여주시겠어요?

●●
flight attendant 비행기 승무원 **announce** (방송으로) 알리다 **passenger** 승객 **turn off** 끄다 **electric device** 전자 기기 **interfere with** ~을 방해하다 **navigation** 운항

19

W Do you want to go to the senior's center this weekend?
M I'd love to go but my mom has to say 'Yes' first.
W Why don't you call her now and ask her about it?
M Okay, I will. [pause]

W What did she say?

M She said it will be a good experience for me.

여 너 이번 주말에 양로원 갈래?

남 나도 가고 싶은데 먼저 엄마가 "그래"라고 말해 주셔야 해.

여 지금 전화 해서 여쭤보는 게 어때?

남 알았어, 그렇게 할게.

여 엄마가 뭐라 하셔?

남 내게 좋은 경험이 될 거라고 하셨어.

① 내 일기장 가져갈게.
② 이곳에서는 조용히 해주세요.
③ 좋아. 지금 당장 갈 수 있겠다.
④ 내게 좋은 경험이 될 거라고 하셨어.
⑤ 나는 그렇게 생각하지 않아. 우리가 거기서 할 수 있는 건 아무것도 없어.

senior's center 양로원 **experience** 경험

20

M Can I get my book back? I need it for the test.

W I'm sorry. I left it at home this morning. If you need it, I will go home and get it.

M Well, you don't have to.

W Are you sure?

M I will just borrow the same book from the library.

W Thank you. It's a long way home.

M No problem. I often forget things, too.

남 내 책 돌려줄래? 시험에 필요해서.

여 미안해. 오늘 아침에 집에 놔두고 왔어. 네가 필요하다면 집에 가서 가지고 올게.

남 음, 그러지 않아도 돼.

여 정말?

남 그냥 도서관에서 같은 책을 빌릴 거야.

여 고마워. 집까지 먼 길인데.

남 괜찮아. 나도 자주 잊어버리는 걸.

① 그렇게 하지 마!
② 사실 나는 Mexico에서 왔어.
③ 맞아, 늦었네. 이제 집에 가자.
④ 괜찮아. 나도 자주 잊어버리는 걸.
⑤ 나도 알아. 그 책은 정말 비싸.

get back 돌려 받다 **need** 필요로 하다 **Are you sure?** 정말?

내신 및 시 • 도 교육청 영어듣기평가 완벽 대비

Listening 올리고 중학영어듣기 모의고사

① 최신 기출 유형의 철저한 분석 및 반영

최근 5년간 전국 16개 시 • 도 교육청 영어듣기능력평가 기출 문제를 철저히 분석하고, 문제 유형, 유형별 출제 비율, 빈출 표현, 소재까지 다각도로 반영하여 완벽한 실전 대비를 할 수 있습니다.

② 영어 교과서 표현들과 소재 반영으로 내신 영어 완벽 대비

영어 교과서의 주요 표현들과 소재를 반영하여 내신까지 효과적으로 대비할 수 있습니다.

③ 영어 말하기 수행평가, 서술형 평가 대비 문제 수록

5지 선다형에서 한층 더 심화된 서술형 문제를 수록하여 모의고사보다 높은 난이도로 듣기 실력을 강화할 수 있습니다. 또한 본문의 주제와 소재를 활용한 다양한 Activity를 통해 말하기 수행평가까지 함께 대비할 수 있습니다.

④ 전 지문 받아쓰기 제공

매회 모의고사마다 전 지문에 대한 받아쓰기를 수록하여 놓친 부분을 꼼꼼하게 점검할 수 있을 뿐만 아니라, 집중력과 듣기 실력을 강화할 수 있습니다.

⑤ 본문 주요 어휘 및 표현 정리

출제 빈도가 높은 본문의 주요 어휘, 표현을 한눈에 볼 수 있도록 정리하여 효율적인 어휘 학습으로 어휘 실력을 향상시킬 수 있습니다.